Amplifying Islam in the European Soundscape

Islam of the Global West

Islam of the Global West is a pioneering series that examines Islamic beliefs, practices, discourses, communities, and institutions that have emerged from "the Global West." The geographical and intellectual framing of the Global West reflects both the role played by the interactions between people from diverse religions and cultures in the development of Western ideals and institutions in the modern era, and the globalization of these very ideals and institutions.

In creating an intellectual space where works of scholarship on European and North American Muslims enter into conversation with one another, the series promotes the publication of theoretically informed and empirically grounded research in these areas. By bringing the rapidly growing research on Muslims in European and North American societies, ranging from the United States and France to Portugal and Albania, into conversation with the conceptual framing of the Global West, this ambitious series aims to reimagine the modern world and develop new analytical categories and historical narratives that highlight the complex relationships and rivalries that have shaped the multicultural, poly-religious character of Europe and North America, as evidenced, by way of example, in such economically and culturally dynamic urban centers as Los Angeles, New York, Paris, Madrid, Toronto, Sarajevo, London, Berlin, and Amsterdam, where there is a significant Muslim presence.

Amplifying Islam in the European Soundscape

Religious Pluralism and Secularism in the Netherlands

Pooyan Tamimi Arab

Bloomsbury Academic
An imprint of Bloomsbury Publishing Plc

B L O O M S B U R Y
LONDON · OXFORD · NEW YORK · NEW DELHI · SYDNEY

Bloomsbury Academic
An imprint of Bloomsbury Publishing Plc

50 Bedford Square	1385 Broadway
London	New York
WC1B 3DP	NY 10018
UK	USA

www.bloomsbury.com

BLOOMSBURY and the Diana logo are trademarks of Bloomsbury Publishing Plc

First published 2017

British Library Cataloguing-in-Publication Data
A catalogue record for this book is available from the British Library.

ISBN: HB: 978-1-4742-9143-9
ePDF: 978-1-4742-9144-6
ePub: 978-1-4742-9145-3

Library of Congress Cataloging-in-Publication Data
Names: Tamimi Arab, Pooyan, author.
Title: Amplifying Islam in the European soundscape: religious pluralism and secularism in the Netherlands / Pooyan Tamimi Arab.
Description: New York: Bloomsbury Academic, 2017. | Series: Islam of the global West | Includes bibliographical references and index.
Identifiers: LCCN 2016039052| ISBN 9781474291439 (hb) | ISBN 9781474291453 (epub)
Subjects: LCSH: Adhan–Netherlands. | Sound–Social aspects–Netherlands. | Loudness–Social aspects–Netherlands. | Islam–Netherlands.
Classification: LCC BP184.3 .T345 2017 | DDC 297.3/8209492–dc23 LC record available at https://lccn.loc.gov/2016039052

Series design by Dani Leigh
Cover image © Brian Stablyk / gettyimages.co.uk

Series: Islam of the Global West

Typeset by Deanta Global Publishing Services, Chennai, India
Printed and bound in Great Britain

In memory of Mohammad and Mehdi

Contents

List of Figures

Acknowledgments

I am indebted, most of all, to Forough Nayeri, my dear mother who never hesitated to make sacrifices for my sake. My explorations in cultural anthropology began as a child when she studied the anthropology of non-Western societies. She and our close friend Halleh Ghorashi were able to pursue their degrees thanks to the support given to them by the University Assistance Fund in the Netherlands. If it was not for this much-needed support for the exiled and the vulnerable, I would not have had the opportunity as a child to be inspired by my mother, by Halleh, and by their friends.

The research for this book was funded by the Netherlands Organization for Scientific Research. I would like to thank all the people who agreed to be interviewed for this project, without whom I could not have conducted research on Islam in the Netherlands. I am also particularly thankful to Patrick Eisenlohr and Martijn Oosterbaan for giving me the opportunity to do anthropological research at Utrecht University, and for introducing me to new styles of thinking. I cannot name all who supported me in this period, but I want to mention the names of Ben Visser, Victor Kal, Kootje Willemse-van Spanje, Christoph Baumgartner, Birgit Meyer, Veit Bader, Rajeev Bhargava, Peter Jan Margry, Daan Beekers, Ammar Maleki, Kamel Essabane, Hamed Khosravi, Ernst van den Hemel, Paul Mepschen, Jan Willem Duyvendak, Oskar Verkaaik, Mehmet Yamali, Jaap Kapteyn, Manon Tiessink, and Corina Duijndam. A special thanks goes to Rasna Dhillon, who did a fantastic job brushing up my English, and to Lammert de Jong, who never complained about reading yet another version of the text. I am also indebted to Bloomsbury for publishing this book, to Frank Peter for his comments on the manuscript, and especially to Kambiz GhaneaBassiri, with whom it was a pleasure to work thanks to his clarity of thought as well as his kindness. My wife Sara put up with a lot during the entire research and writing process. For our honeymoon, we booked a room next to one of Istanbul's many mosques so that I could enthusiastically listen to the azan in the mornings. Our sweet daughter Shiva learned to walk and speak as the book manuscript reached its completion.

My older respondents often said that they found the call to prayer nostalgic; it reminded them of their youth. During this research, in 2013, I visited my family in Shiraz for the first time since childhood. I was woken early in the morning by a soft azan in the distance, and felt what so many of my nostalgic respondents had: I had finally returned home. Although European memories and experiences are central to the thinking that led to this book, the concern for religion and politics was forced on me personally by the history of my country of birth. That is why this book is dedicated to my late father, Mohammad Tamimi Arab, and my uncle, Mehdi Tamimi Arab, who lived in dark times and suffered great injustices. Even though they are dead, I feel like they are here with me now.

Pooyan Tamimi Arab
Spring 2016, Amsterdam

Introduction

Amplifying Islam

Farouq Alzouman took a deep breath and recited the *azan*, the Islamic call to prayer, for the first time in history, on top of the world.[1] The Saudi hero conquered Mount Everest in 2008. Though not the first Muslim to scale the summit, a privilege earned by the Turk Nasuh Mahruki in 1995, the pious Alzouman was the first to carry a Qur'an with him. His courageous romanticism and Islamic pride left young Muslims across the world gaping in awe. Alzouman subsequently traveled to various countries to tell his story and give self-realization pep talks with an Islamic flavor. On one of these journeys, he ended up in a former Protestant church in Rotterdam, the Netherlands. I was there to listen to him in the new Islamic center, and to observe his interaction with the audience. The room was packed. Sitting on the benches of the former church were young Muslims, women to the left and men to the right, of Moroccan, Turkish, Somalian, and Afghan descent. There were also a few Iranians, several Dutch converts, and others. A majority of them were either born or raised in the Netherlands, and all of them were burning with a passion to practice Islam in a different way than their parents' generation—less bound by racial and ethnic categories; brothers and sisters in a predominantly non-Muslim land. They conversed in Dutch and often inserted the exclamations *inshallah* (God willing) and *alhamdullilah* (praise to God), crafting a new Dutch-Muslim piety. Despite being a Persian speaker and accustomed to these phrases, and aware that many of these youngsters' parents also used these expressions in the Netherlands, I felt as if they were overdoing it, being "more Catholic than the Pope." From my perspective as a "skeptic" and "disbeliever" of monotheism, I thought they undoubtedly romanticized their religion, that they could not hear the silence of God, the proper perception after the *Religionskritik* of the Enlightenment, and were too vulnerable to kitsch. What I identified as their "Islamic enthusiasm"—failing consistently in suppressing my own opinions—ensured that, in their view, Islam would under all circumstances present answers to life's difficulties. Echoing within me were memories of the fateful hubris of my parents' generation, many of whom supported the Iranian

Islamic Revolution that in turn strengthened my generation's spiritual enmity and defiance. An upbringing in Amsterdam, including time spent at a high school named after Spinoza and with teachers who made sport of religion by poking fun at its absurdities, especially Christianity, reinforced these feelings of repulsion for monotheism. While university learning nuanced this negative relation toward religion, it also reinforced a skeptical attitude toward the very notion of transcendence or the divine. Clearly, if "cultural anthropologist" was going to be my identity, I was a very biased one.

Listening to Alzouman, however, I also had a change of heart. Perhaps because, just like everybody else, I had come from elsewhere—from a Muslim country—and was sometimes perceived as different. Although intellectually privileged because my mother was a cultural anthropologist, just like many of the attendees I too had grown up in mixed and migrant neighborhoods and knew something of how it feels to be the "other." This common background helped me to appreciate Alzouman when he energetically said to his audience: "I am so proud of all of you." This was not a sentiment I had heard often and it stood in sharp contrast to the usual disdain for Dutch-Muslim youth. It certainly struck a chord in me, and I could not help feeling compassion—a skeptic would say pity—for his listeners. Alzouman was around thirty years old and spoke with a flawless American English accent. He appeared modern, educated, handsome, strong, and wealthy. And he was a proud Muslim from Saudi Arabia, a country hated by the anti-Islam populist politician Geert Wilders, who had dominated public discourse in the Netherlands a great deal during this Dutch audience's life span. Speaking to the young Muslims in a way that their old-fashioned parents could not hope to fathom, Alzouman was a shining example of what a successful Muslim could be in a globalizing, contemporary world. He was proud of them, he said, because he knew that it was not always easy being Muslim in a non-Muslim land. In his eyes, they were not the pitiful children of migrants lost between worlds, walking the earth in confusion like headless chickens. They were pioneers of Islam who would create a contemporary story of Islam as a source of strength and honor, demanding universal respect through deeds rather than by begging for recognition. Being raised in an era of intense criticism, if not outright anti-Muslim racism, many of these youngsters had always been mere "allochthons"—within, but never truly part of, the Kingdom of the Netherlands. Misunderstood, unaccepted, and above all, too often sorely missing the encouragement, passion, and confidence that Alzouman convincingly displayed. He used his story, of chanting the Muslim call to prayer on the peak of Mount Everest "to call out Allah's name from the highest point on Earth and to pray where no other human had prayed before," as a metaphor for being someone in the world, someone courageous, successful, powerful.[2] This was a vision of Islam, and of what a believer could be and accomplish, that was very, very different from the everyday social reluctance to love and accept Dutch Muslims as equals. For a moment, the azan symbolized spiritual empowerment, not by going back to an era in which it was a victory cry, but through its connection to what Immanuel Kant defined as "the sublime."[3]

The indispensability of forms

Alzouman's performance on top of Mount Everest prompts a question that is of central importance to this book on amplified Islamic calls to prayer in the Netherlands. Did it make sense that this wanderer sang the azan out loud, even though he was not with a group of believers ready to perform the *salat*, the Islamic ritual prayer? And what if he had been all alone? Why should his inner faith manifest itself in sound in a place where the air is pure and undisturbed by the clamor of mankind? In the Netherlands, such a question betrays or harks back to a rigid Protestant style of thinking in which religious content is associated with the mind, conceived as a sealed inner space of cognition and associated with the social concept of the private, while religious form is separated and associated with being outside the mind and located in a social public. In such a spirit we could argue, as Kant did, that the essence of religion lies within the "invisible church" of the heart.[4] Such an interpretation would be in line with Islam, since God is repeatedly described in the Qur'an as the Knower of Human Hearts: "And We have already created man and know what his soul whispers to him, and We are closer to him than [his] jugular vein" (Qur'an 50:16).[5] This is comparable with Kant's *Herzenskündiger*, or one who knows the heart,[6] whom we cannot deceive by outward activities and appearances. What is the point of expressing piety through external means, Kant demanded, when all we truly need is the inner moral law, that is, the essence of religion? What are practices such as calling others to prayer and prostrating oneself to worship other than wishful thinking? "Even prayer," the great Enlightenment philosopher wrote, "is no more than a wish, inwardly uttered in the presence of a Searcher of the Heart."[7] From his pietist perspective, and with a conception of religion that resonates well with Protestant-influenced sentiments in the Netherlands, religion must limit itself to the limits of reason alone. The mediation of religion through forms—worshiping in a special building, chanting, praying, sacrificing, healing, dancing, and so forth, all the activities that anthropologists of religion find worth studying—become secondary at best and meaningless at worst. Although such a logic is clearly inspired by a Protestant history, it goes far beyond Protestantism, rejecting all claims to supernatural hearing, dividing immanence and transcendence as sharply as possible. In other words, the invisible "church of the heart" is also an inaudible one. A man who claims to speak to a transcendent deity or who claims that it speaks to him has not studied the proper limits of reason and, in some cases, as when a father believes that he must sacrifice his innocent son, should be considered insane. In this line of Enlightenment thinking, a man chanting the call to prayer on a dangerous mountain may well also be a madman. A cultural anthropology of religious experience, from this perspective, adds nothing to the knowledge of true religion. One does not need to seek out faraway peoples, nor climb great heights, to study religion. The result of such investigations, wrote Kant, "is one which, even without traveling to the mountains, everyone could have met with among his fellow citizens—indeed, yet closer to home, in his own heart."[8] But this was not true for those such as the mountain climber Alzouman or, even better, the Malaysian astronaut Sheikh Muszaphar Shukor, who heard the call to prayer in outer space:

> Everyone will experience a miracle in space. I heard a "call to prayer" in space. I actually heard the "call to prayer" in the Space Station. Other astronauts had no idea . . . but I physically heard the call. . . . [The call is not surprising] in space as you feel the presence and strength of God in every second. . . . I felt very close to God while in space.[9]

Shukor, who heard where there can be no sound, and Alzouman, who recited aloud where no one could hear, wondered like Kant about "the starry heavens above" and "the moral law within," but not quite in the same way.[10]

Even after the Enlightenment critique of religion, which unmasked religious voices as illusory (Schmidt 2000), hearing has remained fundamental to religious experiences in modernity. This *indispensability of forms*, propagated by anthropologist of religion Birgit Meyer (2012: 11), was anticipated in Kant's *Religion Within the Limits of Reason Alone*, where he suggested that the ideal Enlightened religion, a pure universal Christianity, requires "a total abandonment of the Judaism in which it originated" (Kant 2001: 156). He viewed the latter as too cultic, too concerned with external, public attachments such as rituals, specific clothing, and arbitrary rules. But despite his radical intent and critical analysis, Kant came to the conclusion that a visible church building, a material manifestation of religion, a mediation through forms, cannot be avoided: "A church which is the union in a moral community of many human beings of equally many dispositions, needs a *public* form of obligation, some ecclesiastical form that depends on experiential conditions and is intrinsically contingent and manifold" (Kant 2001: 138, 6:105). For believers all over the world, including Muslims, this is as plain as day. A religion "of pure religious faith" (Kant 2001: 138, 6:105) can in the end resemble historical Islam only remotely, regardless of believers' claims. Believers are engaged with both form and content, ritual and belief, the body *and* the mind, which are furthermore embedded in a community. Rather than adhering to Enlightenment iconoclasm, focusing on revealing the absurdities, insincerities, and illusions of religion, scholars of religion from various disciplines have recently renewed the interest in the senses and the materiality of religions, in an effort to better understand what is at stake for believers.[11] The point of this appreciation for religious aesthetics is "to study religion through the vector of practices, i.e. concrete acts that involve people, their bodies, things, pictures, texts, and other media through which religion becomes tangibly present" (Meyer 2012: 7) and to move "away from a mentalist understanding that locates experience in a silent interior toward one that places it in a body practically engaged with the world" (Hirschkind 2006: 29).[12]

The very notion of content as idea and form as merely a configuration of sensuous material which presents that essential idea, a view espoused most literally by Hegel, must be rejected.[13] But neither should form, as an antithesis to the Hegelian view, be promoted to the essence of religion. The ideal of a private, inner conviction should not, therefore, be replaced by a conception of a Muslim other as obsessed with ritual, praxis, and form. It would be a perverted, orientalist reversal to juxtapose Protestants, supposedly characterized by a focus on beliefs, that is, the mind,[14] with Muslims (or before them, Jews) stereotyped by a focus on rituals, that is, the body. The same can be said of equating a particular sensory dimension with a particular religious tradition. Relativist claims that the Western tradition has traditionally been focused on the rationalist eye, whereas non-Westerners have been more bound by the emotional and primitive ear, also need to be rejected. Protestants have been captivated by the ear, Muslims by the eye, and the other way around. We must always resist the simplistic reduction and association of a particular religious tradition with only one of the human senses, which is not only historically false but also creates a divided world of "us" and "them." We should instead aim for a multisensory interpretation. It is worth repeating that the indispensability of form entails that we take religious aesthetics seriously without excluding private, inner convictions or abstract theological principles. Muslims have, as a matter of fact, separated religious form from content, most famously in works by jurists, philosophers, and poets that predate the European Reformation.[15] To this day, it is well known among believers across the globe, and frequently asserted, that the Qur'an warns against insincerity, that is, the reproduction of religious form without cultivation of the proper religious mental contents: "Indeed, the hypocrites [think to] deceive Allah, but He is deceiving them. And when they stand for prayer, they stand lazily, showing [themselves to] the people and not remembering Allah except a little" (Qur'an 4:142). And to be absolutely clear: "Woe to those who pray [but] who are heedless of their prayer" (Qur'an 107:4–5). Such verses remind us of Kant's Enlightenment perspective, in which form or enforced obedience to ritual and law is regarded as insufficient to establish "a Kingdom of God on earth."[16] Likewise, if the ideal community of Muslim believers, the imagined *ummah*, is to be an ethical Islamic community, it cannot abandon ritual nor reduce its religion to mandatory praxis alone. As an anthropologist, I have to tread carefully here, because it is not my intention to define what Islam is *really* like. I only want to argue that, to different degrees, believers can and do distinguish religious content from ritual form, while the same or other believers may at other times refuse or simply be unable to do so. In this book, we encounter Muslims who say that they can separate the audible call to prayer from its spiritual meaning. They insist that their wish to amplify the azan, to consider this practice as of the highest importance, is not caused by an inability to separate religious form and content.

In any case, a strong and traditional consensus does exist among Muslims all over the world that at least some ritual practices are in fact essential. Calling to prayer using the human voice is one of these very important, ordinarily considered indispensable, practices. We read in a *hadith*[17] of Bukhari, widely considered to be one of the most reliable religious sources on the deeds and sayings of the Prophet, that even when one is without other believers, such as in a desert or, we may add, on top of a mountain, the call should be made out loud:

> Narrated Abdur-Rahman: Abu Sa'id al-Khudri told my father, "I see you liking sheep and the wilderness. So, whenever you are with your sheep or in the wilderness and you want to pronounce azan for the prayer raise your voice in doing so, for whoever hears the azan, whether a human being, a jinn [spirit/daemon] or any other creature, will be a witness for you on the Day of Resurrection." Abu Sa'id added, "I heard it [this narration] from Allah's Apostle." (translation by Muhsin Khan, Nr. 583)

The fundamental importance of the ear, hearing the Islamic call to prayer even when alone, is not surprising since it is a practice connected to the first two pillars (out of five) of Islam. The verses of the call contain the primary principle and first pillar of Islam, the *shahada* or bearing witness that there is no deity except God and that Muhammad is his Prophet. Because it is a call to prayer, or *salat*, it is also connected to the second pillar, namely the obligation to perform a ritual prayer five times a day. In addition, the very act of calling to prayer dates to the time of the Prophet Muhammad himself and is considered mandatory inside a mosque when Muslims gather to pray.[18] It is so essential that Muslims in countries as different as Morocco, Iran, and Indonesia pronounce the azan in a newborn baby's right ear. In Pakistan, the azan is even called into the right ear of foals that are brought up to parade in the Shi'ite 'Ashura processions as *Zoljaneh*, the horse of Imam Hussein (Frembgen 2012: 181). And if possible, a believer's dying words should be the last verse of the call to prayer: *la ilah illa Allah*, the proclamation that there is no deity but God.

Amplifying Islam

If the outward call to prayer is considered meaningful in solitude, its reach to a public outside, a community of believers, is even more highly recommended, indispensable, and widely practiced in Muslim-majority countries across the world. But whereas calling and praying on Mount Everest is the soul's summit of purity, and in that sense uncomplicated, things are quite different in our human world below, in the well-organized flat land of the Netherlands. Famous for turning sea into land, no less than a quarter of which is protected by dunes and dikes, the country is densely populated. Unlike France, the Netherlands is known, not for grand cathedrals and revolutionary fervor, but rather for iconoclasm, sober churches, and schisms. It was a seventeenth- and eighteenth-century bastion of religious toleration, but in the minimalist sense of allowing religious others to coexist and worship in clandestine fashion. During the nineteenth and twentieth centuries, Catholics slowly acquired freedoms and were granted permission to construct churches and organize a public presence, but their emancipation coincided with social segregation in so-called pillars. This book shows that these historical struggles over public worship have shaped, both culturally as well as constitutionally, ways of dealing with both visible and audible manifestations of Islam in the present. Despite the contemporary religious diversity of the Netherlands, today on a par with the most secularized nations of the world, can Muslims call to prayer out loud here? In the impure, messy, reality on the ground, the call does not lend itself to neat categorization qua form and content, or orthopraxy and orthodoxy. And, as a sound that travels inside and outside the Muslim house of worship, the *masjid* or mosque, but also neighboring homes, nor can it always be captured by a sharp distinction between private and public. Heard only now and then, if at all, by most Dutch citizens, the azan is as fleeting as it is thought provoking because it is not merely the call to prayer which is amplified but, in a way, Islam itself, questioning the limits of religious toleration and civic decency in the Netherlands. The title of this book, *Amplifying Islam in the European Soundscape*, therefore refers to the politics of Islamic soundscapes in a globalized Western world, to the *Islam of the Global West*.[19] This title should not mislead readers, however, to believe that the pronouncement of the Islamic call to prayer in Europe is a totally new or recent phenomenon, nor are the politics of regulating the sounds of those perceived as religious others. Whether or not the azan is "European" is in fact as old as, if not older than, the idea of Europe itself.

In 1311, for example, Pope Clement V decreed that Islamic calls to prayer, which could be heard in parts of contemporary Spain and Italy, should be generally prohibited in "Christian lands":

> It is an insult to the holy name and a disgrace to the Christian faith that in certain parts of the world subject to Christian princes . . . Saracens [i.e. Muslims] meet to adore the infidel Mahomet, loudly invoke and extol his name each day at certain hours from a high place, in the hearing of both Christians and Saracens, and there make public declarations in his honor. . . . These practices cannot be tolerated any further without displeasing the divine majesty. We therefore . . . strictly forbid such practices henceforth in Christian lands. (cited in Constable 2010: 74)

Besides complaints about the symbolic, territorial meanings associated with religious sounds, the late medieval period also reveals other parallels with the contemporary situation such as the thought that church bells can be compared to Islamic calls to prayer (Ibid.: 91). Today, these ideas return in the context of the globalization, diversification, and also standardization of European religious diversity. This context was shaped especially in the second half of the twentieth century, after the destruction of Dutch Judaism during the Second World War, when the Netherlands witnessed the arrival of postcolonial citizens from Suriname and Indonesia, unprecedented secularization, and the arrival of migrant laborers, refugees, and others, bringing together a great variety of religious experiences and practices. The desire to understand these continuing transformations has brought scholars of religion and globalization together.[20]

Religious globalization produces not only new landscapes but also soundscapes—a term coined by composer Raymond Murray Schafer (1977)—in places that are not intuitively associated with those sounds. Anthropologists have studied such contexts, opening up the "ethnographic ear" (Clifford 1986: 12) for the politics of hearing, including religious soundscapes.[21] Qualitative anthropological research is particularly well suited to interpreting sounds that acquire meanings through social practices. This is so because, with a little exaggeration, we could say that there are no noises at all, only interpreted sounds. The point here is not to "unmask" experiences of hearing as false or superficial, but to emphasize how the meanings of sounds are powerfully shaped by nonacoustic, social, and political factors. This is especially the case with amplifying Islam, given the loaded meanings attached to public forms of Islamic aesthetics that are contested all across the Global West. "The other offends the senses," writes Leigh Eric Schmidt (2000: 67). That sums up, in a nutshell, what the issue of the azan in the Netherlands is all about: a certain religious group is perceived as "other" and the sounds that this group makes are experienced as offensive by the (diverse) non-Muslim majority, hence the disputes over "noise pollution." On the other side, demanding the right to amplification and listening to the azan brings Muslims together. Other ethnographic accounts of the politics of the technologized azan usually dealing with loudspeakers, radio, and television also show that the azan is part of home and community-making strategies for local Muslims, whether in Singapore or London.[22] In the Netherlands too, the politics of amplifying Islam is a "politics of home" (Duyvendak 2011) and, as the azan is transformed from a "foreign" traditional practice into a contentious element in Dutch anxieties over national and cultural identities, part of the "perils of belonging" (Geschiere 2009).

In the Netherlands, loudspeakers for the azan have been in use since the 1980s, for example in The Hague,[23] but demands to amplify the call have increased since the 1990s and through the 2000s and the number of purpose-built mosques has risen in the same period. Together, Muslims in the Netherlands have around 450 mosques, but of these some 300 are housed in makeshift (as distinct from purpose-built) locations such as former schools (FORUM Verkenning 2012: 12). Half of all the mosques are run by Turkish Muslim organizations, almost 40 percent by Moroccans, and the remaining 10 percent have a Surinamese migration background. Less than 1 percent of Dutch mosques are owned or run by a different group.[24] It has been estimated that less than 10 percent of all Dutch mosques amplify the call to prayer, usually once a week on Friday afternoons but sometimes once or twice daily. Many mosques and Muslims report that if it could be done without a fuss, they would like to amplify the call, but just not at all costs.[25] By the time this book was finished, the azan could be heard in many small towns across the country, such as Middelburg, Deventer, and Zutphen, but also major cities like Amsterdam, Rotterdam, and The Hague.

While this research is mainly focused on the Dutch case, a transnational trend is discernible across North America and Western Europe where Muslim communities have begun to use loudspeakers for the azan more often. The call is amplified in Brooklyn[26] and is being considered in Ottawa.[27] In 2003, the call could be heard in Granada for the first time in half a millennium.[28] Loudspeakers were utilized for the first time in Stockholm as recently as 2013.[29] Though I have not heard of azan amplification in France, where praying in the street has been officially banned since 2011, the television channel La Locale broadcast the azan for the holy month of Ramadan in 2013.[30] So did the much more popular British Channel 4, which ran a specially produced azan video for the same occasion.[31] To protest anti-Muslim sentiments, Swiss artist Johannes Gees came up with a provocative "sound bomb" performance entitled *Salat* (prayer) in 2007, broadcasting the azan through loudspeakers and megaphones from churches in Bern and Zurich but also in the Alpstein, a popular, romanticized part of the Swiss Alps.[32] The toxic politics of xenophobia prevailed, however, and after a controversial referendum Switzerland went so far as to ban minaret construction in 2009. A year later, Dutch artist Jonas Staal had a megaphone installed on the roof of the Centraal Museum in Utrecht, which called for prayer five times a day for a period of three months, not to propagate the azan but to question anti-Muslim sentiments across the West.[33] Resistance to the azan by non-Muslim residents is indeed a general phenomenon. In her introduction to *Making Muslim Space in North America and Europe*, Barbara Metcalf already noted the absence of Islamic sounds (1996: 8). For example, the Queens Muslim Center in New York City received permission to construct minarets and domes but not to amplify the call to prayer, "out of deference to the secular authorities" (Slyomovics in Metcalf 1996: 210).

I hasten to add that complaining about noisy Islam is not an exclusively Western phenomenon. That is another reason why we must reconceptualize debates over the azan in Europe and North America as part of a Global West. In India, for example, the call to prayer has been criticized for fostering "communal tension."[34] In Egypt, "Articles in secularly oriented newspapers routinely complain about the 'assault on the ears' produced by mosque loudspeakers and cassette recorders, perceived as the violent imposition of religious discourse onto the nonreligious space of public life" (Hirschkind 2006: 125). In Iran, reports of emptying mosques are accompanied by the observation that the call to prayer is heard less often "because people complain about the noise."[35] In Morocco, a similar battle for the meaning of Islamic soundscapes is taking place, where debates over loudspeakers are not merely about noise but about ideas concerning the future public presence of religion in the country. For example, Olivier Roy, the well-known scholar of Islam, has said that recent uproar over the Moroccan azan is tied to a web of complex social relations including class inequality, divisions between liberals and conservatives, and transnational Islamic movements.[36] In a way that recalls the Dutch fear of an encroaching public Islam, but within an evidently wholly different nexus of power relations, there have been calls in Morocco to ban the amplified azan "on the grounds that they disturb residents in the neighboring areas not only because of the sound, but also owing to the ideas they spread." Even though loudspeakers for the azan have become much louder than in the past, and in that sense represent a rather recent practice, critics of "modernist" azan opponents respond that silencing the azan is equal to "strip[ping] Morocco of its Islamic identity."[37]

Whereas the amplified azan dominates Istanbul via the city's three thousand mosques, it is just as consistently present—but much softer—in Isfahan. To Muslim ears, the reciting style of a muezzin[38] in Fez differs in tone and feeling from one in Tunis. And while Cairo is famous for a cacophony of competing calls to prayer, in Kuala Lumpur a single azan covers the shopping district at the iconic Petronas Twin Towers. Everywhere in Muslim skyscraper cities, loudspeakers have allowed mosques to catch up or even compete with the everyday noisiness of urban life. Some religious scholars have historically disputed amplifying the call by loudspeakers as an inauthentic innovation, for example in Pakistan (Khan 2011), but in a noisy postindustrial world it has become common Islamic practice. Less noisy solutions are, however, widely used in all Muslim-majority countries. Calls to prayer can be accessed on television, radio, private azan clocks, and—how could it be otherwise—handy applications on smartphones connected to the internet. Complaints about loudspeakers, which were introduced all over Muslim-majority countries in the twentieth century, are most often about the early morning call in countries as diverse as Morocco, Turkey, and Indonesia. In the West, however, the azan is—as far as I know—never amplified in the morning or very late in the evening.

Religion and equal rights to the city

As in other parts of the world, stories about complaints of noise pollution alone give a misleading impression of how Western Muslims were—and still are—transforming their homelands, and are assisted by their governments in that process. As with resistance to Islamic aesthetics, accommodation is a transnational phenomenon. We read in Metcalf's 1996 volume that the East London Mosque was permitted to broadcast calls to prayer, which sparked "public debate about 'noise pollution' when local non-Muslim residents began to protest" (Eade in Metcalf 1996: 223). More recently, not only in Boston, but also in small towns such as Hamtramck (near Detroit), Muslims have successfully negotiated for the right to broadcast the azan (Perkins 2010 and 2015; Weiner 2014), while Duke University's decision to reverse its standpoint to allow the call from a campus chapel tower sparked a heated controversy.[39] In the Netherlands, mosques made national headlines in 2013 when their right to amplify the azan on a daily basis was (re)affirmed by local authorities after non-Muslims complained.

There is no doubt that the positive accommodation of Muslim aesthetics is not without difficulties and this book shows many instances of bitterness and misunderstanding. This should not surprise us, since feelings of home are determined by strong and competing emotions such as nostalgia—elder Muslims of Turkish origin, for example, feel nostalgic for the azan in their country of birth, whereas elder non-Muslim Dutch residents may feel nostalgic for their small town as it was in the not yet so pervasively global past. In this context, xenophobic politicians such as Geert Wilders mobilize the idea of a clash of so-called "Muslim" and "Judeo-Christian" civilizations against the public presence of Islam in the Netherlands. Criticizing this ideological opposition is not to say that European Muslim and Christian rule, for example in medieval Spain, never involved silencing each other's religious practices (Constable 2010). But if one were to claim that, today, Islam cannot "fit" in "Christian Europe," or that "the West" singularly oppresses "Muslims," viewing these as incommensurable entities, it would grossly ignore historical and present complexities and revive both xenophobic and xenophile versions of Samuel Huntington's widely criticized clash of civilizations thesis.

Instead of a simple clash, the story of the azan in the Netherlands is about the resistance to public expressions of Islam and hesitance in accepting the wishes of Muslim citizens, but, so far, also a positive account of slow, pragmatic accommodation. Rather than a process toward banning these sounds, as in late medieval Spain (this too did not occur overnight) the Dutch norm today is an increase in amplification of the azan. In this context, where Muslims have often faced the critical question of why they insist on amplifying the azan and why they cannot simply keep their religion to themselves, the azan has acquired an additional meaning alongside its traditional religious one, as a symbol and mediator of the status of Muslims as equal citizens. Like other contested practices, such as male circumcision and the right to ritual slaughter, the azan has sometimes come to stand for equal rights. As will become clear in this book, Dutch Muslims successfully demand azan amplification based on strict legal notions of equality rather than on subtler ideas about accommodating otherness, which are poorly developed in the Netherlands in comparison with the United States.

In the Netherlands, as in the United States, the right to broadcast the azan is constitutionally protected. But from a secular cultural perspective informed by Dutch-Protestant and Catholic memories, the azan can be experienced as agitating. It recalls relatively recent stories like those of Maria, a senior citizen from the picturesque village of Ouderkerk aan de Amstel, who told me about Catholic priests knocking on her door to ask if and when the family would welcome a new child. "Two or three children were not enough! And they did their best to interfere with our lives!" she often exclaimed with great indignation. Although for years Maria had no or barely any contact with Dutch Muslims, she imagined that they too could interfere with her family's life. "Religion should stay behind the door of one's home" was a motto that she defended vigorously and in a tone that implied this was age-old wisdom. But in fact such particular conceptions of the proper place of religion have always been under pressure in the history of the Dutch Republic (1588–1795) and the Kingdom of the Netherlands (since 1815). The presence of others, especially of Muslims, has slowly shifted such thinking on religious manifestations, not only about the present but also to reinterpret the past. In an era of both rapid secularization as well as the flourishing of migrant churches and mosques, purpose-built Hindu *mandirs*, and Buddhist temples, the many voices that come together enable a rethinking of secularism, usually referred to in the Netherlands as the "separation of church and state" (*scheiding van kerk en staat*).

Over the years, I myself have witnessed a shift toward questioning the assumed limits of secularism and public religion among ordinary citizens, but also among secular intellectuals who have become more sensitive to religious citizens' rights to public expression. An instance that comes to mind is a meeting in 2006 in a house near the Oudemanhuispoort, part of the University of Amsterdam's campus and a bastion of its secular left intelligentsia. A host of Dutch academics and intellectuals had gathered to discuss a book in a private, homely atmosphere. Fouad Laroui was presenting his book *De l'islamisme: Une réfutation personnelle du totalitarisme religieux*, which had been translated into Dutch (2006). One of

Laroui's key arguments was that a religion that goes public or infringes on the rights of others to be left alone is dangerous and should be avoided. His tone and critique of public religion was nicely summed up in a review article in *Vrij Nederland*, an influential Dutch magazine:

> Against everybody who calls himself Muslim, or Catholic, or believer, I say: please keep it to yourself and the world will become a better place. My whole life I have never answered personal questions about what I believe or don't believe. Twenty years before I read Wittgenstein, I already knew that you don't have to, shouldn't or can [even if you wanted to; *niet moet, mag of kán*] talk about that.[40] I ask everyone: please, I don't want to know anything about your religion, it does not concern us, do not shout [your beliefs] from the rooftops. That is a personal matter and that is how the Netherlands became the Netherlands. I don't care if people pray five times a day. I wish for them all the freedom of the world. But if one demands of others to do things just as they, then it has to be clear that Islamists do not have that right. That has nothing to do any more with faith, but with decency among citizens.[41] [my translation]

The ideal that religion should be private and stay within the home, as Laroui defended, and that a religion that is concerned with form and ritual is backward, remains one of the dominant and recurring responses to religious others. On the other hand, Laroui's French-sounding ideas were received critically by several of his likeminded secular listeners, including myself. For some decades now, old-fashioned critiques of and sentiments surrounding highly ritualized religion, which historically developed in Europe as a reaction to the pompousness of the Catholic Church, have been changing. Today, the times in which secular intellectuals could be *a priori* expected to wish religions away from the streets and the public sphere have passed. Laroui asked religious citizens to "leave religion behind the home door," but others present, me included, objected that this was simply not possible. It was a secularist wish, not an empirical possibility. The amplified call to prayer in the Netherlands is de facto actually all about claiming public space by shouting one's beliefs from the rooftops.[42] The average Dutch-Muslim citizen rarely seeks an essence of religion in a way, if at all, that sharply excludes such traditions of public worship. To defend his position, Laroui had referred, for example, to Spinoza's normative concept of religion as essentially about universal ethics, an idea that he shared on a highly abstracted level with thinkers as different as Immanuel Kant and Mahatma Gandhi.[43] But such conceptions of religion are insensitive to the variety of ways in which people actually practice and experience their religion. Such great ideals of political philosophy must reckon with empirical analysis, in this case at the very least with the insights of historians, legal scholars, and anthropologists on the dynamics of contemporary religiosity. For a Muslim who may want to amplify the call to prayer or a Christian who wishes to organize a procession in the streets, keeping religion behind closed doors is a form of suppression, whereas for nonreligious or nonpracticing individuals such as myself and Laroui, being asked on the street why I was eating or being called on the telephone to ask whether he was fasting during Ramadan was a breach, albeit a mild one, of the right to be left alone, a cornerstone of liberal ethics. These boundaries, then, needed to be critically reexamined in a way that did justice to both sides. Banning religions from the city, I and others thought, could not be a solution to this predicament.

After key publications such as Jose Casanova's *Public Religions in the Modern World*, in which he argued that the modern process of secularization did not have to contradict the de-privatization of religion in contemporary contexts (Casanova 1994, 2009),[44] debates on expanding space for religious discourse in the public sphere[45] have, since the 1990s, been accompanied by an academic concern for the study of public forms of religious organization and worship in urban settings. This shift is clearly traceable in the field of social and cultural geography, among others, and is part of a broader, and normative, conversation about rethinking religion and equal rights to the city.[46] By 2010, when I began research for this book, studying the spatial manifestations of Islam in the West had become increasingly relevant. Minarets had just been banned in Switzerland's highly controversial referendum (Stüssi 2008; Mayer 2011), in New York City the so-called Ground Zero Mosque controversy sparked protest and debate (e.g., Nussbaum 2012), while in Rotterdam the Essalam Mosque opened after years of disagreement, erroneously hyped in Dutch media as the "biggest mosque of Europe" and epitomized by the successful leader of the Party for Freedom, Geert Wilders, as a "palace of hatred" (Tamimi Arab 2013a). As these anti-Muslim sentiments grew stronger, so did the steady academic interest in European mosque construction.[47]

A review of the literature on mosque construction in the Netherlands shows that, especially from the 1990s onward, more and more purpose-built, and therefore visible, mosques have been constructed. This development has attracted the attention of art historians, who have increasingly included the mosques of Europe and North America in art historical narratives of Islamic architecture (e.g., Frishman and Khan 2002). But although mosques may be located "in" Europe, according to critiques such as Talal Asad's (2003) they are not truly conceived as being "of" Europe: not truly accepted by wider society, controlled and unfairly regulated by government, and very often protested and discriminated against. Indeed, as mosques became "un-sheltered" and more visible, they also became widely unwanted in the West (Cesari 2005).

Simultaneously, however, with the benefit of hindsight, early accounts of the geography of the Islamic religion in the Netherlands (such as Doomernik 1991) now reveal a consistent accommodation process. Nico Landman's book *Van mat tot minaret: De institutionalisering van de Islam in Nederland* (from prayer rug to minaret: the institutionalization of Islam in the Netherlands) contains the most important research done in the 1980s and early 1990s. "The time that Islamic guestworkers rolled out their prayer rugs in factory halls lies far behind us," Landman wrote in his conclusion. And he added:

> Slowly, the realization that most immigrants will stay permanently in The Netherlands has settled in. Their religious organizations as well are beyond their temporary phase. The minarets arising here and there in the townscape symbolize that Islam is becoming one of the established religions of the Netherlands. (Landman 1992: 348)

Metcalf's 1996 volume showed, a few years later, that Landman's observation was connected to a wider, inter- and transnational development. Much of the literature on mosque construction that was produced thereafter is normatively loaded, implicitly insisting on the right of Muslims to construct their mosques, and focuses on the difficulties worshippers faced. Criticizing and mapping the production of marginal Islamic spaces, particularly in relation to mosque construction in the West, has persisted as an academic concern (e.g., Schinkel 2009, Kuppinger 2010a and 2010b). In the spirit of Landman's work, I have taken note of positive mosque construction developments as well (e.g., Tamimi Arab 2013b), and do so in this book with regard to the amplified azan.

The intellectual currents described above—empirically and normatively cautious and less dogmatically anticlerical than before—have coalesced in a veritable boom in studies of the complexity of what is often called political or constitutional secularism, that is, the manifold ways the state governs and regulates religion.[48] Following Bowen et al. (2014), in this book secularism is investigated from the perspective of actual practices of regulating religion on different levels such as media, law, and policy, and municipal interactions with locals. Although I aim to give an ethnographic account of what can be called the Dutch national model of secularism, the ways in which different countries handle religious diversity partly overlap, depending on the practices under question, the sociological level that is analyzed or the (socio-)logic of a particular institution (schools, armies, and hospitals, to name some). That is why I inevitably build on and refer to secularism as it is practiced (or not) in other countries as well.

Overview

My analysis of "Amplifying Islam" is divided into four chapters followed by an epilogue on religious tolerance. The first two chapters cover contemporary religious pluralism and its history in the Netherlands. The primary concern in these chapters is first to show the importance and specificity of the material manifestation of Islam as sound, and then to embed the call to prayer in a broader history of Dutch religious pluralism.

Chapter 1, "'A Minaret of Light': Transducing the Azan?," deals with the question of why the azan has to be amplified with loudspeakers and emphasizes the particular importance of hearing—rather than seeing—in the search for alternatives that are less disturbing or more acceptable for those who are not used to a Muslim call or would not like to get used to it.[49] The remarkable architectural proposals to use light signals instead of loudspeakers are discussed as a public alternative. The association of light with inaudible spirituality is investigated from the perspective of mosque aesthetics negotiations by describing these light-azan proposals and then analyzing the extent to which they have been actually adopted. I argue that aesthetic technologies of ordering physical spaces, in this case a transduction of sound into light, but also the use of glass in mosque architecture, can regulate the extent and the quality of Muslims' presence in European cities. Whether the medium of light can faithfully convey the human voice, however, is bound with questions of religious authority.

Having introduced the question of the azan in the Netherlands and having begun discussing the aesthetics of religious pluralism, Chapter 2, "A History of Public Worship: From Procession Prohibition to Amplified Azan," takes the reader deeper into the Netherlands's religious past and shows how the azan is embedded in a longer history of religious pluralism. Taking two contested public rituals as case studies—the Catholic procession and the amplified Muslim call to prayer—I show that the historical trajectories of Dutch Catholics and Muslims became explicitly connected to one another in a constitutional change that signaled a shift from a Protestant hegemony to a more pluralist model of governance of religions. The 1980s Public Manifestations Act ended the so-called Procession Prohibition of the nineteenth century, thus emancipating public Catholic practices, and simultaneously allowed the use of loudspeakers for the Muslim call to prayer and other forms of audible public worship. The chapter ends by documenting how mosques in various cities and towns in the Netherlands each began broadcasting the call to prayer for the first time.

The third and fourth chapters move to the main issue of this book, namely amplification of the azan with loudspeakers today. Chapter 3, "Conflicting Secularisms: Nativism and the Constitutional Protection of the Azan," describes the contemporary political spectrum of Dutch resistance against the use of loudspeakers for the azan, from the liberal People's Party for Freedom and Democracy to the orthodox Calvinist Reformed Political Party. Criticizing Talal Asad's influential conceptualization of "secularism," which I have found to be too expansive and unidirectional in terms of analyzing the power relation between the secular and the religious as well as insufficiently based on empirical evidence, the chapter shows that observable connections between constitutional secularism and governance of religious diversity on the one side, and a culturalist secularism that excludes Muslim rights to public worship on the other, are shown to be far from straightforward and in tension with one another. Rather than formulating a negative critique of "secularism," I attempt to show how the Netherlands deals with the particular question of amplifying the azan with the varieties of secularism and practices of governing religions in mind.

Chapter 4, "Regulating Nostalgias: Azan Negotiations in a Dutch Town," departs from the domains of law and policy and political parties and delves into the ethnography of a single case of local mosque negotiations for the azan. In 2012, the Turkish Center Mosque in the small city of Deventer in the eastern province of Overijssel expressed its wish for a daily azan. This resulted in a series of tense meetings and negotiations that lasted more than a year. The chapter provides data for understanding how an abstract concept such as "constitutional secularism," a context-specific mode of regulating religion, actually works in the field. In actual practice this term, and the more popular Dutch expression of the separation of church and state (which is absent in the Netherlands Constitution), was either never used or barely mentioned by respondents. I describe how the municipality, mosque, and protesting neighborhood residents interacted to finally reach a consensus. The chapter is not in the first instance concerned with political party labels of left and right, because that distinction can give us a simplified image of both Dutch opposition and practices of accommodating Islam. This chapter describes the desire for the azan as a kind of nostalgia as well as a demand for cultural recognition, while resistance to the azan, often nativist in character, was equally accompanied by nostalgia for a lost home in situ. Opponents experienced the azan as noise pollution, as sound out of place. The azan is therefore analyzed as a case of "defilement" of native local space on the one hand, and as a homemaking strategy on the other.

Based on the findings gathered in this book, I suggest in the Epilogue that a sober, minimalist conception and practice of tolerance is necessary for a just handling of the future of religious pluralism. While during some unique events the azan has been amplified in churches to promote mutual respect and interfaith understanding, such strategies can only complement but not supersede what is found in everyday life. In the Netherlands, tolerance legitimized by strictly equal rights, granted by benign forms of secularism, is more decisive in the actual accommodation process of the azan than utopian conceptions of living in harmony with difference.

"A Minaret of Light": Transducing the Azan?

It is He who made for you the night to rest therein and the day, giving sight.
Indeed in that are signs for a people who listen.

Qur'an, Surat Yunus 10:67

***

The idea that the truth of religion must be heard, that truth consists of the response of believers to a call, is fundamental to religions such as Christianity and Islam. Having faith means adhering to the truth of the call, and this truth is a matter of trust or submission, of being true to the call. The Islamic call to prayer, the azan, is a practical way of calling believers, but it can also be understood as a spiritual metaphor for the turn and change in orientation that takes place in the believer's soul. This reorientation of the soul toward a transcendent good—Muslims take great pride in emphasizing that Islam teaches monotheism in the strictest sense possible—is reminiscent of Plato's account in the *Republic* of the turning (*periakteon*) of the soul toward the good. The Platonic metaphor for the reorientation of the soul presupposes a body that must turn to see a kind of bright light or a lantern (*phanos*) (518c). Similarly, the Qur'an repeatedly demands that its believers both listen to divine words and bear witness to a divine truth. Studies of actual ritual practice, however, reveal that hearing cannot be so easily conflated with seeing (Erlmann 2004). In this chapter, I examine the importance of the ear by discussing the physical transduction[1] of the Islamic call to prayer, from sound to light, in a European context. Even though it can be said to be a marginal development in European Islamic architecture, the proposal to use light signals instead of loudspeakers for the azan reveals the fundamental issues at stake: European Muslims would like to amplify their call to prayer, what does this mean and entail, and what are the options on the table?

The same sound can have multiple meanings that are worlds apart depending on the listener, in a metaphysical sense but also of the social and the political. The emergence of the amplified Islamic call to prayer in European countries is bringing hidden sentiments to the fore and creating new "soundmarks" which, like landmarks, demarcate emotional boundaries for distinct communities but do so aurally rather than visually (cf. Weiner 2014: 163). According to a Dutch Muslim interviewed by a local newspaper, the problem is that "for [a believer] the call can sound like streaming water, whereas I can imagine that for local non-Muslims it can be like a cannon."[2] This divergence of opinion and experience is part and parcel of the *fact of pluralism*, the (historical) *a priori* condition and product of constitutional liberal democracy (Rawls 1987). In an age of globalization, religious pluralism is a "permanent feature of the public culture of modern democracies," wrote John Rawls, and only "the oppressive use of state power" (1987: 4) can, or can attempt to, undo this condition. It is not only reasonable to assume pluralism, but pluralism itself is reasonable, the outcome of the myriad life stories of persons and groups in contemporary society. As a political principle, reasonable pluralism only requires citizens to be able to relativize their own position, practices, and beliefs, but does not go so far as to require citizens to regress into metaphysical relativism. How then should people deal with religious pluralism in practice, especially if, on the basis of their backgrounds, different individuals and groups can legitimately disagree over such matters as whether or not listening to the azan is agreeable? One way is to limit or change the nature of pluralism in public life, to search for alternatives that can ameliorate agonistic relations. Of the many questions I was asked during my fieldwork, one of the most recurrent was whether Muslims in the Netherlands could use an alternative to amplifying the call to prayer. "Can't they just use a watch?" is still a frequent response among azan opponents, but also among people who have not given the meaning of religious sounds in urban settings much thought. As I will show, alternatives to the use of loudspeakers for the Muslim call to prayer are limited in their success.

In order to situate the demand for the amplified azan in the Dutch context, we need to grasp the issues of pluralism and material religion and their history in the Netherlands, which form the topic of this chapter and the next. Before looking at the cultural history of visible and audible expressions of religious pluralism in Chapter 2, this chapter expounds the contemporary situation by focusing on the thought-provoking attempt in the Netherlands to transduce the call into light, precisely because sound can be experienced as intrusive. This idea has come up in response to European discrimination or ambivalence toward Islamic aesthetics; Muslims and involved non-Muslims such as architects and local officials are adapting to find solutions to the strained relation between Islam and Dutch society. It shows that we need to pay attention not only to aesthetic formations (Meyer 2009; see Introduction) to understand how European societies are dealing with religious pluralism, but also to attempts to switch between different media—and thus bodily senses—by aesthetic transductions.

Below, I will begin with a brief review of the anthropology of the technologized azan and its relation to globalization and religious innovation. I then explain how the idea of a light-azan originated in the context of European debates about Islam. This, however, raised questions of religious dogma among European Muslims. What is the place of aesthetics, sound, and innovation within Islam itself? Are alternatives such as the light-azan acceptable to Muslim scholars and everyday worshippers? Finally, I end this chapter with a discussion of the extent to which the light-azan has been adopted and associated with inaudible spirituality, and conclude that the aesthetic transduction of the azan is mainly a "spiritualizing strategy" (cf. Margry 2000: 393–94; Chapter 2), a creative attempt to discipline Islam into publicly accepted forms of piety.

Globalization and the technologized azan

The broad term *globalization* encapsulates both migration flows and modern technological advancement, both of which have impacted the call to prayer. Globalization not only transforms how we relate to our time, it also changes our perceptions of space (Anderson 2006: xiv; cf. Robertson 1995). Thanks to the variety of global flows, today new multi- and trans-ethnic religious spaces have emerged so that traditional "religioscapes" intersect and cross with each other in unprecedented ways. The concept of the religioscape,[3] building on Arjun Appadurai's original intention to theoretically dissect the impact of globalization on culture, provides an approach to some key questions: what do we mean by the adjective cultural in our time, why is the noun culture misleading in the way it posits culture as something fixed, and how does religious pluralism manifest itself in localities in the present time? By using the metaphor of "scapes," this approach automatically leads to the aesthetics of globalization, expressed in changing land-, sound-, and smellscapes. Thus, amplifying Islamic calls to prayer in European countries where the practice is still widely associated with "the East" challenges how "the West" is conceived of today.

Most studies on technologized religious sounds, however, primarily focus on the impact of modernity as technological advancement, for example how new technologies can reduce the meaning of calls to prayer to a practical function. American churches faced such issues when city clocks and pocket watches were introduced, making church bells appear pointless and at best nostalgic (Weiner 2014: 55). In a premodern world that was much quieter than our globalized one, church bells dominated city soundscapes as much as church towers dominated the skyline. As cities became noisy and industrialized, the meaning of church bells changed dramatically. The great Dutch cultural historian Johan Huizinga contrasted modernity's clamor with the Middle Ages' silence. In *The Waning of the Middle Ages*, he wrote:

> The contrast between silence and sound, darkness and light, like that between summer and winter, was more strongly marked than it is in our lives. The modern town hardly knows silence or darkness in their purity, nor the effect of a solitary light or a single distant cry. . . . [In the Middle Ages] One sound rose ceaselessly above the noises of busy life and lifted all things unto a sphere of order and serenity: the sound of bells. The bells were in daily life like good spirits, which by their familiar voices, now called upon the citizens to mourn and now to rejoice, now warned them of danger, now exhorted them to piety. They were known by their names: big Jacqueline, or the bell Roland. Every one knew the difference in meaning of the various ways of ringing. However continuous the ringing of the bells, people would seem not to have become blunted to the effect of their sound. (Huizinga 1924: 2)

The religious ambition to amplify sounds beyond bells, however, is an old wish. As early as the seventeenth century, the Jesuit Athanasius Kircher "experimented with mammoth speaking trumpets to beckon devotees from the surrounding countryside to a hilltop shrine" (Schmidt 2000: 107). In Islam too, amplification has existed prior to the invention of the loudspeaker. The great Shah Mosque of Isfahan, currently known as the Imam Mosque, found an impressive architectural solution to amplifying the call: when standing directly under its dome, the human voice echoes far beyond it, making even very subtle sounds audible to a public audience. The reach of these solutions was, however, limited until, in the twentieth century, the dream of amplifying religious calls became a technological reality. In 1934, a Dutch newspaper reported how King Ibn Saud of Saudi Arabia established a radio broadcasting of the call to prayer: "Believers in the entire world will be henceforth called to prayer from the microphone."[4]

Technological innovation not only amplified but also changed the meaning of religious sounds. For instance, in the nineteenth century, it became possible to produce bells that sounded exactly alike; in a similar way, in Egypt, before the fall of Mubarak in 2011, there were plans to introduce one master call to prayer for the entire city of Cairo through the use of radio and loudspeakers. In such cases, aural homogenization can shift power from religious organizations to the regulatory powers of the modern state. The transition to modernity has therefore often implied a fundamental shift from "qualitative time" toward the homogeneous, "quantitative time" of the modern state (Corbin 1998: 110). From such a perspective in which time is nothing more than desacralized measured time, calls to prayer can sound not only *out of place* (Chapter 4) but also *out of time* (Chapter 2). Alain Corbin notes, for instance, that French clergy in the nineteenth-century countryside were suspicious of private clocks. They worried that the profane private clock would challenge the church's monopoly on regulating time through bells and have a negative impact on the public community of worshippers and, indeed, on the power of the Catholic Church.

Similarly, contemporary Muslim scholars are ambivalent toward the suggestion that private smartphone applications and other innovations can replace the public call to prayer and thus make the traditional call appear old fashioned. The move toward quantitative time implies both a privatization and a disciplining of Muslim ritual practice to make it adhere to standards that a nonreligious society may want to respect, rather than engaging with the way in which a Muslim minority in that society would like to practice their religion, namely in public. The state regulation of amplified calls to prayer is one way of determining the extent to which a religious community is publicly present. When a prohibition is in place, as in contemporary Singapore, listening to the call to prayer at home via the radio can "reunite each member of the Islamic community and create an abstract communal Islamic space without the encroachment of non-Islamic social spaces" (Lee 1999: 94). Islamic sounds have indeed been significantly recreated in private settings across the world, for example with digital azan clocks, which are often shaped like a miniature mosque and can set the time for the five daily prayers (Metcalf 1996: 8), or with smartphone applications that call to prayer and often reproduce mosque architectural iconography. On the other hand, Muslim scholars have been ambivalent about technological innovation for public calls to prayer. In Pakistan, for example, the introduction of loudspeakers in the twentieth century prompted debates on the question of whether loudspeakers could authentically reproduce the human voice (Khan 2011).

In our case study, the question of authenticity returns, although the idea of a light-azan deviates from the studies mentioned above because it is a European proposal to use *transduction* as a "translation" of the azan from sound to light rather than merely reproducing sound in private contexts. We will see that the proposal for a light-azan is part and parcel of a cosmopolitan and avant-garde development in Islamic architecture. The sources from which architects and their patrons draw inspiration for mosque proposals in the Netherlands have many local as well as transnational connections. By studying the light-azan, we also get a glimpse of the volatile nature of the aesthetic formations of globalization. Scholars of globalization have pointed out its chaotic, contingent nature, following no single line and resulting in social constructions that are strongly dependent on the many perspectives and interests of involved groups (Casanova 1994; Appadurai 1996; Beyer 2006). As Peter Beyer puts it, "The development of the religious system is not the outcome of some inevitable evolutionary process, but rather something historically arbitrary, constructed, and in that sense even odd" (Beyer 2006: 115). The light-azan is one of those odd, unexpected outcomes of the volatile process of globalization.

The idea of a light-azan

The azan has been heard in the streets of the Netherlands since the 1980s (the early history of the Dutch azan is described in Chapter 2). Even though some mosques in cities and small towns have amplified their call to prayer for about three decades, most mosques refrain from doing so or do so only once a week. Because the volume is usually limited, so that it is audible only in the immediate surroundings, the majority of Dutch citizens rarely hear the azan. One of the mosques that does amplify the call is the An Nasr Mosque in Rotterdam, visited primarily by Moroccan-Dutch Muslims. The building was originally constructed as a Protestant church, but because of rapid and enduring "de-churching" (*ontkerkelijking*) after the Second World War, it is now a mosque and broadcasts the call to prayer on Friday afternoons. As with most mosques in the Netherlands, the building is only recognizable as a Muslim house of worship thanks to an entrance sign in Arabic, which is decorated with the shapes of a dome and minaret, and through the people who gather there and look stereotypically "Muslim." But the amplified call to prayer proclaims the existence of the mosque in a way that is often experienced as much more pervasive than its visual characteristics (Chapter 4).

The environment is lively, with people of different backgrounds continuously passing by on foot, on bikes, and in cars. There are veiled women who just went shopping, young Moroccan-Dutch boys wearing jeans and caps, and men wearing *djellabas*. A blond-haired woman walks alongside the mosque as the muezzin, the one who recites the azan, continues to call loudly, *hayya 'ala 's-salat*, "hurry to prayer"; *hayya 'ala 'l-falah*, "hurry to salvation"; *la ilaha illa Allah*, "there is no deity but God." Adolescent schoolchildren, wearing heavy rucksacks filled with schoolbooks, are crossing the street. A woman wearing a black veil that covers her hair and chest is cycling and takes a turn in the bike lane. A brown-skinned woman, perhaps originally from Suriname or the Dutch Antilles, passes by. Everyone is moving as if they cannot hear the call to prayer. They do not appear to be disturbed by its amplification.

And yet, non-Muslims in Rotterdam have protested mosque constructions as well as the amplified call to prayer. The protests are against the call *an sich* and not because one dislikes the voice or style of the muezzin, which is one of the responses among skeptical Muslims and non-Muslims from Muslim-majority countries. International students from Iran, for example, expressed the view that Moroccan-Dutch muezzins did not perform well. A Tunisian-Dutch Muslim said that he thought the Moroccan call was "aggressive," which was not far from the judgment of a Moroccan-Dutch Muslim who described the Moroccan call as "severe and manly, without too many ornaments such as the Turkish and Iranian versions [have]."[5] There were often complaints about the poor quality of the loudspeakers too. The same students from Iran also remarked, "Of course the Dutch don't like the call when the loudspeakers make screeching sounds." However, conversations in Dutch about the call with people who did not grow up in a similar acoustic context usually do not delve into these subtleties.

A few Dutch and English comments to a YouTube post about the An Nasr Mosque's amplified call give us an impression of the anxieties that the call arouses: "Is that allowed like that, blaring like that? This isn't normal!" Someone else asked, "How could we have ever let this happen to our country!" There were also those who defended the call, but most comments in Dutch were negative, some even threatening the mosque. During my fieldwork in 2012, over 50 percent of four million individuals who voted in a national election poll agreed with the statement, proposed by the Party for Freedom (PVV, *Partij Voor de Vrijheid*), that "the construction of new mosques must stop."[6] Earlier, in 2010, the PVV's leader protested the construction of "megamosques" and "palaces of hatred" (Tamimi Arab 2013a). The PVV came out of the 2012 elections as the nation's third largest party, with one and a half million votes (out of roughly ten million). The winner of the elections was the People's Party for Freedom and Democracy, or Liberal Party (VVD, *Volkspartij voor Vrijheid en Democratie*), which appointed Henk Kamp, who previously served as Minister of Defense and

Minister of Social Affairs and Employment, as the Minister of Economic Affairs. Earlier, in 2007, Kamp had suggested that the Muslim call to prayer should be banned because it was not part of the cultural heritage of the Netherlands (Chapter 3).[7] Such electoral outcomes resonate with my fieldwork observation that both mosques and the amplified azan are widely unwanted among non-Muslim Dutch citizens (as I will discuss in Chapter 4).

In another district of the city, Rotterdam-South, stands the Essalam Mosque (Figure 1). The mosque, which opened in 2010, follows a conventional dome and minaret plan. With a height of 50 meters, the two minarets are the highest in the Netherlands, but the mosque's call to prayer can only be heard inside. Ibrahim, a middle-aged man who is a regular at the mosque, said that it is right that the

Figure 1 Molenaar & Van Winden architects. The Essalam Mosque, Rotterdam. Photograph by the author, Spring 2012.

mosque does not have an amplified call: "For me, the call is beautiful. A mosque should call to prayer. But it's better not to do it here, because the others [non-Muslims] would be provoked." Ibrahim was particularly worried about the amplified call because the Essalam Mosque had been subject to intense criticism during its planning and construction. It was one of the most discussed mosques in the country as well as abroad, for example in Switzerland where minarets were banned in 2009.[8] The Essalam Mosque's minarets were discussed on television—in both 2010 and 2012, it figured prominently in video advertisements for the Party for Freedom's anti-Islam campaign. Moreover, the process of construction, which spanned more than a decade, had been very tedious, with conflicts within the Moroccan community and with the municipality. The building's style has been scorned by local politicians, but also by architecture critics such as Christian Welzbacher, who thinks that the "traditional" appearance of the mosque emphasizes the otherness of Dutch Muslims—it is a mosque built in the Netherlands, and by a Dutch architect, but it is not of the Netherlands (Welzbacher 2008). For Ibrahim, who did not follow these intellectual debates, the media fuss around the mosque was wearisome. Using loudspeakers for the call to prayer would again attract negative attention to the mosque and could provoke conflict in a neighborhood that he described as otherwise "calm, green, and nice," a way of looking at the environment that contrasted sharply with the national perception of Rotterdam-South as marginal and unpopular (Tamimi Arab 2013b).

In his polemical book *Euro Islam Architecture*, Welzbacher defends the critical approach of the design for the Poldermosque in Rotterdam. The Poldermosque was designed in 2003 by architecture students with a Muslim background as a more "contemporary" alternative to the Essalam Mosque, which they considered uninspiring and orientalist. One of the principal designers of the Poldermosque was Ergün Erkoçu. Here, we will focus on an aspect of the Poldermosque that has been neglected in debates about mosque aesthetics, namely the proposal to transduce and replace the outward call to prayer by using light. Loudspeakers were not attached to the Poldermosque's "minaret" tower, which functioned and looked like an elevator shaft connected to the dome in an L-shape. Instead, the tower could emit an upward-going light signal that was supposed to replace the azan. From an interview I conducted with Erkoçu about this light-azan, we can conclude that it can be interpreted in at least three intersecting ways—a model for discussion, a compromise, and a religious experiment:

PTA: You've said that the light-azan is part of a "discussion model" for contemporary mosque designs. How did you come to this idea?

EE: It started in 2003 as a graduation project. Three other students and I at the Rotterdam University of Applied Sciences had the idea to design a mosque, the Poldermosque. We wanted to make something from scratch, and we wanted to redefine the meaning of "mosque." What kind of building is it, and what is its meaning here in the Netherlands, not only in its appearance but also in its functionality? If you begin from scratch and look at the functionality, what could such a building look like?

There are a few ingredients, so to speak, that are functionally necessary for a Muslim house of worship. There are specific wishes regarding the direction of prayer, ablution spaces, the fact that people take off their shoes, and usually a separation of men from women. But there are also aesthetic wishes, and we wanted to put particularly those aside and begin from the beginning. At the time, we chose as a site the challenging location of the Essalam Mosque because there was already a plan for a mosque there. And in its appearance, the mosque was, to put it [in] black and white, "traditional," namely with a dome and minaret. Throughout the years we have learned that this is, in fact, much more nuanced. Having a dome and minaret is not just about being "homesick." There is much more attached to it, a sort of truth.

PTA: Yes, what are often seen as "traditional" mosque designs can for example be seen by Muslims as connecting to a transnational, "cosmopolitan" Islam, a way to religiously distinguish a community from other varieties of Islamic experience. It is tied to the phenomenon of people desiring to separate "culture" from "religion," for example from "Moroccan" mosques in this case, which are perceived as less "pure" and "universal."

EE: Indeed. We did not know such things at the time, but what we wanted was to juxtapose something to the "standard" mosque. But then you start thinking about the dome, and about the minaret. What are these things? Where do they come from? At the time there was a lot of discussion about a possible ban on constructing minarets and whether they were too high.

Erkoçu mistakenly thought that in the Netherlands it is ordinarily not allowed to amplify the call to prayer, and that a permit from the municipality is required for amplifying the azan. I explained that, in the past, mosque boards often did not know that there were legal guarantees for religious calls to prayer, and that they did not need a permit for amplification (see Chapters 2 and 3). In practice, many mosques chose not to use loudspeakers to avoid trouble. This uncertain situation had made Erkoçu consider alternatives:

At the same time, there are also other ways to call to prayer. There are paper timetables to see when the prayers begin. There are SMS reminders and iPhone applications. There are possibilities on the Internet that are very accurate. These were ingredients for us to take a good look at the minaret and wonder what its meaning is today and whether a mosque really needs it. We tested that for the first time when we designed the Poldermosque.

Reactions to the Poldermosque design varied. The light-azan proposal was not worked out in detail; it was mainly proposed to evoke discussion. Two years later, in 2005, Erkoçu also made a design for the An Nasr Mosque in Rotterdam. It was (and still is) housed in a former Protestant church and the mosque board was interested in erecting a completely new building. The mosque's amplified call had distressed those who feared "Islamization" and there was heated national debate about minarets.

Erkoçu's first sketch for a new An Nasr Mosque did not include any minarets at all, but did include an empty space for the absent minaret. The idea was to have a beam of light in the sky instead of a minaret. The "non-space of the minaret" would be provocative because it appropriates contemporary commemoration iconography, particularly that of Ground Zero in New York City. However, the mosque board members who were thinking in more practical terms did not agree with this plan. They wanted a recognizable symbol, a physical minaret, and were not interested in commemoration iconography, which would have been too provocative for their needs. The discussion model had drifted too far in experimenting with religious functionality.

Figure 2 Ergün Erkoçu, CONCEPT0031. 2006. Design for the An Nasr Mosque in Rotterdam.

So Erkoçu designed a minaret that visually recalled the square minarets of Morocco, but which had new functions such as allowing fresh air to enter the mosque from the open top (Figures 2 and 3). As in the Poldermosque design, but with a more recognizable minaret, the idea now was to emanate light instead of sound for the call to prayer and not to try to replace the minaret. Furthermore, the light should be "translated," de facto transduced, from the call to prayer:

> EE: We didn't choose to call to prayer using loudspeakers, but to translate the call into a play of light patterns. The fact that the minaret is opened up from above is used to communicate with light, but also to circulate air through the building.
>
> PTA: How and what does the light communicate?
>
> EE: The live call to prayer is sung into a microphone. The electric signal is then transformed via a machine into fragments of light. We chose to use only one color, a warm white color. The frequency is directly connected to the call, to the words. In a sense one can "see" the call. . . . It would also be possible to translate the flickering light back into a "text" from the outside. There are already smartphone scanner applications that can do that.
>
> PTA: But can it be seen during the day?
>
> EE: Yes, because we envisioned [making] a slit in the minaret that creates a shadow so that the light could be seen. Of course, at night it would work better.
>
> PTA: And why the warm white color; why not green, the color of Islam?

Figure 3 Ergün Erkoçu, CONCEPT0031. 2006. Light-azan for the An Nasr Mosque.

EE: We thought white would reflect an open experience. It is a pure color. Green is often used, but [is] not very aesthetically pleasing. We also thought it shouldn't be blue or RGB disco lights, because we tried to keep the design as pure as possible.

As a discussion model and a religious experiment, the idea of the light-azan is also colored by the arts. Erkoçu took his inspiration not just from religious iconography and architecture but from indirectly and distantly related artworks such as a tower installation at the University of Milan, which refers back to the form of the tower but also to our technologized age, thanks to its use of LED lights. He showed me an image of the tower to explain what a light-azan could look like.

Above all other considerations, and especially at first sight, the light-azan could be interpreted as a compromise between the demand for the amplified call and local resistance to what is seen as an alien practice:

PTA: You said that you want to begin designing "from scratch," but of course the An Nasr Mosque does broadcast the call already, and they are doing so in a politicized situation where ordinary people, sometimes even Muslims, react negatively to having the call in what is often described as a "non-Muslim country." To what extent is the discussion model a reaction to this context? Should we interpret it as a compromise?

EE: No, no . . . well, many elements of the original Poldermosque have been explained as a compromise. And that is perhaps also intended a little. The name Poldermosque comes from the Dutch practice of "polderen," looking for an agreement, looking for a consensus. But that is then one of the questions of the discussion: Should one always look for a so-called polder-model solution? Should one always choose the middle? The design of the Poldermosque is very explicit and unique in the way it looks, so on the one hand it could be seen as a compromise, but on the other it is also very unconventional.

Reactions to the design are different every time. There are proponents and critics of all kinds and sizes. There are those who like it or don't within conservative Islamic movements, just like there are different opinions among the older as well as younger generations.

The Poldermosque is not supposed to replace all other Dutch mosque designs. It is one way to conceptualize a mosque next to several others. And we thought this model was still missing in the architectural spectrum of possibilities. When I talked about starting from scratch, I didn't think about a compromise, but I asked myself what could be done differently. You can see it as a compromise, but also as a new function of what a minaret could be. From a political perspective, when one is looking for social and political solutions, it could be seen as a compromise, while at the same time it can be functionally—qua religion—very pure.

The plans for a light-azan in a new An Nasr Mosque were presented in 2006 to a broad audience, including the mayor of Rotterdam and city council members. The public event was a celebration of the thirtieth anniversary of the An Nasr Mosque held at the Doelen concert venue and conference center. Erkoçu presented his design alongside speeches by the mayor and the famous Muslim scholar Tariq Ramadan. The mosque board members approved of the design and were especially sympathetic toward the idea of building a new mosque from the ground up, but in the end the project turned out to be too expensive and so they opted instead for a more modest renovation, to be carried out by the Dutch architect Rokus Visser. This idea was dropped again in favor of constructing a new building, but the municipality has until now refused to permit the bulldozing of the former church, which has the status of a heritage monument.[9] The unrealized idea of a light-azan, however, has slowly spread to other parts of the Netherlands and has come up in France as well, where the Marseille Grand Mosque—if it is built in the future—is planned to have a minaret that lights up specifically for the call. In 2009, the year of the Swiss minaret ban, the *New York Times* stated: "The minaret of the new Grand Mosque of Marseille, whose cornerstone will be laid here in April [2010], will be silent—no muezzin, live or recorded, will disturb the neighborhood with the call to prayer. Instead, the minaret will flash a beam of light for a couple of minutes, five times a day."[10]

Glass and light

Ideas such as the light-azan and related elements such as the use of glass and the color white in order to be more "open" impact Dutch mosques and their aesthetic negotiations.[11] Almost a decade after the first Poldermosque design, Oskar Verkaaik noted that young Muslim students in the city of Almere held the view that a "minaret of light" could, in theory, replace the constructed minaret. They liked the idea of a minaret "with lots of glass" that would make it "light and transparent" (Verkaaik 2012: 168). Light from the outside would enter the mosque through the minaret during the day, and at night the light would emanate from within the mosque. As the discussion about the light-azan evolved, some of these ideas were realized.

The Al Ansaar Mosque in Delft is based on a design similar to the one described by Verkaaik—the minaret can light up in green on special occasions and is made of brick and glass. It is thought that one way to make a mosque appear more "Dutch" is to use brick. The elaborate use of bricks in mosques has a centuries-old history in countries such as Turkey and Iran, but they are chosen in the Netherlands because they are reminiscent of Dutch architecture. In Delft, I talked to a former board member of the mosque about the use of light and the call to prayer. Not only was he a *hafiz*, someone who can recite the Qur'an by heart, he told me that he had also performed as a muezzin and that his son was the building's architect, an achievement of which he was very proud. Some of the non-Muslim residents in the neighborhood had visited the mosque on open days and had heard the call inside the mosque, but there was no amplified call: "No, we don't broadcast the call. It would create trouble, but you know what, I will have a conversation about this again with the mosque's board. Maybe we should have an amplified call." It became clear to me that the use of light here had in no way replaced the need for a call. Merely being asked about the call prompted the man to reconsider its absence, and to acknowledge that the only reason was fear of aggravating the neighborhood.

In another small town, Hoofddorp, a minaret in the Ar-Rahman Mosque was constructed entirely out of glass. This minaret functions at the same time as a shaft for the elevator provided for elders, an idea that Erkoçu had already presented in his Poldermosque design, and that has also been applied to the bigger Ulu Mosque in Utrecht. There was local resistance to the Hoofddorp mosque when it was being built, and while granting permission for construction in 2006 the municipality stated that the plans did not include sounds that could cause annoyance (*geen geluidsgevoelige bestemming*). During a public meeting to explain their plans, one of the mosque's board members, Donald Karamet Ali (of Surinamese descent, d. 2011), expressed his regret that local residents had not shown up. He assured the municipality and the local media that the mosque would not amplify the call to prayer, but would use "light signals" coming from the "transparent," glass minaret.[12] This was necessary "to preserve the peace with our neighbors. . . . We [have] already [been located for] fifteen years in a residential area and have never had any trouble. But if we would use a sound installation, that would be assisting those who support people like Geert Wilders and Ayaan Hirsi Ali."[13] A chairman of an overarching Dutch Islamic organization, Arslan Karagül, gave his support for the light-azan: "I find it an enlightened solution [*een verlichte oplossing; sic*] in more than one way. It will not change the meaning of the call to prayer."

Karagül also thought that, in every town, the local context should determine whether or not the azan is amplified.[14]

I visited Hoofddorp's Ar-Rahman Mosque (Figure 4) in 2012 and had a conversation with Atef, a man of Egyptian origin who spends much of his time at the mosque. He was happy to give me a tour of the mosque, which had been completed only a year ago. Atef was enthusiastic about the mosque's facilities and the decorated prayer space, but he had no idea about the light-azan. The glass

Figure 4 The Ar-Rahman Mosque, Hoofddorp. Photograph by the author, Fall 2012.

minaret does not light up, contrary to other mosques in the Netherlands that have this feature. For Atef, it was mainly the minaret elevator that was important because it was helpful for an elderly friend.

Moreover, the use of glass and the metaphor of transparency should be taken with a grain of salt. In my conversation with Erkoçu, I broached the subject of the extensive use of glass: should it be seen as a religious innovation that has been provoked by European political pressures? For example, Wael Farhat, a Muslim mosque architect in Italy, told me in an interview I conducted in Venice that he used a lot of glass because he thought it stood for a more pure, universal Islam. At the same time, however, he talked about pressures from Italians who were against mosque construction. It was my impression that he did not want to admit that his mosque designs, and his concepts of transparency and a cosmopolitan Islam, were strongly influenced by local politics. In reality, alternative conceptions of Islam as well as local political pressures intersect and shape the final design. It would be an exaggeration to describe this particular form of globalized Islam as essentially reactive, as Olivier Roy (2004) has suggested, nor would a description of Farhat as totally immune to non-Muslim pressures and as essentially proactive be convincing. We should constantly remind ourselves of the fact that the globalization of religion is messy and deeply perspectival, and therefore unpack or nuance any simple explanations. Erkoçu's own explanation was that of an architect who wants to promote his design needs to use a language that is understood by non-Muslims:

> We also used a lot of glass for our design of the Poldermosque and explained it every time [by saying] that there is nothing to hide, that it's open, while actually we made the prayer space very closed because that is something personal. Because when one passes by a church, it's not like you can see the people praying inside. And that is something that is being used in the discourse surrounding the acceptance of mosques, that they are closed. But it makes sense that they are closed off.

Indeed, the idea of a light-azan or the use of new materials such as glass has not fundamentally altered the traditional meanings of the call or what is, from the perspective of a religious minority group, the private, secluded experience of prayer. Kareem, a young Muslim intellectual who lives in Rotterdam, told me that he thought the physical effect of using light signals to call to prayer would be different, and thus also its religious meaning, particularly "because the function of sound is to make one turn toward the call, whereas a light-azan is something that one is confronted with when already facing that direction." As

I have already mentioned, for Plato the reorientation of the soul was primarily explained with an optical metaphor, but this may not always capture the importance of techniques of listening in Islam that enable believers to become "auditory receptacles of divine speech" (Hirschkind 2006: 39).[15] Similarly, the captives of Plato's cave were not only unable to properly see each other, they could equally only hear each other's echo (515b). In other words, we should reject the stereotypical opposition of seeing versus hearing, and say that what is lost without sound is a part of the synergetic experience of the mosque building itself.[16] Kareem was not against the idea of a transduction, but was skeptical about its possible value as azan in practice. The amplified call turns the mosque into an actor and people into objects of its attention; would not the light-azan mosque lose agency in the process of transducing the call?

It is worthwhile to distinguish the related discussion on glass from the light-azan in terms of the production of actors and their objects of attention. The material specificity of glass and the concomitant social idea of transparency create outsider subjects who are less sharply excluded from the mosque building. Muslims inside must perform their prayers while being (potentially) watched, in order to become more trustworthy to a skeptical, non-Muslim society. The light-azan, however, "rescues" non-Muslims outside the building from being touched by unwanted religious sounds and in that sense disempowers the mosque. In other words, different materials and strategies are used in response to power relations: the transduction is a transformation of hierarchies, changing who touches who, albeit in a soft way through sight and hearing. However, that does not mean that Muslims themselves wholly reject the use of light and glass because of different interpretations and experiences of material religion (see the Introduction). Kareem did indeed say that he considered the effect of light important for generating an aura of spirituality: "When I drive by the Essalam Mosque at night and see that it is lit up, I feel something, a pleasing sense of spirituality." Erkoçu had also told me that he intended the use of light to enable a spiritual experience for mosque users.

Spirituality and religious authority

Puzzled by the varied reactions to the light-azan proposal, I arranged a meeting with three scholars at the Islamic University of Rotterdam, a school that was founded in 1997 and offers degrees in Islamic theology and spiritual care. One of the questions I put forth was whether it was religiously valid to translate the human sound of the call into light patterns. Suat, one of the young teachers working at the school, immediately came up with the word "compromise." When I pressed further and asked him if he was sure that a light-azan should be interpreted as a compromise, he replied that perhaps it was not even a real compromise, in the sense of being fair, but "a necessary solution." His senior, Gamal, did not like the idea. He believed that the technologization of the call was dangerous because its long-term effects could not be predicted. "The roots of Islam," he said, "could be undermined and the azan could lose its importance. I am afraid that the azan will not stay in the hearts of Muslims." Gamal viewed the light-azan as he did the broadcasting of the azan by radio and the Egyptian government's desire, before the 2011 revolution, to replace the cacophony of numerous azans with a unified master azan in Cairo. He disapproved of all these innovations as either too mannerist or too modern.

The younger Suat was slightly more positive about the proposal, particularly because he thought it would be less threatening to non-Muslims. Both scholars said that in "non-Muslim countries" such as the Netherlands and France, it would be wise if Muslims did not challenge their environment too greatly. Muhammad, the third scholar who participated in the meeting, added that, after all, the call to prayer had historical ties to a sense of victory and conquest and that today this could be viewed as problematic. The scholars agreed that the decision to amplify the call should depend on the context; they thought it was more appropriate in a neighborhood with a significant number of Muslims, or in one which is very multicultural. Moreover, they thought that amplifying the azan in the afternoons was not a practical necessity, since most people visiting mosques during weekday afternoons are elders who do not require the azan to be on time for their prayers.

Muhammad said that Muslims should not seek recognition through a demand to amplify the azan:

> We must not force people to recognize us. That will cause pain and resistance. We must look for other ways to be acknowledged. . . . We should engage in dialogue and explanation, but not in force. We could base ourselves on the law and demand our legal rights, but there is at the same time a social reality, the fact that people are not used to the azan. One must take this into account and behave pragmatically.

Gamal added that the history of the azan and that of church bells should be considered in judgments regarding the Dutch case. Although the law in the Netherlands is interpreted to equate the azan with church bells (as I discuss in Chapter 2), he and the others thought that in reality it was slightly different because of the use of words and a specific spoken language. "Could we perform the call in Dutch? What would that mean?" For them, the red line of recognition was not the call, but first and primarily the right to construct recognizably Islamic mosques.

"Can the light-azan be seen as a 'spiritual' translation of sound into light?" I asked, to see whether a reference to spirituality could authenticate the light-azan in religious terms. In the Netherlands, I had not heard of any Qur'anic interpretations to defend the light-azan, but the word "spiritual" had been mentioned. Interestingly, according to Maxime Repaux, the architect of France's Marseille Grand Mosque (Figure 5), French Muslims interpreted the spiritual aspect of the light-azan by referring to the Qur'an's verse on divine light.[17] Verse 35 of the *Surat an-Nur* goes as follows:

> Allah is the Light of the heavens and the earth. The example of His light is like a niche within which is a lamp, the lamp is within glass, the glass as if it were a pearly [white] star lit from [the oil of] a blessed olive tree, neither of the east nor of the west, whose oil would almost glow even if untouched by fire. Light upon light. Allah guides to His light whom He wills. And Allah presents examples for the people, and Allah is Knowing of all things.

According to Repaux, the use of light symbolizes "a passage from the material to the immaterial," toward the "spiritual," from stone to sound, and from sound to light. During the interview he mentioned a very similar design for a mosque in Algeria that aims to be one of the largest mosques in the world and has a

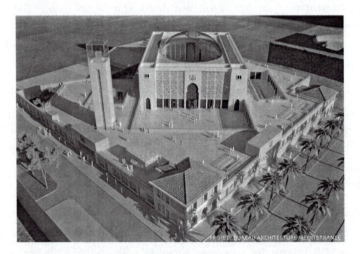

Figure 5 Bureau Architecture Méditerranée. 2008. Design for the Marseille Grand Mosque.

minaret that can function as a "lighthouse," though not one that would replace the azan. There are also other mosques that use light—the Hassan II Mosque in Casablanca, for example, has a 210-meter-high minaret that can shoot a green laser beam toward Mecca, and the 600 meter-high Mecca Clock Tower blasts unprecedented glittering light upon the holy center of Islam—but none of these are meant to replace the call to prayer. Repaux portrayed the passage to light as going from the material to the less material and therefore spiritual, whereas both sound waves and light rays belong to the domain of physical phenomena. Following Webb Keane's discussion of the religious work of transduction, we can say that the azan is first materialized as sound, but then "dematerialized" as light, which is, in fact, a rematerialization (Keane 2013: 2). A similar notion of spirituality as a transcending of the material, or even a denial of the material, can be found for example in classical Islamic philosophy[18] and also abounds in Protestant theologies. The point that I want to make is not genealogical, but that even though religious reasoning may deny materiality, in reality quite the opposite can be the case.

Repaux admitted that the idea of the light-azan had also come up in France—"to keep the neighborhood happy"—because of great resistance to the mosque. He claimed that the light-azan did not have any opponents and is often considered an interesting approach for preventing conflict. Yet, despite these intentions, significant local opposition to the very idea of building the mosque led the city to cancel the project's construction permit; the cancellation had to be overturned by an appeals court in 2012 before the first stone could be laid symbolically. At the time of writing, in 2015, the site for the future mosque was still a car park.

At the Islamic University of Rotterdam, Gamal thought it was strange to want to replace the azan. "It belongs to the Islamic tradition, but it is much more than just that, it is a part of Islam and mandatory inside a mosque." Though initially sympathetic, Suat also thought the idea of a translation was awkward: "It would be good if one could actually read the words of the call if they were to be projected, but still . . . if we start doing this then maybe in the future one will argue that a [particular] piece of a pig can be eaten and another piece cannot." Gamal added that the *Surat an-Nur* refers to a spiritual, divine light, and that the intention of the Qur'an was in no way to equate physical with divine light and certainly not to designate it as a replacement of the call. Moreover, being allowed to translate the words and the Arabic language cannot be simply taken for granted, as these are of importance to the sacred character of the azan.

The conversion from one sensorial dimension to another, the transduction, just like the translation of a text, raises issues of accuracy and authenticity. In order to be experienced as authentic and immediate, a medium must erase itself: "Can light as a medium faithfully convey the human voice, without its own specificity coloring the process of mediation to an unacceptable degree?" (Patrick Eisenlohr, private correspondence; also see Eisenlohr 2009a and 2009b). The question of immediacy is bound with that of religious authority. For a scholar of religions, it is revealing to analyze religions *as* media, recognizing the intertwinement of sensational forms and theological content, but for a religious, Muslim scholar such as Gamal it is important to distinguish Islam *from* media, although without denigrating rituals as inessential. A successful process of mediation, from a worshiper's perspective, requires that a religious practice be experienced as immediate. In other words, the general observation that religious sounds are socially acceptable when they fade into the background and go unnoticed (cf. Weiner 2014: 206) also holds from the intrareligious perspective of Islamic authority that, in the twentieth century, has widely come to accept the immediacy of a call broadcast on loudspeakers. The key question, therefore, is whether the transduction of the azan can ever be experienced as an immediate, spiritual way of calling to prayer.

Although they had doubts about the light-azan, the Muslim teachers in Rotterdam could easily accept the link between spiritual light and the call to prayer. Indeed, many scholarly accounts of the minaret across the world describe it as originating in a lighthouse, and its development is widely seen as intertwined with that of the call to prayer. In 1880, Alfred J. Butler, an English historian, published an article in which he defended the hypothesis that the minaret developed from an antique lighthouse.[19] The German orientalist Friedrich Schwally suggested that the use of the Arabic word *manar* to describe the minaret was related to the practice of the muezzin holding a light, for instance an oil lamp, while reciting the call (Schwally 1898).[20] The Iranian-American Muslim philosopher Seyyed Hossein Nasr has also stated that the connection between the call to prayer, the minaret, and light is valid. In his book *Islamic Art and Spirituality* Nasr writes of the call from the minarets emanating a divine, spiritual light into the city: "It is certainly not accidental that the place in the mosque from which the Word of God in the form of the call to prayer reaches the community, namely the minaret, is called in Arabic *al-manarah*, literally the place of light." The message of Islam, its language, is not just contained in sound; the revealed word is "a light which shines upon the otherwise dark path of human existence in this world" (Nasr 1987: 51). However, Muslim scholars often deem the intentional replacing of sound by light unacceptable. The influential Egyptian al-Azhar University has declared that the light-azan cannot replace or translate the call to prayer in Marseilles, and that Muslims should inform French citizens of the importance of the call.[21] In this case, the connection between the spiritual and the political compromise was too direct and too close, while the deviation from tradition was too great.

Spiritualizing strategies and pluralism

To conclude, I want to make a general comment on spirituality in modern, pluralist societies. Peter van der Veer argues that "the gradual transformation of a transcendent hierarchical order into a modern egalitarian immanent order has displaced institutional religion, while freeing a space for spirituality" (2008: 790). This free space allows for peaceful interactions between worldviews: "An embracing, vague term like spirituality has been adopted precisely to make peaceful communication between different conceptual universes possible" (2008: 793). Such dialogue is much welcomed in highly diverse settings. However, the implementation of the light-azan shows that, in daily practice, the relation between freedom and spirituality can also be one of religio-aesthetic negotiation, spatial struggle, and political compromise. Thus, the light-azan, and spirituality in general, has a disciplinary aspect; as Weiner put it, they "[discipline] religious adherents into practicing more restrained forms of piety" for the sake of "public order" (Weiner 2014: 73). This prompted Tariq Ramadan to once exclaim at Erasmus University in Rotterdam that spirituality, often proposed as a kind of Sufism, is not a final answer to the question of living with religious difference, though it could be one among others. Similarly, the light-azan cannot solve the problem of Islamic sounds in a Muslim-minority space, but it can be one among several options to address the issue. Architects like Repaux and Erkoçu use the language and iconography of spirituality to open up new religious possibilities, as suggested in van der Veer's analysis. Such "spiritualizing strategies," however, are not entirely new (Margry 2000: 393–94). For centuries, Dutch Catholics held silent processions, prayed in clandestine churches, and could not ring the *Angelus* call to prayer. Through innovations such as the silent procession (*stille omgang*), they kept the memory of the abundant procession alive (Chapter 2).

These silent processions functioned as an immanent protest against religious intolerance from within a religious tradition. Similarly, the acceptance among some Muslims of the aesthetic transduction of the azan is not merely tied to a desired spiritual experience but is in fact a spiritualizing strategy, an attempt to balance religious obligation on the one hand and compromise with local situations on the other.

During my interviews, when I showed Dutch Muslims pictures of the Empire State Building lighting up green to celebrate the end of Ramadan, they reacted with enthusiasm and awe. In contrast to New York City's recognition of religious diversity, the Mevlana Mosque in Rotterdam has been lit up in orange to celebrate the Dutch soccer team, performing its allegiance to the nation. And yet, the idea of using light in a light-azan here in the Netherlands is often met with great reluctance. For those who were aware of the Empire State Building's subtle role in New York City's everyday life, it turning green was an impressive sign of recognition, while the European idea of a light-azan was mainly a sign of negotiation. This is an ongoing process: the recently constructed Ulu Mosque in Utrecht (Figure 6) has glass minarets that light up every night, and even before its opening voices were raised in protest against a possible amplified azan in Utrecht with suggestions that a smartphone application could replace the public call. The same holds true for the new mosque in Enschede, whose remarkably unorthodox mosque design was revealed to the public in 2014 and consists of white surfaces and glass to be lit at night. The architect, Erdal Önder, explained that the building

Figure 6 Architectenbureau Önen BNA. The Ulu Mosque, Utrecht. Photograph by the author, Winter 2016.

will have a very "open" and "inviting" aura (Figure 7).[22] At the time of writing, the municipality had performed an azan test by placing loudspeakers on a tripod in a street in the neighborhood, which immediately attracted neighbors in opposition to it.[23] These examples show that Muslims of diverse backgrounds are sensitive to aesthetic formations, creating a common, cosmopolitan, European ecumene for Islamic architecture. At the same time, ordinary worshippers rarely embark on the avant-garde style of questioning that motivates architects like Erkoçu. This can lead us to questions regarding the relationship between recognition and compromise, and between religious experiences and their regulation, through aesthetic technologies of ordering physical spaces, shaping what we see and hear in private as well as in public domains.

As we will see in the next chapters, for the ordinary worshipper the demand for the amplified call in the Netherlands and Europe has grown in the past decades. It asks non-Muslim hearers to be certain kinds of people, who accept the public presence of Islam, visually and aurally. Such ethical calls, as Plato envisioned, reorient our souls. The way in which we respond to such calls determines who we are and, perhaps more importantly, who we want to be. Although Muslims may freely engage in religious innovations such as the light-azan, it has not been successful in fully addressing the concerns that arise in a diverse country such as the Netherlands. To the extent that it is a move toward greater spiritualization, the light-azan privatizes the call and yet retains some of its public, communal character. Modern religion is caught between these two poles, a privatized personal experience and a public, group-oriented conception of religion (cf. Taylor 2002). The light-azan is an attempt to straddle both poles

Figure 7 Erdal Önder, ENA Architecten. 2014. Design for the Turkish Cultural Center in Enschede.

but underestimates the importance of an aural presence for worshippers. For a greater understanding of their demand for the call to prayer, in Chapter 2 we will look back on the history of the Netherlands and trace its movement from a Protestant hegemony toward a pluralist constitutional liberal democracy. We will then move on, in Chapters 3 and 4, to see how the demand for the azan is played out in practice under contemporary Dutch secular government.

A History of Public Worship: From Procession Prohibition to Amplified Azan

If solemn assemblies, observations of festivals, public worship be permitted to any one sort of professors . . . neither Pagan nor Mahometan, nor Jew, ought to be excluded from the civil rights of the commonwealth because of his religion.
John Locke, A Letter Concerning Toleration, 1689

***

For a greater understanding of religious pluralism in the Netherlands, we need to embed the call to prayer in a broader cultural history of public religion. To do so, I compare the emancipation history of Dutch Catholics with that of Dutch Muslims, and observe that Catholic and Muslim emancipation are juridically and historically connected. After dealing with the public debate over what can be named the Catholic-Muslim emancipation analogy, the Protestant history of opposition to public Catholic rituals is considered in order to understand the historical background to the emancipation of Dutch Muslims today. First, I describe how the Procession Prohibition (*processieverbod*) for Dutch Catholics came into existence in the nineteenth century. I then explain how the Procession Prohibition came to be abolished as recently as 1988 with the implementation of the Public Manifestations Act. Leading up to this change were court cases which resulted in a juridical negation of the Catholic right to processions, followed by parliamentary debate, and finally constitutional change. The formal end of the prohibition on processions not only concluded a history of Catholic-Protestant enmity, but also signaled the arrival of religious newcomers. A point of particular interest for our purpose is that during the debates in the 1980s, there were explicit references to the right to the Muslim call to prayer, and this right was eventually codified in law. That is why this chapter focuses on the Catholic procession and the Muslim call to prayer, rather than on Muslim processions in the Netherlands, which are very rare. Furthermore, there is the important analogy between the azan and Catholic church bell ringing, which I also discuss, because it reveals the falsity of the popular narratives of church bells as inherently Dutch. Finally, I provide an overview of the history of the Muslim call to prayer in the Netherlands.

The consequence of the emancipation of both Catholics and Muslims in the Netherlands is that public religion has become much more "accepted" in recent Dutch history, not in a maximalist moral sense but in the minimal legal sense of indifference to what religious others do publically. This may strike the reader as strange, given the intense criticism—if not outright racism—against European Muslims in the last few decades. Yet it is the historical reality. In Chapters 3 and 4, we will see that, despite protests by politicians and citizens, public Islam has acquired more space today than in recent times, while this historical chapter reminds us that the emancipation of religious groups can proceed alongside persistent discrimination and mutual animosity. Before delving into the past, however, I begin with two stories of public religion today, one about a procession and the other about an amplified azan.

Two stories of public religion

The Passion

In 2011, the small town of Gouda in the province of South Holland celebrated Easter with a Christian procession in its streets. During the event, which was called The Passion—the English term was used—and has been repeated annually ever since, a 6-meter long cross was carried through the town as a crowd watched a live outdoor musical performance; people at home could follow the proceedings on national television. Participants' responses were positive and viewer ratings were good,[1] so the following year The Passion was held in one of the Netherlands' major cities, Rotterdam. The event attracted visitors to the city and reached more than a million viewers at home.[2] It was an unusual public display of religion in the Netherlands, and participants frequently expressed their surprise to the television presenter that such a procession was possible at all.

In 2013, The Passion was held in The Hague, the political capital of the Netherlands. The organizers included the Evangelische Omroep and the Omroep Rooms-Katholiek Kerkgenootschap, two Christian media platforms, as well as the Dutch Protestant Church and the Roman Catholic Church. The Netherlands Bible Society and local municipalities, including the police, were also co-organizers. This time, it reached over two million viewers at home and attracted thousands to the procession at night.[3] The same long cross was carried throughout the city, glowing white in the dark. The musical, with spectacular lighting effects and amplified sounds, was staged in a modern, urban, and everyday setting, accompanied by kitschy pop music in Dutch that was familiar to the crowd. The stage was based at the Hofvijver, a pond in the city center adjoining the medieval building complex of the Binnenhof that houses the Dutch Parliament. Jörgen Raymann, a famous television presenter of Surinamese descent, was the evening's host. "Good evening Netherlands," he said, and the crowd consisting of young and old cheered. "We are here at the Hofvijver, the center of power of the Netherlands." If Jesus were here today, would he have clashed with the established order, Raymann asked, "or would he have been 'tolerated' (*gedoogd*) in Dutch fashion?" The procession had "a special significance this year," he continued, because The Hague was a "city of peace and justice [referring to the UN's Peace Palace and the International Criminal Court], a world city where different nationalities, cultures, and faiths have lived together for centuries."

The procession passed by the Peace Palace and went on from there toward Plein 1813, the square of 1813 with a monument that commemorates the victory against Napoleon and the subsequent establishment of the Kingdom of the Netherlands. A statue depicts King William I taking an oath to the constitution. Ironically, it was the same Protestant king who, in the early nineteenth century, initiated what came to be called the Procession Prohibition or *processieverbod* for Dutch Catholics. This did not matter; the square and government buildings indicated to viewers at home that the procession was part of the nation. The history of the prohibition was not mentioned, and the procession marched on to Palace Noordeinde, the current working palace of the Dutch monarch, before finally returning to the Hofvijver.

Several politicians participated in the musical as actors, and Dutch police officers also played a part. The latter's uniforms and cars, symbols of authority, were used as a metaphor for the soldiers of Rome. The police also accompanied the procession on motorcycles and on foot. In contrast, in the nineteenth century, authorities on horseback had used force to prevent Catholics from holding processions. Such aversion against a public display of religion seemed entirely absent in The Passion, a forgotten ghost from the past. And yet, a presenter following the procession told the television audience that she had never seen such a procession, and that she could see how special the event was for participants. When she asked one of the cross bearers why he was there, he replied that he was a Protestant who wanted to be in the procession together with others. Throughout the event, no connection was made between Catholicism and processions, which had been an ordinary association in the time of William I but also during much of the twentieth century. Moreover, a nonbeliever and a Muslim were also interviewed on television, to demonstrate the diversity of the crowd. A young lady marching expressed her thoughts about televising the procession in "such a grand way" to the presenter: "I think it is very special. I think it is beautiful to show to all the people in the Netherlands, who are here or watching at home, that the cross still has meaning in our time." A student walking with the procession said that he had not expected it to have "such an impact." These surprised reactions testify to a past in which abundant processions were taboo, but in this case the story of Christ was told by overtly appealing to the senses through storytelling, music, and visual arts, and shared carrying of the cross. The evening ended with the figure of Jesus literally standing on the water of the Hofvijver, singing in glimmering light as the crowd cheered.

The call to prayer in Terborg

Umar Mirza and his television crew visited the Mimar Sinan Mosque of Terborg in 2012. One of the many episodes of *Mijn Moskee is Top* (My Mosque is Great), a Dutch show about mosques in the Netherlands, was on this very small Muslim community in a mostly rural area close to the German border. Terborg has two churches, one belonging to the Dutch Reformed Church[4] and the other to the Catholic community, and, since 1983, one mosque. After the Reformation, local Catholics continued their services in a clandestine church. Not until the nineteenth century could they construct a purpose-built church for themselves, and the current St. George Church was realized in the early twentieth century. The Mimar Sinan Mosque, named after the principal architect of the great Ottoman mosques of Istanbul, was housed in a former industrial building, described by *Mijn Moskee is Top* as a "former garage-ish looking building." By adding two minarets, one of which has two loudspeakers on top, the building was made to appear like a mosque on the exterior. "How did a mosque come to be in a place like Terborg?" Mirza asked the mosque's spokesman, a board member and former chairman. "Our parents came here in the 1970s to do ironworks [at a local factory]." Other Turkish guest workers had come as early as the 1950s. Their need for a space for prayer resulted in what Mirza called a "guest worker mosque." The Turkish community had to raise funds at the time of construction but could not do so without the help of their non-Muslim neighbors. Despite this assistance, locals objected to the mosque's wish to use loudspeakers for the call to prayer five times a day. As a compromise, the spokesman said, "We came to an agreement that the mosque could amplify the call every day in the afternoon." Mirza was surprised: "What did you just say?! Once a day?! . . . Do you know how special that is?" The mosque spokesman smiled: "There is nothing special about that. For us that's normal." Mirza: "This is not Turkey! In The Hague, in Amsterdam, in the entire country, it is only allowed to call to prayer once [a week]! But here you can do it every day!?" Mirza was not exactly right about what is and is not permitted with regard to the call in the Netherlands, but many Dutch Muslims I spoke with between 2011 and 2015 assumed the same thing, namely that a daily azan was out of the question. The mosque in secluded Terborg had been using loudspeakers on a daily basis for years, but thanks to a television show with a national audience, Mirza was now bringing to the attention of other Dutch Muslims that it was indeed possible to amplify the azan on a daily basis in the Netherlands. An agreement was reached based on "good relations with our neighbors," the mosque spokesman explained. To verify this, Mirza knocked on the door of one of the mosque's Dutch neighbors. An elderly lady came to the door and told him that the mosque had always amplified the azan. "It does not disturb you?" Mirza asked. "No," she replied calmly, "in the beginning it was several times a day, but now [it is] only once in the afternoon."

Although the mosque and television show did their best to depict harmonious relations between mosque and town, there had been a few troubling incidents such as racist slurs pasted on the mosque once and, on September 11, 2001, someone had thrown a brick through one of the mosque's windows. Some in the mosque thought that it was a disgrace that they could not call to prayer five times a day. "Don't the church bells ring during our prayers as well?" a mosque visitor told a journalist in 2002. According to a local alderwoman, negotiations for the call to prayer were a troublesome issue. "We had to get together with the whole neighborhood . . . and they thought that five times a day was getting too crazy. Of course, they [the Muslims] said that church bells could also ring [often]. I then clearly stated to them: you are in the Netherlands. . . . Sounding church bells is a centuries-old practice here. This is a society that has built up each other's rights together. You have no choice but to respect that. Not everything that you ask for is possible."[5] By 2012, the process of "de-churching" (*ontkerkelijking*) was taking its toll on the Catholic church in Terborg. (De-churching is a Dutch word that can simultaneously refer to secularization, rejection of institutional religion, the closing down of church buildings due to dropping attendance rates, and to the pursuit of [alternative] private religious experiences.) The lack of young people after de-churching in Terborg was a significant contrast to the mosque, which remained connected to Turkish-Dutch youth. But even though the church was in decline, its bells still rang louder than the mosque's daily—but only in the afternoon—amplified call to prayer.

Comparing Catholic with Muslim emancipation

The two vignettes above reveal a rather changed Netherlands, one which has shifted over the centuries from Protestant hegemony to a pluralist, constitutional, liberal democracy, disestablishing Protestantism in the process (Bader 2007: 54; cf. Bouma 1999; Hollinger 2003). Declaring independence from Spanish and thus Catholic rule in the sixteenth century, and maintaining this as a founding narrative for most of their existence, neither the Dutch Republic (1581–1795) nor the Kingdom of the Netherlands (1815–present) allowed religious others, in particular Catholics, to unequivocally engage in what John Locke termed "public worship."[6] Tolerance was interpreted strictly and in a minimalist sense: religious others should not exhibit their religion to the public eye (too much). Even the great thinker of freedom, Spinoza, who was born in Amsterdam, focused his attention on personal and private religious liberty. In his *Tractatus Politicus* we find, in contrast to Locke, a rather strong curtailing of religious liberty for the sake of state hegemony in religious matters:

> Although everyone should be granted freedom to say what he thinks, large congregations should be forbidden, and so, while those who are attached to another religion are to be allowed to build as many churches as they wish, these are to be small, of some fixed dimensions, and some distance apart. But it is important that churches dedicated to the national religion should be large and costly, and that only patricians or senators should be permitted to administer its chief rites. ([1677] 2007, TP, section 46)

However, the basic right to or at least the aspiration toward an autonomous *foro interno*, the inner space of religious conscience, was an important achievement in itself. The right to be free from inquisition was a first step toward the right to practice one's religion in public, in *foro externo*. William of Orange, the pater patriae of the Netherlands, is reported to have said, in opposition to Phillip II of Spain, that he could not accept the principle that monarchs rule the souls of their subjects. As early as 1579, the Union of Utrecht—the de facto constitution of the new nation—affirmed religious autonomy against inquisitions:

> Each person shall remain free, especially in his religion, and . . . no one shall be persecuted or investigated because of their religion. (my translation, cited in Labuschagne 1994: 70)

An autonomous conscience, however, did not necessarily include the freedom to act on one's religious preferences in public, and well into the seventeenth and eighteenth centuries it was not an acceptable idea, not even for a radical freethinker such as Spinoza. The public Protestant church of the Dutch Republic allowed only one official and public understanding of Christianity, while Protestant dissenters and Catholics could be tolerated as long as they did not challenge the public church[7] (Rooden 1996: 151–52). The result was that Catholics, defined as enemies by the independent Dutch state, were forbidden to construct churches for over two centuries.

The history of religious toleration in the Netherlands shows that constructing houses of worship has been an important indicator of the social status of Jews and Catholics in the country (Sunier 2004). In that sense, Muslim emancipation through mosque construction is not something that can be compared with the history of Dutch Catholics for analytical purposes alone, but is rather the latest episode in a continuous history that has shifted from Protestant hegemony over public space toward pluralism. Acknowledging that history does not merely repeat itself nor follow a teleological trajectory, it can be argued that Muslims from North Africa and Turkey, who found themselves in a postwar welfare state in the twentieth century, are in many ways in a fundamentally different position than Catholics were in the nineteenth century (Sunier 2004: 565). But while there is "no perfect historical analogy for the settlement of millions of Muslims and the development of complex layers of religious organizations" in Europe (Laurence 2012: 17), mosque struggles over the boundaries between private and public are reminiscent of those of Catholics and Jews in the nineteenth century, and build on the legal rights achieved thanks to a critical remembering of the past.[8]

To illustrate this point with another example, we may take notice of the right to religious education in the Netherlands, a right that Catholics and Protestants successfully defended in the nineteenth century. Muslims have followed suit, basing the right to Islamic primary and secondary schools on the same laws. Making such analogies and juridico-historical connections are not new: Cornelis Klop, a Protestant sociologist and philosopher, proposed a Catholic-Muslim emancipation analogy in 1982. In 1999, he reiterated the importance of accommodating public manifestations of Islam, and compared the fear of Muslims to the public sentiment against Catholics in the nineteenth century (Klop 1999; cf. van Rooden 1996: 45). Others have followed suit in the 2000s, including anthropologists and sociologists, political scientists, and philosophers (e.g., Casanova 2012; Sunier 2004; Laurence 2012; Nussbaum 2012).

Moreover, in the Netherlands the comparison between Catholic and Muslim emancipation has not merely been a scholarly innovation, but a sociocultural phenomenon in itself. Because the memory of Catholic emancipation is still alive, small mosques in factories, homes, and garages have often been described as "clandestine" mosques (*schuilmoskeeën*), even though the Dutch Constitution does not oppose the construction of mosques. So, no mosque needs to be clandestine. In everyday conversations and newspaper articles about Muslims in the Netherlands, references to the clandestine Catholic churches (*schuilkerken*), some of which are now public tourist attractions, show that citizens themselves draw on the history of clandestine Catholic spaces for prayer to interpret Muslim devotional spaces (Beekers and Tamimi Arab 2016).

At the same time, the analogous use of the term "emancipation" for describing Muslims' greater spatial integration of Islam in the Netherlands has been contested. Public expressions of difference are frequently interpreted as failed integration into a dominant culture rather than as emancipation. Therefore, when a Muslim politician in The Hague described the use of loudspeakers for the Muslim call to prayer as "integration," he met with great resistance (Chapter 3). Dutch politicians who declared "multiculturalism" dead, as former Deputy Prime Minister Maxime Verhagen did in 2011, claim that the current anxieties of the populace about "foreigners" (*buitenlanders*) should not only be taken seriously but could be considered understandable and justified (*begrijpelijk, terecht*).[9] In this vision, the Dutch nation must proclaim its *Leitkultur* or guiding culture, and acknowledge the specifically Christian roots of the nation.[10] A decade before European leaders such as the German chancellor Angela Merkel, the French president Nicolas Sarkozy, and the United Kingdom's prime minister David Cameron all declared multiculturalism a failure,[11] the political shift away from Dutch multiculturalism was exacerbated in the year 2000 after the publication of a very influential essay on the "multicultural drama." In hindsight, it is noteworthy that the author Paul Scheffer explicitly distanced himself from the Catholic-Muslim emancipation analogy: "The role of Islam cannot be simply compared to that of Christian religions [*christelijke godsdiensten*] in the Netherlands."

The Dutch Catholics, after all, had a common history with Dutch Protestants and fought their emancipatory battles in the "same language." The Netherlands was pillarized according to religious factions, but shared the "single roof" of the nation. Muslim newcomers, however, are so different that the house itself, roof and all, has become strained. Everyone still fits in the building, but no one really feels at home together. For Scheffer, migration and multiculturalism are acts in a painfully alienating drama. We may compare his critique with the academically popular idea that Europe's religious diversity is new, unprecedented, and of an interreligious nature, rather than merely intrareligious as it supposedly was prior to the arrival of Muslims, excluding colonial histories and the rich history of Dutch Judaism. From such a homogenized perspective of Dutch and European religious pluralism, we could continue to suggest that new conceptions of state governance of religions are required (e.g., Bhargava 2010b).

What can be exaggerated in such lines of thought is Muslim and Catholic religiosity as totally, rather than partially, incommensurable. An anthropology that does not deconstruct such a view of Christian-Muslim difference, making a space for comparison and analogy, will also fail at deconstructing xenophobia and nativism. This is because the Dutch construction of Christian natives (*autochthons*) and Muslim nonnatives (*allochthons*) rests precisely on exaggerating differences and downplaying family resemblances between these groups (cf. Beekers 2014). From a perspective in which there never was a "radical mistranslation" (Hacking 1981), however, Scheffer's claim that Muslims speak a different language than Catholics is a half-truth at best. Therefore, if we consider the severity of past intrareligious hostility between various Protestant and Catholic groups, European and Dutch histories of religious pluralism appear rich in reserves that can be useful for reflecting on contemporary Muslim emancipation.[12]

Scheffer does compare Muslims and Catholics in a book he published after his famous critique of multiculturalism, albeit in an uncharitable way. There he argues that, in the past, the Catholic community's place in the nation was in doubt and that the same holds true for Muslim migrants today, who will nevertheless slowly become part of the imagined Dutch nation (2007: 160). Their situation, he writes, is similar to that of Irish Catholics in nineteenth-century United States:

> [The Irish] resisted against all reforms, whether it concerned the abolition of slavery, the rights of women or the introduction of public education. . . . What is interesting is that resistance against Irish immigrants was one between a reform-minded majority and a traditional minority. It does not require a great power of

imagination to fill in Muslim migrants from Morocco of the twentieth century
for the Catholic Irish of the nineteenth century. (my translation, 2007: 311)

In other words, nativist resentment on the part of the majority is caused by the
migrant's insufficiently progressive values. It is striking that Scheffer makes the
Catholic-Muslim comparison to locate the source of American nativism in the
Irish Catholics' lack of immersion in "Protestant Enlightenment" (2007: 311).
Put bluntly, the enlightened native Dutch of today must tolerate the backward
ways of the Moroccans. Of course, Scheffer claims in his book that a complex
multidimensional phenomenon such as emancipation must originate from, and
be achieved by, all sides. However, his comparison leaves the dominant native
position hardly questioned (in contrast, for example, with Casanova 2012 and
Nussbaum 2012).

Dutch religious histories are vital for understanding contemporary views of
Muslims as not fitting in the nation, because they unravel an all too homogeneous
image of who constituted the Netherlands in the past, an image that leads to the
bifurcation of Dutch and Muslim identities. But generally speaking, to young
adults in the Netherlands today stories of Catholic emancipation seem very
distant. Their grandparents, however, do remember the northern bitterness
toward Catholics,[13] when in the pillarized Dutch society of the late nineteenth
and first half of the twentieth centuries, religious segregation formed the
status quo (Jong 2011: 44). Even though Dutch Catholics possessed a strong
religious identity and constituted at least a third of the population, they were
barely included in the imaginings of the nation as a whole (Rooden 1996: 32).
Protestants and Catholics did not speak to one another, bought their groceries
from different shops, sent their children to different schools, and ran their
own newspapers and political parties. They constituted "heavy communities"
(Dam 2014), which coexisted side by side. Importantly, for Catholics this
meant a continuation of their emancipation and increasing public presence.
All sorts of interactions between religions did take place, as they had from
the seventeenth century when Rembrandt had contact with various religious
groups in Amsterdam. Nevertheless, at times fierce theological debates further
separated people from each other, even within families. At the national level,
Queen Wilhelmina (head of state from 1890 to 1948) openly questioned whether
Catholic citizens were "loyal to the Pope in Rome or the Dutch nation where
they belonged?" (Jong 2011: 44) Catholicism was seen, in the pillarized nation,
as "an obstacle for the moral development of citizens" and as "a false community
within the nation" (my translation, Rooden 1996: 200). Similarly, today's public

discourse questions the loyalty of Dutch-Muslim politicians and citizens of Turkish or Moroccan descent—are they *truly Dutch*? Although this question is now being asked by the populace rather than the royals, former Queen Beatrix or the current and officially Protestant King Willem-Alexander and his Roman Catholic wife, Queen Máxima (cf. Sunier 2004: 559).

When the differences between the so-called pillars (Catholics, Protestants, liberals, and socialists) started to fade, known as the period of de-pillarization (*ontzuiling*) after the Second World War, the Netherlands also witnessed the construction of its first mosques. Slowly, former guest workers, who prayed on mats in factory halls, began to construct purpose-built mosques (Landman 1992). As guest workers decided to stay in the Netherlands, Dutch constitutional secularism also changed. International discussions of the disestablishment of Protestantism from the state were already familiar—for instance the American model of "perfect separation" required "non-establishment"—but it was only after the Second World War, during de-pillarization, that these discussions began to really pressure the Dutch toward constitutional change. Equality in the law resulted, not from moral acceptance in any grand sense but rather from increasing indifference to Catholicism. However, these constitutional changes, which I will discuss shortly, did not merely update an old law to a contemporary situation: in Chapters 3 and 4, I show that the consequences of the constitutional shift in governance of religious diversity are still playing out. A procession such as The Passion, then, is a very new phenomenon that builds on the historical Catholic procession, transforming it into a procession of Catholics, Protestants, and others all together, an unthinkable situation only decades ago. The amplified call to prayer first began in the Netherlands in the 1980s when the constitution was changed to become more pluralistic, and the demand to amplify the azan has only increased since then.

The Procession Prohibition

Like Muslims in the Netherlands today, Catholics in the nineteenth century had the right to construct churches. When religious liberty (*godsdienstvrijheid*) was proclaimed in the Netherlands in 1795, enthusiastic Catholics rang their church bells as a symbol of reclaimed freedom. However, the official separation of church and state (1796) and the constitutional arrangement of religious liberty (1798), granting Catholics the right to construct churches, did not reform the ban on church bells. Even though the more liberal constitution of 1815 allowed openings for church bell ringing, local Protestant complaints quickly led to municipal bans. The purpose of the separation of church and state was not to destroy the power of the Protestant church of the Dutch Republic, which was not a powerful institution comparable to the Church of Rome. Although accepted forms of public religion continued to be limited, the separation was intended to "end social and political discrimination based on religion" (Rooden 1996: 28). In this sense, the development of Dutch constitutional secularism resembles the American model more than the French, where revolutionaries sought to free themselves from the economic, political, and religious grip, among others, from the Church with a capital "C." These historic differences continue to have an impact today: public expressions of Islam in the United States and the Netherlands, though under constant scrutiny, have been more accepted than in France.

As in the French experience of church bell ringing in the nineteenth century (Corbin 1998), in the Netherlands church bells were associated in negative ways with Catholicism but did not involve a similar revolutionary intensity and violence.[14] As is often with the azan today, church bells were experienced as aural intrusion into public spaces, difficult to ignore for those who did not wish to hear the sounds of religious others, namely, Catholics. Church bell ringing was experienced as religiously offensive, as noise pollution, or simply as antipathetic (Margry 2000: 139) and had already been banned several times during the existence of the Dutch Republic in the seventeenth and eighteenth centuries. Opponents of the azan today frequently claim that church bell ringing is and has always been an unproblematic aspect of the national culture. Margry's study shows that this view is far from the truth, and does not take into account the various uses of church bells, the fact that people could distinguish different types of bells, and that ringing was a contested practice. In an exact parallel with contemporary reactions to the anticipated presence of the Muslim call to prayer, announcements of *Angelus* ringing angered residents who complained preemptively about decreasing property values (Margry 2000: 352; also Chapter 4).

After the French Revolution, church bell ringing in the Netherlands was limited to marking time and for funerals, and ownership of church towers and bells was transferred to local municipalities. In practice, though, Catholics did ring the *Angelus* and called for prayer, also as a way to resist authorities. The sound of the *Angelus* would reach non-Catholics as well, and to add injury to insult believers would take off their hats in public or even kneel to pray in the streets. These public displays of religiosity shocked the nation. However, in other parts of the Netherlands, for example Rotterdam, church bells had been effectively prohibited. Only in the nineteenth century did they ring for the first time since the Reformation (Margry 2000: 141), and church bell ringing in general increased in the second half of the century. It is worth citing Margry at length here:

> How highly Catholics esteemed church bell ringing can be seen in a childhood memory from the 1830s of the physician-historian Nuyens. During that time he was confronted with what was according to him one of the most intense emotions among Catholics: the fiery wish that their church towers would have bells that were allowed to ring on ecclesiastical occasions. This feeling was further strengthened according to Nuyens because even the boldest Catholic doubted that they would ever be allowed to do so. (quotes are my translations, Margry 2000: 141)

For example, when Catholics applied in 1810 to construct a church in a town in the province of Utrecht, there were complaints that the sounds of the church bells would pervade and disturb services in the neighboring Protestant church (Margry 2000: 152). Although the Catholics had a formal right to build their church, more than four decades passed before it was realized and construction was allowed only after the House of Representatives (*De Tweede Kamer*) decided to interfere. Just like mosque construction negotiations today, antipathy toward Catholic church bell ringing and public displays of religion, such as processions, was used by opponents to obstruct church construction.

Throughout the nineteenth century, Catholics were perceived as "backward" (*achterlijk*) and persisting in "superstitions" (*bijgeloof*) (Margry 2000: 28; Rooden 1996: 116). The Catholic community protested against discrimination but also organized hate speech against Protestants. They saw the procession as militant, a metaphor for a victory march against Protestants (Margry 2000: 35). That a foreign power, Rome, had declared processions to be triumphs against heresy obviously did not help (Margry 2000: 45). The azan has similar connotations today, associated with Ottoman conquest and invading Arabs, or simply terrorists. This was most explicitly the case in the Swiss minaret ban of 2009, in which minarets were depicted as missiles (Nussbaum 2012; Mayer 2011).

Once Catholics acquired larger church buildings, it became more feasible to hold processions inside churches. Processions could also be organized on walled-in church property. What Protestants especially resented was the public procession through urban streets. To Dutch Protestants, Catholic opulence agitated the senses. Where processions were tolerated, they were required to be sober. Singing, for example, was forbidden, as were religious garb (Margry 2000: 81–82). Earlier, in the seventeenth and eighteenth centuries, Catholics were known as "silent citizens" (ibid.: 13). Like the Muslim call to prayer, processions have medieval and even ancient origins,[15] and during this period the memory of local medieval processions was kept alive in a uniquely Dutch way. Catholics did not gather in large groups but informally, individually or in small groups, with an "introvert piety" (ibid.: 129). By going outside and simply walking along the former routes of important processions, the memory of the ritual was kept intact. Margry describes these as imaginary reproductions of the original procession. As early as 1573, only seven years after the start of the Iconoclastic Fury, Catholics in Gouda organized a so-called Silent Walk (*Stille Omgang*), a silent procession (ibid.: 175). In nineteenth-century Amsterdam, which had housed clandestine Catholic churches for centuries, the silent procession grew into the nation's largest public ritual, "a symbol for the national unity of Catholic Netherlands and simultaneously an immanent protest against limitations of public religious rituals" (ibid.: 131). The atmosphere of the silent procession was that of a protest demonstration. Although they were performed in silence, Protestants experienced them as loud (ibid.: 398). This aural aspect of historical processions is easily overlooked but made explicit in the Dutch case by the intentional silence of the Silent Walk, standing in sharp contrast with the rather loud The Passion procession in the twenty-first century.

In the nineteenth century, the connection of Protestant provinces such as North-Holland with the Catholic southern Netherlands, forming a single nation, reinforced and kept the memory of processions alive (ibid.: 178). As we saw in the previous chapter, the silent alternative to the Muslim call to prayer, the light-azan, fails as an attempt to replace the azan. The memory and present consciousness of the aural call is vibrant; it serves as a reminder that the light-azan is inauthentic. In a similar vein, Margry describes the focus on the spiritual aspects of Catholicism, in a context in which public expressions of the religion were taboo, as "spiritualizing strategies" (ibid.: 393–94) that functioned as religious innovations in a time of contested public worship. In a globalized age, however, with easy access to Muslim-majority countries where the azan is common practice, it is unlikely that an innovation such as the light-azan will become anything more than a makeshift solution.

After French rule in the early nineteenth century, the new constitution of 1815 allowed public manifestations of religion which could only be banned for the sake of public order and security. Catholic Belgium also became part of the new Kingdom of the Netherlands during this time, but the biased Protestant

King William I soon decided that public processions should be limited. A period of uncertainty followed, in which it was unclear whether processions were allowed or not (ibid.: 223). Although the constitution seemed to allow processions, a royal decree of 1822 functioned as an effective obstruction and even ban on processions. Processions could not be held more than a few times a year, and were banned in locations where a procession tradition had not existed during the Ancien Régime. The latter requirement was especially difficult for Catholics to prove. In addition, troops were deployed to intimidate Catholic churches to prevent processions (ibid.: 228). Rather than becoming a civil right, the allowed procession thus acquired a nativist-culturalist character. Where it had or was believed to have existed in the past, it was permitted, but innovations were forbidden. In Chapter 3, we will see that this style of thinking has persisted into our time and is evidenced in critiques of those who equate the right to ring church bells with the right to amplify the call to prayer.

By allowing processions in the southern provinces and banning them in the north, differences between Protestants and Catholics were emphasized and strengthened. Margry notes that during this period, the king and his government followed an Enlightenment tradition of state control of religion. Influenced by the French Revolution and the modernizing policies of Joseph II, the enlightened Habsburg monarch, the separation of church and state was primarily interpreted as a one-sided exclusion, especially of Catholic churches, rather than a mutual exclusion of powers as was the ideal in the United States. The attempts of William I to enforce his Protestant preferences backfired, however, and were among the causes of Belgium's secession in 1830.

After repeated conflicts between Catholics and Protestants, in which Catholics were deemed to have provoked non-Catholics with ornate processions and church bell ringing, a new and general government perspective needed to be developed. Johan Rudolph Thorbecke, the Netherlands' greatest liberal, achieved a milestone in virtually single-handedly drafting the new constitution of 1848 that limited the powers of the Dutch monarch, effectively turning the Netherlands into a parliamentary democracy. A commission led by Thorbecke followed the very open formulation of the constitution of 1815 and did not include clauses that could easily limit processions. In contrast, public opinion held that the "Protestant Netherlands" was not used to processions and that the constitution should not facilitate Catholic expansion. Dominant Protestant pressures finally led to what became known as the Procession Prohibition (*processieverbod*) in the constitution of 1848. The Procession Prohibition, which allowed the government to ban processions in the entire country, was one of the new laws that Thorbecke vehemently opposed. He thought that the government would be regarded as a "bigoted and intolerant or intolerance empowering lawgiver" (cited in Margry 2000: 292). Nevertheless, the majority of the House of Representatives considered processions to be anachronisms in an enlightened age, and resisted Thorbecke's criticism. The new Law of Church Societies of 1853 (*Wet op de Kerkgenootschappen*) gave teeth to the Procession Prohibition by adding a clause that included the possibility of prosecuting disobedient Catholics. In the 1870s, the legal persecution of procession organizers escalated with Catholic allegations of power abuse against the government, for example when a priest was pressured to publicly repent for organizing a procession but was still convicted. In response, Catholics sometimes reacted with violence against authorities (ibid.: 300). Not only were allowed processions limited, the wearing of Catholic clothing in public, even for funerals, was also banned. Religious clothing was banned not just for Catholics, but also for Protestants who preferred not to wear church clothing themselves rather than being forced to see Catholics in religious garb!

The right to ring church bells, however, was accommodated. In addition, in order to uphold the Procession Prohibition but also manage Catholic desiderata, the Dutch High Court decided in 1856 that a private or "closed-off" space (*besloten ruimte*) could be defined broadly to include church perimeters (ibid.: 136). This made it possible to hold processions outside church buildings on what was often publicly visible church terrain. Processions that could be proven to have been part of a legal and continuous tradition prior to 1848 were also allowed. But in 1875 the Dutch High Court made a decision that furthered the prohibition: the routes, times, and number of processions should follow an exact scheme in accordance with state authorities (and were therefore limited). By documenting and expanding existing lists of permitted processions, made in the 1850s, the government attempted to entirely control and regulate the "sacral infrastructure" of public spaces (ibid.: 325). This led to a messy situation in which it was once again unclear which Catholic rituals were allowed and which were not. At the same time, new nonreligious "processions" such as fanfares were allowed, while police and troopers were deployed to block processions, if necessary by force. The police came to be known as "hunting" for processions (*processiejacht*) that attempted to circumvent state control (ibid.: 319). Margry describes how violence against police officers and convictions of Catholics made it painfully clear that a better modus vivendi between religious factions was necessary (2000: 321). In contrast, in our vignette of The Passion in The Hague in 2013, we saw that police officers not only accompanied but also participated in the show as actors. In the nineteenth century, such a "neutral" police presence during processions was impossible (ibid.: 333).

Margry describes Catholic emancipation as a paradoxical process: on the one hand, church construction was permitted, but on the other, as the Procession Prohibition exemplifies, religious segregation and curtailment of religious liberty intensified (ibid.: 371). Peter van Rooden similarly observes that the redistribution of church buildings after the separation of church and state, and the emancipation of Catholics compared with the situation prior to the nineteenth century, led to "sharp conflicts" and "strong anti-Catholic feelings," particularly in the south where Protestants had been using, not a few or some, but all old church buildings, that is, formerly Catholic buildings (Rooden 1996: 29). Persecution of Catholics led to a stronger Catholic identity (Margry 2000: 377), ultimately with a quantitative increase in Catholic public rituals, while Protestants were appeased by the formal Procession Prohibition. Although church bell ringing and processions were often banned, Dutch authorities practiced pragmatic and consensual negotiation strategies, tolerating many exceptions (ibid.: 373). This conflicted, of course, with the above mentioned hunt for processions, and led to critical questions in the House of Representatives. How could it be that violence was used in one case and pragmatic accommodation applied in the other (ibid.: 278)?

The Catholic struggle for public space was extended from church buildings to bell ringing and, more controversially, processions, in the same way that Muslims have defended their right to use loudspeakers for the azan after fighting the more important struggle to construct mosques. The further emancipation of Muslims, when more purpose-built mosques were constructed and the azan was amplified, has coincided with greater resistance to and friction with public manifestations of Islam. In similar fashion, Protestant resistance to Catholic rituals did not decrease but rather intensified with the latter's emancipation. Conflicts were often experienced by Catholics as caused by stubborn Protestants who could not get accustomed to a new Netherlands in which religious liberty applied to all. Dutch Muslims have pursued the call to prayer in an activist manner (discussed in Chapters 3 and 4); processions were similarly important for Catholic self-consciousness and higher emancipatory expectations. Protestants, on the other hand, pointed to the dangers for the nation when Catholics glorified Pope Pius IX, who explicitly rejected religious liberty (Forst 2013: 395). For example, in 1871, they held a public feast in Amsterdam to mark his silver anniversary.[16] Even though Dutch Muslims today do not follow a single central leader or institution, their incorporation into the nation has faced similar resistance, especially when mosques have invited conservative foreign imams to the Netherlands.

From Protestant hegemony to pluralism

One of the ways in which the histories of Catholic and Muslim emancipation connect is by a significant change to Dutch constitutional secularism in the 1980s. A new law, the Public Manifestations Act (*Wet Openbare Manifestaties*), simultaneously marked an end to the long history of discrimination against Catholics and opened up possibilities for hitherto unfamiliar religious rituals such as the Islamic call to prayer. The most important aspects of this constitutional change, ending the ban on processions, pluralizing the idea of public religious manifestations, explicitly equating the Islamic call to prayer with other protected practices such as church bell ringing, and favoring a decentralized approach in which municipalities are given space to negotiate with local religious organizations and their neighbors, will serve as a backdrop for the argument of the following chapters.

Bart C. Labuschagne, a philosopher of law, introduces his 1994 dissertation on religious liberty in the Netherlands with a question about the azan. What if Muslims were to decide in the near future that they wanted to amplify the azan more often?

> In the past years in many cities in the Netherlands mosques have risen. Next to traditionally present church towers minarets help determine the religious skyline in various larger and smaller cities. The established Sunday chimes are more and more acquiring a Friday pendant: the call from the minaret to gather in the mosque. Based on the clear analogy with the weekly ringing of church bells on Sundays, the weekly call from the minaret is protected equally by the power of religious liberty. Indeed, religious liberty does not hold only for established, predominantly Christian religions, but also for traditionally non-established religions such as Islam. It can be questioned, however, whether this religious liberty protects an eventual daily call to prayer, or even several calls a day from the minaret. In Islamic countries the daily call to prayer usually occurs five times a day, beginning before sunrise. In the near future it is not unthinkable that in neighborhoods of large cities where many Muslims live, the need would arise for a more frequent call to prayer. (my translations, 1994: 1)

No mosque in the Netherlands amplifies the azan five times a day or in the early morning, as far as I have been able to determine. But as Labuschagne predicted, the need for a more frequent call or at least a weekly call has grown, and not just in large cities (see Chapters 3 and 4). According to him, the Christian-Muslim analogy is clear. He specifies this later in his dissertation: "This history [of public religion in the Netherlands] can give an insight into the way a dominant culture frustrated the expressions of another religion (in this case the Roman Catholic), something that could be of interest especially for 'newer' or less dominant religions" (1994: 131).

Constitutional change in the Netherlands proceeded slowly throughout the twentieth century. In 1918, Charles Ruijs de Beerenbrouck became the nation's first Catholic prime minister, and the Dutch High Court altered the conditions for a legal procession. Before this change, Catholics had to prove that such a tradition had historically existed in that location. Now the burden of evidence was placed on the prosecutors, who had to prove that such a procession had *not* existed (Labuschagne 1994: 136). Margry described this change as a "time bomb under the Procession Prohibition" because situations prevailing before 1822 and 1848 were very difficult to prove, as there were poor archives and no living witnesses (2000: 387). In 1919, after decades of reluctance, Dutch Catholics organized the first National Catholics Day (*Nationale Katholiekendag*). In the ensuing years, as the event came to be repeated annually, the celebration shifted from having a more defiant emancipatory character to a public liturgical-theological one (Margry 2000: 162).

In the 1950s, Catholics interpreted historical processions so broadly that virtually all places where processions had existed during the Middle Ages could be included in the right to conduct processions. In the same period, the State Commission Van Schaik, led by the prominent Catholic politician Josef van Schaik, prepared a report for revising the constitution.[17] The commission rejected the Procession Prohibition of 1848:

> The constitutional lawgiver must not take as [a] norm the contingent relations, which existed a century ago, but that which in our society should be just [*recht*].
> (cited by Labuschagne 1994: 118)

The state commission held that public manifestations of religion do not limit the freedom of members of other religions or persuasions. Religious manifestations could only be curtailed for the sake of public order and peace. However, as late as 1957, a procession in the Netherlands caused an uproar. The Catholics involved in organizing it were prosecuted and a pastor was found guilty. The case was brought to the Dutch High Court (Margry 2000: 419; Labuschagne 1994: 136), which had to decide whether the Procession Prohibition was compatible with Article 9 of the 1950 Treaty of Rome, the Convention for the Protection of

Human Rights and Fundamental Freedoms. The treaty article has two parts and runs as follows:

1. Everyone has the right to freedom of thought, conscience, and religion; this right includes freedom to change his religion or belief and freedom, either alone or in community with others and in public or private, to manifest his religion or belief, in worship, teaching, practice, and observance.
2. Freedom to manifest one's religion or beliefs shall be subject only to such limitations as are prescribed by law and are necessary in a democratic society in the interests of public safety, for the protection of public order, health or morals, or for the protection of the rights and freedoms of others.

The High Court decided that the Procession Prohibition did not contradict the European convention on human rights, even though the latter explicitly mentions the right to manifest a religion in public. It did not see why the nineteenth-century prohibition was in contradiction with what could be "reasonably" done to preserve "public order" (Labuschagne 1994: 138). With this judgment, the Procession Prohibition was again legitimated. Meanwhile, advice for a constitutional revision in 1969 prepared by the State Commission Cals-Donner,[18] led by Jozef Cals, who was Catholic and had briefly served as prime minister, and Andreas Donner, a Protestant jurist who had served as President of the European Court of Justice, again recommended that public manifestations of all religions be allowed and that all religions should be treated as equal before the law (ibid.: 123). An interesting addition was that a "religious conviction" (*godsdienstige levensovertuiging*) was accorded the same protection as the right to "behave" (*gedragen*) according to that faith. Only the preservation of public order could be considered a reason to limit or ban a public religious practice.

Finally, a new constitution with a revised understanding of the freedom to worship was agreed on as late as 1983, to come into effect five years later. With this, the Procession Prohibition was finally abolished, a century and a half after the first royal decree against processions by William I. For Dutch Catholics, Labuschagne notes, this was a step forward in terms of religious toleration and a recognition of the rights of a traditionally nondominant religion. In addition, "This could mean a great deal for other nondominant religions, which may have expressions and practices that can likewise penetrate public life deeply" (ibid.: 139). Proposals for the new law of 1983 treated the variety of religions in the Netherlands in principle on an equal footing.

Not only was the ban on processions abolished, but rules regarding church bells were also softened. In the Law of Church Societies of 1853, church bells could be banned "in municipalities, where there are churches of more than one denomination [*kerkgenootschap*], for the sake of public order and peace" (Article 8.1). This clause was eliminated in the 1980s, but municipalities retained the right to ban religious sounds in case of disturbance of public order or for the sake of traffic or public health. It is questionable whether an issue such as traffic constitutes a justifiable limit to a fundamental right such as religious liberty— indeed the base issue of parking spots has been often used to obstruct mosque construction (e.g., Landman and Wessels 2005; Maussen 2009; Erkoçu and Bugdaci 2009)—and the Netherlands is unique in this formulation of the law. Public order and health, however, are more serious concerns that may be justifiably used by a municipality to limit a particular religious practice. What if, for example, riots would ensue if a mosque decided to amplify the call to prayer five times a day? Or what if the call to prayer, supposing it was very loud in the early morning, caused psychological or even physical health issues for non-Muslim neighbors or even Muslims themselves? These are quite extreme hypothetical situations, but are not unthinkable for lawgivers. In more practical terms, Labuschagne predicted that if it came to pass that Muslims wish to amplify the call more frequently, the "big question that remains is of course how to weigh the interests of believers against the interests of neighboring residents" (1994: 163).

In the first formulation of the 1983 Public Manifestations Act, the azan was not mentioned specifically but interpreted a posteriori as "sounding bells" (*klokgelui*), namely, as analogous and translatable to the existing Christian practice. However, at the time some members of Parliament feared that the new law could be used to ban the Muslim call to prayer, since it was not explicitly mentioned and its coverage within the law required an interpretation that allowed for comparison and translation. In 1988, House of Representatives members Gerrit-Jan van Otterloo (Labor Party) and Jacob Kohnstamm (Democrats 66) suggested that the new law should be amended to include religious practices similar to church bells, such as the call to prayer from a mosque. Kohnstamm also argued that, in the case of a procession or other expressions of public religion, municipalities should be reluctant to make too many formal demands of religious organizations. When a religious organization wants to hold a procession or amplify the azan, "a single notification is the maximum which can be demanded."[19] In Chapter 4, I discuss the case of a mosque in Deventer that sent such a notification to its neighbors, and the response of the neighborhood that deemed this approach inappropriate. In practice, the legal equation of church bells with the azan turned out to be very significant. Kohnstamm and van Otterloo anticipated as much when they argued in parliament against Minister Kees van Dijk (CDA, Christian

Democratic Appeal) that it was necessary to explicitly mention the azan, rather than rely on a charitable interpretation of what is thought to be an acceptable religious expression equivalent to church bells. Referring to the greater religious diversity of the Netherlands, van Otterloo stated that municipalities should not be given too much power to regulate public religions in an arbitrary manner. Recent municipal practice, van Otterloo stated, showed that the Muslim call to prayer needed explicit protection.[20] During the parliamentary debate, Jan-Kees Wiebenga (VVD, Liberal Party) pointed out that the Muslim call to prayer is amplified with loudspeakers and that this was not mentioned in van Otterloo's proposed amendment to include the azan, which he had described as "oral" (*mondelinge oproep*):

> No doubt an imam [the term muezzin was not used in parliament] in other countries takes care of an oral call from minarets. . . . As far as I know that happens very often mechanically. The phrase "oral call" then does not represent reality.[21]

Van Otterloo agreed with Wiebenga that the inclusion of "oral" in the amendment could be abused to prevent the amplified azan and it was decided that the phrase would be deleted from the amendment. Minister van Dijk agreed to have a vote in the House on whether the amendment would be accepted. The House accepted the amendment the following day, January 28, 1988. Only three small orthodox Protestant parties, the Reformed Political Party, the Reformed Political League, and the Reformatory Political Federation, voted against the amendment.[22] The final Article 10 of the Public Manifestations Act, which came into effect in April that year, states that the

> sounding of church bells [*klokgelui*] for religious or philosophical [*levensbeschouwelijk*] ceremonies and funeral ceremonies, including calls to practice [*belijden*] religion or philosophy of life [*levensovertuiging*], are permitted.

It is worth mentioning the comment made by the Minister of Justice, Frits Korthals Altes (VVD, Liberal Party), during the technical discussions about processions, church bells, and the call to prayer. There was a sense that the new constitution had definitively ended a period of religious intolerance:

> It delights me that there is now complete agreement in the entire House and the government about the fact that the Law of Church Societies shall be withdrawn, and with it a period of turmoil in our nation's history was brought to an end.[23]

In its final form, however, the law does leave room for municipalities to determine whether or not the volume of the azan is "reasonable," so that in principle they can restrict the amplified call but cannot ban it without very strong local political pressure and consensus. (A ban is considered unreasonable if it means that a religious group cannot profess its faith and also cannot perform the rites and practices of that religion.) Even though van Otterloo made sure to protect the azan constitutionally, a decentralized pragmatic approach in which municipalities could make contextual judgments was agreed upon as necessary.

The Islamic call to prayer in the Netherlands

In the next two chapters, we observe how municipalities navigate the space they were given, not to ban the azan in toto but nevertheless to regulate it.[24] Since there are no scholarly studies of the practice of the call to prayer in the Netherlands, I proceed with a brief history. There are four phases in the history of the Dutch azan: first, colonial encounters; second, post-Second World War migration; third, the first use of loudspeakers for the azan in 1986 and the Public Manifestations Act; and fourth, the increased construction of purpose-built mosques since the 1990s to the present. Long before the general public acquired some familiarity with the Muslim call to prayer, however, the Dutch had been in contact with Muslims at least as far back as the sixteenth and seventeenth centuries (Kaplan 2007; GhaneaBassiri 2010: 9–12). It is impossible to discuss the early history of Dutch-Muslim contact here; a few words must suffice, merely to indicate the complexity of this issue.

Colonial encounters

The Ottoman Empire under Sultan Ahmed I was the first political entity to recognize the independence of the new Dutch Republic, which could trade in Istanbul under its own flag. In the same period, Morocco too allied itself with the new country; after all, they shared a common Spanish enemy. In 1610, a "Treaty of Friendship and Free Commerce" was signed between the Moroccan Sultan and the Republic. Even though Muslims rarely visited the Netherlands in this period, they were sometimes included in representations of Dutch religious diversity, for example in paintings and poems, and played a part in constructing the ideal of Dutch religious toleration (Kaplan 2007: 10). Having brought Turkish and Moroccan workers to the Netherlands after the Second World War, such historical bonds have become more interesting for Dutch citizens. In 2010, the Dutch state officially celebrated the four hundredth anniversary of

Moroccan-Dutch diplomatic relations, and in 2012, the Netherlands and Turkey celebrated four hundred years of Turkish-Dutch relations. In 2013, there were approximately 400,000 Turkish-Dutch and 370,000 Moroccan-Dutch citizens residing in the Netherlands (Central Bureau of Statistics 2013).

Familiarization with the call to prayer, however, first became pervasive through colonial encounters with Islam. Though merchants and others may have heard the call to prayer, not only in Istanbul but also among the few Muslim visitors to the Dutch Republic, the scale of the colonial encounter of the Dutch Republic—and later the Kingdom of the Netherlands—with Islam was of another order altogether. That is why we can broadly designate the colonial era as a first phase of familiarity with the azan and then proceed to greater historical precision, namely, how the azan was received in the homeland in subsequent periods. Indonesia, the country with the largest Muslim constituency in the world, was a Dutch colony until after the Second World War, but so were Suriname and the Dutch Antilles, which are home to Muslims, Jews, and Christians to this day. We can infer from newspaper articles, however, that before the Second World War there was minimal familiarity with the call to prayer in the homeland.

Dutch articles about the azan from the 1920s and 1930s are often about the use of loudspeakers in Mecca and Istanbul but also in Singapore, described as a sign of the modernization of Islam.[25] An article from 1934 stated that King Ibn Saud of Saudi Arabia had ensured a radio broadcasting of the call to prayer: "Believers in the entire world will be henceforth called to prayer from the microphone."[26] Another article from 1930 announced that in "Constantinople," the muezzin had "died for good" due to the modern use of loudspeakers. "The tradition of the muezzin, prosaic sign of the times, must now make place for the lifeless loudspeaker!"[27] Earlier, in 1908 and 1909, the famous Dutch orientalist Christiaan Snouck Hurgronje, who converted to Islam to gain access to the holy city of Mecca, had given instructions to the Dutch consulate to record the everyday sounds of Jeddah. These wax cylinder recordings included the call to prayer and are among the oldest if not *the* oldest recordings of the call to prayer in the world. They reveal a far softer, distinctly human sounding and unamplified call to prayer, in an otherwise much quieter, but not silent, urban soundscape than what we are used to today. The cylinders are kept at the National Museum of Ethnology and Leiden University, where the unamplified call to prayer was silently preserved until interest in Islam intensified in the twenty-first century.[28] A few decades after Snouck Hurgronje's recording of the call to prayer, Dutch journalists visiting Cairo and Istanbul in the 1930s reported disappointment at finding modern and "European" looking cities with neon lights and loudspeakers.[29] They had hoped for an oriental setting suggestive of the *One Thousand and One Nights*. Some Muslims also responded to the modernization of the call to prayer with hesitation. For example, in 1938 a Dutch journalist wrote that "the Mohammedans in Singapore were at first surprised about this violation of the old customs, but the sound of traffic had become so loud that no one could hear the call to prayer; now it can be heard again."[30]

Also often mentioned in Dutch newspapers is the translation of the call to prayer from Arabic to Turkish, by order of Atatürk, from 1932 to 1950.[31] The Arabic word "Allah" was replaced with the Turkish "Tanrı" until more than a decade after Atatürk's death, and the call is also mentioned in the Republic of Turkey's national anthem: "These azans, whose *shahadas* [my italic; declaration of the oneness of God and prophethood of Muhammad] are the foundations of my religion, May their noble sound last loud and wide over my eternal homeland." In Chapter 4, we will see that the azan has a nostalgic dimension for Turkish-Dutch Muslims. It comes as no surprise that such feelings of nostalgia are interwoven with nationalist notions of the Turkish homeland.

The call in Indonesia is also mentioned in Dutch newspapers of the first half of the twentieth century, for example in an advertisement about a musical performance.[32] In colonial exhibitions on Indonesia, however, the role of Islam was generally downplayed (Shatanawi 2014) and interest in the azan was minimal if present at all. There was no "civilizing mission" as was explicit in the French colonies, no serious attempt to Christianize Indonesia, and unlike the French, before the Second World War the Dutch did not build a mosque on their home soil. Nevertheless, there are articles about Islam written in Dutch by Indonesians, introducing basic aspects of Islam to a Dutch audience: "The imam delivers his *khutba* [my italic] (sermon) on Friday. Furthermore, each mosque has a muezzin that calls to prayer. . . . For the very indispensable good relation between Dutchmen and Indonesians it is necessary that Islam and its professors are in no way disturbed."[33]

Post-Second World War migration

The second phase of Dutch familiarity with the azan is that of post-Second World War migration and the period after Indonesian and Surinamese independence, a time when orientalist fantasies about Muslim rulers continued to abound.

In a Norwegian story that was translated and published in a Dutch newspaper in 1966, the call to prayer in Cordoba was described in the style of adventure fiction. The "Moors" had "wondrous customs," among which was the azan.[34] But the globalization of Islam had begun to reach the Netherlands. The first Dutch mosque was established in 1955 by a small community from Pakistan. Over the next two decades, Muslim guest workers, mainly from Turkey and Morocco but also former colonial subjects from Suriname and the Moluccas, came to the Netherlands and created makeshift houses of worship and gradually, from the 1970s onwards, designed mosques (Roose 2009). However, there were not many mosques during this period, so the call to prayer was performed mostly privately, at home, inside what were called "garage mosques" (*garagemoskeeën*), or simply in a small space inside a stationary train or a factory that was for workers' use. At the same time, television and increasing access to air travel introduced the call to the Dutch population. In 1967 a journalist wrote about his experience in Istanbul listening to what was "for our ears such a strange sounding call to prayer."[35] Another wrote about the call to prayer in Cameroon, which opened up a "strange [*vreemd*] world."[36] A retired high school teacher recalled, while speaking to me, his first visit to Istanbul in the late 1970s: "When I heard the call to prayer for the first time in the morning, I was completely surprised and even frightened by the sound. I was disappointed in Islamic culture at the time. I thought many of the mosques were not beautiful and I missed the frescos of Giotto, the Theresas in ecstasy, the requiems. . . . How those Muslims had maimed the Aya Sofia [in Istanbul] by destroying Byzantine mosaics, not to mention putting up hideous-looking lamps. . . . 1453 [the Ottoman conquest of Constantinople] was a tragic year. I have fonder memories of the call in Cairo, and later when I visited Indonesia, I heard the call from a distance in the dusk and thought it had a beauty to it."

While Muslims were migrating to the Netherlands, the Dutch began their 1960s rebellion against authority, particularly against church authority (Verkaaik 2009, Chapter 3). In 1968, a journalist wrote that both church bells in the Netherlands and the Muslim call to prayer in Indonesia were "anachronisms," because "they were symbols of being forced [*moeten*] rather than allowed [*mogen*] [to decide on one's life]." These religious rituals were considered too "schoolish," too traditional and didactic in their approach to religion. They did not belong in a world becoming enlightened [*mondig wordende wereld*]: "In a modern society one specific church may not impose its will on all people. It must take into account that there are people of other persuasions. Indonesia too is becoming a modern society in which Islam must learn to live with other believers." He had been woken up by the azan in Sulawesi at 4:30 am, and had "for the first time" realized how disturbing church bells could be for non-Christians, though he had to hear the azan to come to this realization.[37] By describing church bells and the azan as anachronisms, the author implied that there was an ongoing process of secularization in which religion retreats into the private sphere, reminiscent of the nineteenth-century idea that Catholic processions are unenlightened and therefore anachronistic. To describe this normative stance, which did not coincide with the reality of public religion, the author ironically uses the same verb *moeten,* being forced to do something, to criticize being forced to tolerate noisy religion: religions "will have to" (*moet er rekening mee houden; zal moeten*) learn to respect others. This view, which was and still is prevalent in the Netherlands, is similar to American Protestant and post-Enlightenment notions of the properly interiorized faith, as described by Isaac Weiner in his study of religious sounds in the United States: "Noisy religion has been criticized for placing too much emphasis on material form rather than substantive content. It has been considered the sign of an immature faith, overly concerned with external behavior rather than interiorized commitment and insufficiently respectful of the rights of others" (Weiner 2014: 6).

The Public Manifestations Act

In his study of the United States, Weiner shows a movement toward a more pluralist secularism that is capable of criticizing and undoing a historical Protestant bias. Such a shift also occurred in the Netherlands in the 1980s, the third phase of the Dutch history of the azan. In this period, the revised legal understanding of constitutional secularism and the Public Manifestations Act of 1988 enabled the amplifying of the Islamic call to prayer. Prior to this, the small town of Tiel in the middle of the Netherlands and larger cities such as Leiden and The Hague had begun to allow the amplified call in 1986, but not every day.[38] Mosques and municipalities often came to an agreement on amplification once a week on Friday for the *jumʿah* or congregational prayers.[39] In 1986, a loudspeaker was installed in Leiden at a Turkish mosque (i.e., one attended by Turks) at the Hooigracht and another at the Moroccan mosque on the Rembrandtstraat.[40] They broadcast the azan on Fridays for a test period of six months.[41] The volume reached the mosque's direct environment only, which explains why many non-Muslim residents of the city, to this day, have never heard the call. According to the Leiden municipality official Snouck Hurgronje (not to be confused with the Dutch orientalist), Tiel was the first town in the country to allow the call to prayer. Leiden was at the "forefront," he said, of a "special experiment," when it decided to allow the call to prayer. The Turkish organization of the mosque visited Mayor Cees Goekoop to thank him.[42] Neighborhood residents were informed about the experiment by letter, and there were no complaints against the azan during the six-month public notice period. The municipality concluded that the Muslims in Leiden could continue to call coreligionists to prayer on Fridays, but the latter had expected otherwise: "You have misunderstood us," they wrote in a letter to the municipality. "Normally we call to prayer five times a day; we are, however, satisfied if we could do it three or four times a day." Snouck Hurgronje responded that that was not part of the agreement. "No, three or four times a day. That's not likely. They should not expect so much." He made a comparison with Catholic churches that called for prayer only once a week on Sundays, in order to justify why the Muslim call should also be heard only on Fridays. Mr. Guneji, representing the mosque at the Hooigracht, persisted and said that they would like to amplify the azan several times a day. He would make an exception for the morning and evening prayers, though, so as not to disturb people. The goal, however, of calling to prayer several times a day was never achieved.

The Aksa Mosque in The Hague was also one of the first mosques to construct a minaret and use loudspeakers for the call to prayer. A 1988 newspaper article that made reference to the mosque described this change as follows: "In a society with more cultures and religions, tolerance towards each other is a necessity. That has been an important motive for the House of Representatives [in making] the call to prayer from the mosque legally equal to the sounding of church bells."[43] The article also quoted Christian organizations that, despite some reluctance, supported the change in the name of freedom of religious worship. Pastor C. A. ter Linden in The Hague thought that the amplified azan was a "consequence of the freedom of worship." He advised that, as with church bells, the volume of the azan should be adjusted so that others may not be disturbed, "not out of fears for a lack of tolerance, but . . . from respect for each other and keeping the other in mind. We live after all in a plural society."

According to the newspaper article, the mosque did not receive any complaints at the time. However, there were voices of dissent against equating the azan with church bells. For example, Klaas Beuker of the (small and now dissolved) Roman Catholic Party of the Netherlands said that it was a disturbing sign of the times that "we have to consider this [the azan] normal and must accept everything." House of Representatives member Meindert Leerling, speaking on behalf of the Reformatory Political Federation, stated that because of the "Christian culture" of the Netherlands, the government should prioritize calls to prayer through church bells: "That has nothing to do with discriminating [against] Muslims and is also not a limitation on the freedom of worship." Despite these views, the city allowed the mosque to amplify the call in anticipation of changes in the law that came later that year, equating church bells with the call to prayer. Abdulwahid van Bommel, a Dutch-Muslim convert, was skeptical at the time. He believed that municipalities would still exercise power to prevent mosques from making the call to prayer. In the next two chapters we will see that in hindsight his view, although understandable, was exaggerated, because in practice a municipality cannot easily ban the azan, although it may disallow the azan if Muslims do not actively demand and insist on their rights.

Today the Aksa Mosque lies at the heart of The Hague, close to the central station and the city hall and next to the main shopping district. It is located in Chinatown, which began with the settlement of Chinese immigrants in the 1970s and continued to flourish after the mosque had opened in 1979. Not far from the mosque is the seventeenth-century New Church that preserves the cenotaph of Spinoza, one of the figures who is glorified in Dutch narratives of toleration and freedom of thought. Spinoza's former house and a statue of him are in the neighborhood as well, right across from The Hague's red light district. In short, the city center boasts a highly diverse population and iconography. Less than four decades ago, neither Chinatown nor the Aksa Mosque existed. A monument in the neighborhood reminds visitors of the historical presence of a Jewish population. The mosque had originally been built as a synagogue, but during the Second World War around 14,000 of the 17,000 Dutch Jews in The Hague were murdered. Although a few thousand survived, secularization and migration to other cities and countries led to the synagogue's closure. Turkish guest workers squatted in the abandoned building and the city eventually gave them permission to turn it into a mosque, adding two minarets to the neoclassical building in 1985.

Now, men come from around the city to perform ritual prayers or *salat* on Friday afternoons. Young, middle-aged, and old men come together on their bikes and scooters. Some wear hip, fashionable jackets, skinny jeans, and sneakers. The elders ordinarily wear suits. The mosque is filled to capacity, including the second floor which was originally meant for Jewish women, and people also find a niche for prayer on the staircase. The first call to prayer echoes from the loudspeakers and one of the mosque's active members starts laying mats on the floor outside for those who will not be able to find a place inside. It is his weekly ritual. Bystanders sometimes look curiously into the mosque's alley to see what is going on. On one of these occasions, a middle-aged man standing and watching told me about his grandfather, who used to be one of the board members of the synagogue. "Thank God my grandfather is not here to see what has happened," he said, looking at the Muslims performing *salat*. When I asked him what he thought about the amplified azan, he responded that "they have their right to a house of worship, and why not include the right to call to prayer?" Not everyone agreed. A local Chinese shopkeeper was not necessarily fond of the mosque. "I'd rather have a Buddhist temple in Chinatown," he joked with the television crew of *Mijn Moskee is Top*. Another young passerby looked at the people praying, listened to the call, and said indignantly: "This is not normal anymore. This is not the Netherlands anymore." This despite the fact that the Aksa Mosque has called to prayer consistently for all his life.

Constructing visible, mostly silent, mosques

The fourth and current historical phase of the azan in the Netherlands, from the 1990s onwards, is characterized by the construction of more visible mosques with minarets. Other strategies continued as well, such as turning unsustainable churches into mosques. For example, the mosque in Leiden at the Hooigracht moved into a former church in 1993. It began to broadcast the azan in its new location once a week on Fridays, as it had done for several years, but there were complaints from the neighborhood. A municipality official responded: "Our current standpoint is that the mosque does not need a permit for the [sound] installation. After all, churches do not require a permit to sound church bells, so why should mosques?" After a test week, the mosque proceeded as before without receiving new complaints.[44]

Although the law allows the amplified call, Muslims often choose not to exercise this right because of strong negative reactions from their non-Muslim neighbors. The demand for the azan is usually made after receiving permission to construct a mosque or after construction is complete. Most Muslims in the Netherlands who wanted to use loudspeakers initially agreed not to amplify the call at all or to do so only on Fridays, out of fear that resistance to the call would result in mosque construction being blocked. For example, the Haci Bayram

Mosque in Alphen aan den Rijn, a small town close to Leiden, was opened in 1997. The mosque's single minaret was described as having "symbolic value" and the call to prayer was to be amplified only once, on Fridays.[45]

Since the start of the twenty-first century, demands for amplification on Fridays alone or daily in the afternoons increased. Several political parties have made objections to the azan (Chapter 3), including the Liberal Party, whose member Jan-Kees Wiebenga, as noted above, made sure to remind van Otterloo in parliament to consider the use of loudspeakers. Despite a change of course in the Liberal Party, in practice the current phase has been mainly one of ongoing pragmatic negotiations. Renewed and explicit challenges by Dutch politicians to the concept and reality of multiculturalism have coincided with an increase in mosques that amplify their call, or demands to do so. Chapters 1, 3, and 4 show how challenges to Muslim belonging in the Netherlands have exacerbated the desire for a public call to prayer, whether audible or visual, as a way to manifest one's religious identity. This is not fundamentally different from the case of Dutch Catholics who fought for their right to processions and church bell ringing. Indeed, one of Margry's important conclusions about conflict between Protestants and Catholics is that greater visibility and audibility resulted in greater public outrage and passionate debate about what can and cannot be tolerated, and who belongs or does not belong to the nation (2000: 371–377).

The new Dutch pluralism

Since the continued existence of "pillars" in the Netherlands became uncertain due to an ongoing de-pillarization (*ontzuiling*),[46] public expressions of the Catholic faith have, for the first time in Dutch history, become fully accepted in Dutch law and are no longer deemed problematic by Dutch society at large—an "emancipation completed,"[47] according to Peter Jan Margry. Dutch Muslims' emancipation, however, is still in a process of unfolding. The azan's equal legal status to church bells and processions does not mean that the sound of the azan is the same, physically or culturally, as that of church bells. (It seems unlikely, for example, that the azan could be used to raise the alarm for firefighters as church bells once did.) People do often think that church bells and Islamic calls to prayer are comparable as religious practices, an idea that underlies the legal right to broadcast the azan. In Chapters 3 and 4, I deal with the strengths and limitations of this constitutional protection.

Less controversial than the call to prayer are the loud and visible processions that Muslims in the Netherlands have sometimes organized. The Surinamese-Hindustani Taibah Mosque has celebrated the birth of the Prophet by fusing "sound car religion" (cf. Weiner 2014) and a traditional walking procession. Occasionally driving through Amsterdam is a convoy of honking cars, with megaphones, flowers and balloons, and bearded men carrying two flags, the flag of the Netherlands and a green flag to represent Islam. They are accompanied by police, while unsuspecting bystanders often have no clue what the fuss is about. The megaphones proclaim in Dutch: "Today we Muslims celebrate. Today we commemorate the birth of the Prophet Muhammad, peace be upon him."[48]

In 2013, the traditional Catholic silent procession in Amsterdam attracted seven thousand people[49] and was also guided by the Amsterdam police. According to the Society of the Silent Walk, "Through the silence and the absence of outward display, the participants feel bound to each other and [set] apart from the worldly city through whose attractions they pass."[50] In other words, the contemporary examples with which this chapter began, The Passion procession and the Muslim call to prayer in Terborg, are not exceptions to a nonreligious secular society per se. Margry has noted an increase in processions since the 2000s and believes that the visual and audible presence of Muslims has also motivated others, such as Catholics, to perform their religion out loud and in the streets.[51] Next to Christian and Muslim rituals, there are organized interreligious walks, and almost everyone in Amsterdam has at least once seen and heard the colored robes and chants of a Hare Krishna procession in the city center. Besides the construction of mosques and new migrant churches, purpose-built Hindu mandirs, synagogues, and even a Sikh gurdwara and a Mormon temple have all been realized in the past two decades. Combined with continuing secularization and de-churching among the majority of Dutch Christians, a simple conception of the contemporary kingdom as essentially Christian has become empirically untenable, while the new religious pluralism is simultaneously pushing the Netherlands far beyond the Protestant Fatherland of the Enlightenment.

Conflicting Secularisms: The Constitutional Protection of the Azan and Nativism

It's our right to amplify the azan, we live in a democracy!

A Turkish-Dutch Muslim, 2013

You can jump high, you can jump low, you can stand on your head, [but]
the mosque is coming. All procedures have been followed, as it should be
in a democracy.

A columnist in a Dutch newspaper, 2014

***

The anthropology of secularism has been vociferous in its critique of the subjugation of Muslim minorities in Europe. The deconstructivist approach to secularism (Cannell 2010) that came into prominence through the work of Talal Asad views "modernity," which includes "secularism" as one of its key concepts, as the force responsible for this subjugation (Asad 2003). The implications for normative conceptions of justice as well as empirical perspectives on European Islam are many. I criticize and complicate this view on the basis of my case study of the amplified azan in the Netherlands. In this chapter I look at the azan and secularism mainly from a political perspective, and in the next chapter I present an ethnography of contemporary azan negotiations on the ground. But before we proceed to the specifics of this case, some discussion of the larger debate on modernity that looms behind the anthropology of secularism is in order.

In *Formations of the Secular: Christianity, Islam, Modernity*, a book that remains influential in academic discussions of secularism, Asad did not eschew grand claims such as the following: "Modernity is a project—or rather, a series of interlinked projects—that certain people in power seek to achieve" (2003: 13). The generalized "modernity" and "secularism" are subsequently loosely related to further generalizations such as their relation to "the West" and to "modern colonialism." In a similar spirit, Wendy Brown writes that she is interested in "secularism as an instrument of empire" (2007), while in *Being a Muslim in the World*, Hamid Dabashi goes so far as to simply state: "Secularism is colonialism in the guise of modernity" (2013: 128). These authors' juxtaposition of secularism and Islam leaves little space for the Muslim worshiper who identifies as a European citizen and wishes to practice his or her religion under liberal rule, or better yet, who believes that liberal democracy creates beneficial conditions under which religious practices are constitutionally protected and guaranteed.

The context of Asad and Dabashi's criticisms of secularism, inspired by metaclaims about the true nature of modernity itself and about imperialism, is part of a broader critique of the untenable distinction between the West and "the Rest," but they paradoxically keep this crude distinction intact by insisting that secularism is Western (Bangstad 2009). It must be reiterated: secularism is historically and de facto not exclusively Christian, Protestant, European, or Western, nor *should* it be in a globalized world. The strongest critique of Eurocentrist understandings of secularism has been provided by the academic debates surrounding Indian secularism (Bhargava 1999; Needham and Sunder Rajan 2007; Srinivasan 2009), in which political philosophers such as Rajeev Bhargava have defended Jawaharlal Nehru's establishment of secularism as a major achievement of independent India. While Bhargava understands Indian secularism as developed through interactions with the West, he also points out its distinctive historical roots in India itself. An easy divide of East and West, colonized and colonizer, simply does not work to understand Indian secularism. Attention for Indian secularism and the postcolonial history of the formation of the Indian Constitution thus forces us Europeans to disrupt an all too Western understanding of the existence and meaning of what can be called *constitutional secularism.*

Any anthropologist today who cites works on secularism and religious freedom should keep in mind that these perspectives are at least as much products of normative evaluations of state regulations of religions as the result of empirical investigations. Ongoing discussions between analysts of modernity will therefore necessarily continue to reproduce value-laden *and* fact-laden evaluations of divides between the secular and the religious. Each side may claim that the divide is counterproductive (Bernstein 2009) or productive (Eisenlohr 2006), that it must be un-thought (Dabashi 2013) or transcended (Jansen 2013). It is my contention that we cannot hope to isolate the empirical debate from normative political theories, nor hope to be good theorists without being informed by empirical research. My methodological critique of the Asadian perspective, which has been dominant and taken for granted by cultural anthropologists of Islam, is in fact that its normative judgments are insufficiently based on empirical, qualitative research. The discrepancy between his negative evaluation of (liberal) secularism and the realities of governance by actual (liberal) secular states is too great. To rectify this, his attempt at normative critique should not be abandoned at all. Instead, what is required is to learn from actual secular states how they deal with religious pluralism. These states, such as the United States and the Netherlands, are a step ahead of academics who do not take the details of the regulation of religions seriously (cf. Modood 2014). Saba Mahmood has recently taken up this challenge and grounded her critique of secularism and the very idea of religious liberty in empirical research, for example by comparing rulings of the Egyptian Supreme Court with the European Court of Human Rights (2015). Her work shows that, besides the question of empirical accuracy, what matters is the way we understand the notion of critique. While Asad and Mahmood opt for a rather uncompromising critique of secularism in general, I suggest that empirical contingencies require a more modest critique, one that can also engage in constructive theorizing and seriously takes into account the practical question of *what to do* when a mosque in the Netherlands wants to amplify its call to prayer.

We do not need to delve into the extreme case of political theocracy, what Thomas Hobbes dramatically called a "kingdom of darkness" (*Leviathan*, Part IV), to point out the lack of empirical scrutiny in all too sweeping critical statements on secularism. I think that it has been more helpful to enable fellow anthropologists to construct "illuminating contrasts" (Bowen 2012: 157) between a variety of institutional (socio)logics that fall under the container concept of secularism. For example, we observe *how secularism works* in contrasting ethnographic accounts of the French and American armies or by comparing how secularism is practiced in different institutions such as schools and hospitals in different European countries (Bowen et al. 2014). The strength of anthropology is precisely that it allows a critical means of closely examining secularism as it is actually practiced in a specific social context. This approach leads me to the following central thesis: *In an age of anxiety and religious intolerance aimed at Muslims, secularism is a double-edged sword that is used to discriminate against Muslims and, at the same time, limits the power of a Dutch nativist, and still very much Protestant, perspective on religion that leaves little room for public manifestations of non-Protestant religions.*

How can a single sword have such conflicting uses? This contrast between the emancipatory and discriminatory aspects of secularism becomes understandable if we distinguish constitutional from cultural forms of secularism in the Netherlands, and show that they have opposing relations to nativism. Some use "political secularism" instead of "constitutional" here, to stress that secularism is not neutral or an abstract void but rather a presence of power (Calhoun 2010) that regulates, and to a certain extent, defines religions. Although these concepts overlap, I have chosen to emphasize the constitutional because—as we will see—it partially resists and transcends the party politics that the term *political* evokes. Based on Chapter 2, I understand emancipation in this context primarily as increasing the possibility of exercising one's right (if one chooses) to practice religious rituals in public, that is, the right to hold religious beliefs and to act or behave in accordance with a particular (nondominant) regime of rituals. I understand discrimination to be the silencing of the azan or enforced privatization of religion, in law and policy, but also in actual ritual practice. The term *nativism* is borrowed from Jan Willem Duyvendak (2011), among others (Casanova 2012; Nussbaum 2012), who have employed the concept to analyze the emotional dimensions of the Dutch "politics of home." Duyvendak's work echoes previous research on minorities' feelings of belonging in the Netherlands (e.g., Ghorashi 2003) but stands out because it is written from the perspective of the "autochthonous" and "national" majority, who blame the so-called Muslim allochthons or nonnatives for no longer being able to feel "at home" in their homes (cf. Mepschen 2016). My thesis that secularism has resisted such xenophobic nativism hinges on a distinction between constitutional secularism and the study of Dutch secularism as a "cultural phenomenon" (Verkaaik 2009; Mahmood 2010; cf. Taylor 2007).

The turn toward the constitutional has double benefits. It allows anthropologists to critique the "culturalism" of some forms of secularism, and to partake in sophisticated transdisciplinary debates about how states and courts actually regulate religions (e.g., Eisgruber and Sager 2010; Mahmood 2015; Cohen and Laborde 2015). Mahmood, for instance, has asked what the relationship is between the two sides of secularism, the "regulatory reach and scope of political [or constitutional] secularism," as theorized by Asad, and culturalist discrimination of religious minorities (Mahmood 2010: 294). Even though they may overlap, I argue that the distinction between cultural and constitutional secularism helps to unpack the specificities of the relation in the Dutch case and show that here constitutional secularism is capable of resisting its cultural counterpart. Secularism, then, must be seen as a concept with conflicting meanings.

In the next three sections, I explore the variety of nativist arguments against Islamic soundscapes in the Netherlands, focusing on interactions of policy and law with public debates. I begin with the attempt by the liberal People's Party for Freedom and Democracy (VVD, *Volkspartij voor Vrijheid en Democratie*) to exclude the azan from the public ear, before turning to smaller groups of orthodox Calvinists, self-proclaimed secular atheists and humanists, who all agree with the openly xenophobic Party for Freedom (PVV, *Partij Voor de Vrijheid*) on the undesirability of the azan. While, prima facie, there are a variety of stances against the azan, they can all be characterized as infected by nativism. Following up on nativist arguments against the azan, I describe how politically conscious Muslims have mobilized to demand the right to the azan and made use of Dutch constitutional secularism to do so. This will lead to the conclusion that secularism is not an exclusively discriminatory style of governance in the Netherlands, and has been effective not only to regulate, and thus possibly limit, but also to guarantee the emancipation of Muslim citizens.

"The azan is not part of our culture!"

Talal Asad makes the following critical statement about European liberals: "Liberals maintain that it is only the extreme right for whom the presence of Muslims and Islam in Europe represents a potential cultural disaster, and that right-wing xenophobia is rooted in the romantic nativism it espouses, and consequently in its rejection of the universalist principles of the Enlightenment" (2003: 160). He suggests that it is not only the extreme right that cannot conceive of Muslims as being *of* Europe, rather than merely *in* Europe, but also mainstream groups such as the Liberal Party (the VVD) or the Labor Party (PvdA, *Partij van de Arbeid*) in the Netherlands. The weakness in such a grand claim, again, is that it is easy to point out major differences in views on Dutch Muslims between liberals in the Netherlands, members of different parties such as the progressivist D66, and the much more nativist-oriented VVD. In Asad's way of thinking, the variety of Dutch liberals and liberalisms is conflated, so that the argument can be stretched even further to point out an "intrinsic" violence in "liberalism" itself (2003: 26). According to him, the liberal concept of tolerance is likewise intrinsically, or structurally, violent because it places Islam and Muslims in the position of the other who cannot really belong to Europe and must therefore be tolerated. This, I believe, is a simplification of both liberalism and of its principle of tolerance, which is widely debated in the Netherlands. Asad's thesis of the intrinsic violence of liberalism is hard to prove without engaging in philosophical debates on religion in liberalism and with different conceptions of religious toleration (which is done extensively in Forst 2013). What is unquestionable, however, is that liberals in the Netherlands have de facto expressed themselves in romantic nativist, or culturalist, terms. Dutch liberals have indeed sympathized with less than universalist, and even nationalist, notions of "culture." But these notions are also unquestionably at odds with Enlightenment principles espoused by liberal thinkers such as the late John Rawls.[1]

An example of the phenomenon of "liberal nativism," following the spirit of Asad, is Henk Kamp's call to ban the azan in the Netherlands. Kamp, a member of the Liberal Party, has been a member of the House of Representatives since 1994. He was appointed as a minister four times, including, at the time of this writing, the Minister of Economic Affairs. In 2007, shortly after his term as the Minister of Defense, Kamp found himself in agreement with the xenophobic Party for Freedom and the small but occasionally influential Reformed Political Party (SGP, *Staatkundig Gereformeerde Partij*), which is orthodox Protestant. Together they suggested a ban on public broadcasts of the Islamic call to prayer. At the time, a mosque in the small town of Vlaardingen, near Rotterdam, had expressed its wish to amplify the azan and Kamp reacted as follows:

> This is revealing of an obtrusiveness that is not helpful for us. People will experience this as very disruptive, because those calls are in a different language and [at] unusual times. . . . If the municipality can't [stop the azan], the law needs to be adjusted.

Kamp then continued to make a culturalist argument in response to the claim that the right to the azan was equal to the right to church bells, stating that church bells "have already been part of . . . Dutch culture for a very long time and will not be experienced by anyone as disturbing."[2] In a note on immigration and integration to the Liberal Party, he suggested that the law be amended: "The obtrusive presence of Islam in public spaces—as in Islamic countries—is not desired in the Netherlands. The amplified call to prayer from mosques must therefore be banned."[3]

Kamp warned of trouble with radical Muslims who, he claimed, did not respect women's rights and gay rights in particular and democracy in general.

It is in this context of associating Muslims with radicalism and crime that Kamp suggested silencing the azan, one of many proposals by politicians for preserving a native form of Dutch culture as it is conveniently imagined to have existed throughout the centuries. Others included banning the face veil, tightening rules around migration through marriage, and stripping Dutch nationality from criminal offenders with dual citizenship, targeting Moroccan-Dutch citizens, and even deporting them out of the country. Immigrants should not merely respect the Dutch law but rather internalize Dutch culture:

> Immigrants are supposed to show [an] interest [in] the history, culture, traditions, norms and values of the country where they live and the population of that country. They are not asked to distance themselves from their own identity, but they should respect and abide by the letter and spirit of Dutch society. Whoever does not want to do so, must leave.[4]

Kamp's firm conceptualization of Dutch culture as monolithic, and certainly not envisioned as rapidly transforming in the cocktail age of cultural globalization, was in part a reaction to a report by the Scientific Council for Government Policy on citizens' identification with the Netherlands. The report stated that in practice, rather than a singular identity, multiple identifications, for example with a sports club, a company, or a political party, mattered more than "Dutch identity." The report said for instance that dual citizenship was not an issue for the Netherlands, because citizens could increasingly, and easily, identify with multiple nations. The otherwise immensely popular crown princess Maxima, the current Dutch Queen of Argentinian descent, sparked national outrage when she said in public that she had not "found *the* Dutch identity" and that "*the* Dutchman does not exist." In his note Kamp responded that while a broader European or even cosmopolitan outlook was welcome in the Netherlands, this should not endanger the specificity of Dutch identity:

> Denying Dutch identity is false and not wanted. Our country was one of the first modern nations in Europe, [it] has its own territory, language, law and history. The achievements and basic rights that we enjoy today are the results of centuries-long struggle. . . . For most Dutchmen their country is also the land of their ancestors and progeny. The Dutch share their low, flat land and their waters, their freedom, prosperity, traditions and eccentricities. They also share their open [outlook on] the world and their willingness to let others with different cultural backgrounds participate fully. The Dutch have much in common and that binds, characterizes and distinguishes them in a certain sense. That which is common is the Netherlands identity.[5]

It is likely that electoral struggle partly influenced Kamp's description of the Dutch as "those" who may or may not "let others" participate. Here, Asad's critique of liberal tolerance seems to the point, but it is a specific aspect of the concept of tolerance that is problematic in this case, namely the dubious "permission conception" of tolerance (Forst 2013: 27) where a powerful majority gives permission to a minority to express themselves as they wish. Something that seems trivial at first sight, such as the amplified azan, is given significance by interpreting it in a context of encroaching cultural change. The proposal to ban the azan is based on the idea that the permission granted to Muslims to express themselves in public life can be withdrawn, because even though Muslims are living in the Netherlands, according to the nativist position, their "culture" is not of the Netherlands. This can be attributed to Dutch conceptions of "autochthony," a twin concept of nativism (Duyvendak 2011; Geschiere 2009). Indeed, in the same note in which Kamp defended Dutch culture from the public azan, he also insisted on the preservation of the categories of native and nonnative, "authochthonous" and "allochthonous," as well as on the crude distinction between "Western" and "non-Western." His party, however, never submitted an amendment to ban the call to prayer. Doing so was not a serious priority. Moreover, the Senate (*De Eerste Kamer*) would have rejected such overtly discriminatory legislation.

"The azan is blasphemous!"

Resistance to amplifying the azan in the Netherlands has also come from the orthodox, and Calvinist, Reformed Political Party (SGP, *Staatkundig Gereformeerde Partij*). The SGP and the Dutch Liberal Party are often viewed as natural enemies because of the Liberal Party's predominantly nonreligious and even atheist perspectives on life, and because of the SGP's radical conservatism, for example their belief that women should not be allowed any political participation.[6] Embodying the maxim that politics makes strange bedfellows, the SGP and the Liberal Party agreed on the undesirability of the azan in the Netherlands, but for different reasons.

In 2004 Pieter Oskam, SGP chairman of Zeist, a town in the province of Utrecht, wrote a letter of protest against azan amplification, which he personally delivered to the board of the local El Moslimen El Mathakine Mosque. Oskam and neighborhood residents maintained that mosque construction had been allowed on the condition that the minaret would have a purely decorative function. After several years the mosque board asked for permission to broadcast the azan, which was granted by the municipality. Non-Muslim residents reacted strongly, arguing that they felt less at home in their neighborhood and even felt threatened. "One gives them a finger, and they take the whole hand," Oskam said. According to local media, he succeeded in gathering 174 signatures from the residents of the 236 homes in the small community in protest to the amplification of the azan. The complaints were similar to those in other cases: the call was in a foreign language, and residents feared that the mosque would eventually push to amplify the call five times a day. Specific to this town, however, was the residents' complaint against the blasphemous and discriminatory content of the call, namely that Allah is the only and greatest god.[7] Christian residents felt threatened because they saw the azan as an Islamic statement addressed to them, a battle cry against their own religion. Oskam also criticized the municipality of Zeist which, in his opinion, had not done enough to prevent the public azan. The "further Islamization of our society and our beautiful town must not be allowed. A boundless naivety is not proper here."

The violation of Christians' rights in Muslim-majority countries was another of Oskam's concerns, and he asked the mosque board to discuss this matter with its peers in those countries. The chairman of the mosque, however, interpreted this last request as an attack on the mosque's identity as actually being "Dutch" and not merely located in the Netherlands. He replied that the mosque board "had nothing to do with attacked churches in the Middle East" because they lived in the Netherlands: "Here we know religious liberty. I can't do anything about the sounding of the church bells in front of my door either."

As we saw in Chapter 2, the Dutch Constitution explicitly mentions the right to call to prayer, which was guaranteed in an amendment passed in 1988 after parliamentary debate on the Muslim call. Only three small orthodox Protestant parties voted against this legal change, among them the SGP. More recently, Oskam and his Protestant supporters in Zeist still did not agree with the de facto legal equation of azan and church bells. He thought that this was "short sighted and [revealed] a lack of historical understanding." He admitted, though, that Dutchmen have also successfully protested against church bells, but insisted that the Netherlands has a specifically Christian heritage that makes it impossible to equate the azan to church bells. "Unfortunately, the Netherlands is a secular country," he lamented. The orthodox Calvinist had also protested against a local sex shop to no avail in what he experienced as a godless country. "But church bells belong to our culture," he maintained. "It is essentially different when someone is chanting texts in [a] language other than Dutch."[8]

The SGP's argument that the azan violates religious liberty by discriminating against Christians did not receive much support other than in its own small circles. The added religious dimension to the SGP's complaints against the azan resulted in a further exacerbation of the dispute. Local Muslims felt insulted during a meeting at the mosque when Oskam stated that Muhammad was a false prophet. On an earlier occasion, the SGP chairman had urged the mosque board to take an interest in the Christian gospels: "We would like to invite you . . . to get acquainted and open yourself [to] the Gospel which teaches that God sent his Son to the world to save its sinners."[9] Eventually, the SGP in Zeist did accept that the call to prayer would be amplified, after their complaints failed to convince the municipality of the need for a ban.[10]

In 2007, however, the SGP protested the azan again. The VVD and the PVV had raised questions in Parliament regarding the azan and Kees van der Staaij, SGP member of the House of Representatives, joined the debate. He worried about the "alienating" influence of the azan and the possibility that tensions between groups in the neighborhood would intensify: "Is it not wiser to forgo such calls to prayer?" He also asked whether the call would indeed be allowed, and to what extent the constitution allowed municipalities to restrict amplified calls. "Are these possibilities sufficient? Are you willing, if necessary, to give municipalities more instruments to prevent such calls to prayer?" The Minister of the Interior and Kingdom Relations, Guusje ter Horst of the Labor Party, responded to these questions, also on behalf of the Minister of Integration and Housing:

> The calling to the professing of a religion or conviction is protected by article 6 of the Constitution. . . . The law is capable of making rules for the exercise of this right outside buildings and closed spaces, for the protection of health, [in] the interest of traffic and to prevent disorderly conduct. It has been determined in article 10 of the Public Manifestations Act that church bells, for the occasions of religious ceremonies and funeral rites, or belonging to other philosophies of life [*levensbeschouwelijke*], as well as calling to profess a religion or conviction, are allowed. The municipal council is authorized to make rules on the duration and sound level.[11]

The minister added that, when directed at nonmembers, the amplification of calls for the profession of a religious community's faith is not directly and explicitly protected by article 6 of the constitution on religious liberty, but by its connection to the third section of article 7, which concerns freedom of speech:

> No one shall be required to submit thoughts or opinions for prior approval in order to disseminate them by means other than those mentioned in the preceding paragraphs [press, radio and television], without prejudice to the responsibility of every person under the law.

Restricting a call to prayer thus turned out to be complicated because, according to the minister, the "limitation cannot be related to the contents of the profession," and because these restrictions cannot go so far that "nothing remains of the meaningful exercise of the right" to call to prayer. In addition, the minister referred to the official "Decision [regarding] environmental management and residence buildings" (*Besluit woon- of verblijfsgebouwen milieubeheer*) of 1996, which set rules for managing noise pollution. This document states that, in general, the maximum allowed sound level from 7:00 a.m. to 7:00 p.m., is 70 decibels. Since most mosques do not amplify to such a high volume, and only broadcast the call during the day, they do not require a permit. Moreover, religious sounds are to be "left out of consideration" when determining appropriate sound levels, so in theory mosques could broadcast the azan at much higher levels than 70 decibels, though if residents complain municipalities have the right to demand that the volume be lowered. The exemption of religious sounds can serve, as Weiner has noticed, to elevate them and signal their broader authority (2014: 24). This still applies to churches in the Netherlands. For example, the churches of Delft ring their bells loudly on Sunday mornings to call congregants, while the Western Church in the center of Amsterdam has a secular clock function, ringing every fifteen minutes all day, all night, seven days a week. However, the exemption of religious sounds has not been applied in the same way to mosques, which never amplify at night or in the early morning, or at volumes comparable with the main churches of the Netherlands. In theory, the exemption could include azans since they are defined as soundings "for the purpose of calling to profess religion or conviction [*godsdienst of levensovertuiging*] or to attend religious or philosophical [*levensbeschouwelijk*] meetings and funeral rites, as well as . . . for the preparation [of] these meetings or ceremonies."[12] More importantly, Weiner notes that such an exemption implies that religious sounds cannot be categorized as "unnecessary noise" (2014: 95). The exemption does not allow the questions asked by many non-Muslims—Do Muslims really have to amplify the azan and can't they use pocket watches or smartphone applications instead? (see Chapter 1)—to have any legal force. And since the minister interpreted the general references in the law to "religion" or "philosophy" as "applicable to a mosque," her conclusion was that residents who experience the azan as disturbing their personal sphere of life cannot claim that this call is unjust, at least not from a legal perspective. The minister was therefore not willing to grant municipalities further power to limit the azan and suggested that, rather than rules, an approach to "manage" the issue, in which "dialogue" between parties is central, should be used to resolve such matters.

That religious sounds can be considered exempt from laws banning loud sounds does not mean, however, that they are exempt from regulation in all possible situations. The case of pastor Harm Schilder of the Margarita Maria Church in Tilburg is a good indicator of the limits of the right to produce religious sounds. For years, Schilder argued with the municipality and local residents about his loud church bell ringing early in the morning at 7:15 a.m. After negotiations between the municipality and the pastor failed, a local court determined, in 2007, that he had not violated any law, that any imposed fines were to be annulled, and that he could ring as he wished. This led the municipality to amend its local ordinance to prohibit church bell ringing between 11:00 p.m. and 7:30 a.m. at a volume above 80 decibels.[13] In comparison, nonreligious sounds above 70 decibels are prohibited at night. While religious sounds can be exempt from secular ordinances, as stated in the 1996 "Decision [regarding] environmental management and residence buildings," and in the 2007 "Decision [regarding] general rules for environmental plans [and] management" (*Besluit algemene regels voor inrichtingen milieubeheer*), according to the courts, the Public Manifestations Act in combination with the constitution allows for a "reasonable" interpretation of this exemption, and allows municipalities to draw up their own ordinances based on negotiations with the local community, so long as bell ringing is not banned.

Schilder insisted on early church bell ringing and continued as before. This again exacerbated the conflict, because the municipal council had determined that each violation of the local ordinance could result in a fine of 5,000 euros that could go up to 50,000 euros. The pastor then put a sock around the bells to dampen the sound and thus bring the volume below 80 decibels in order to avoid the penalty but continued the ringing, which worsened the conflict with the locals. The matter was taken to court again in 2010, and this time the pastor lost because the judge did not agree with him on the main arguments that it was impossible to lower the volume of the bells or that such a limitation would contradict religious liberty. Moreover, if the pastor rang the bells just fifteen minutes later, at 7:30 a.m., the municipality would allow the ringing without sound dampening. Meanwhile, the case had made headlines and the pastor tried his luck again by appealing the 2010 verdict. Much to his dismay, the Council of State upheld the verdict in 2011 and judged that a "reasonable" interpretation of religious liberty does not entail that any and all volumes or any and all durations of church bell ringing, no matter how loud, are allowed.[14] The church could continue calling for prayer in the early morning, but had to dampen the sound. In other words, religious sounds can be regulated as long as the right to ringing bells for religious purposes is maintained. This precedent shows that a loud Muslim call to prayer in the early morning would probably be banned if neighbors complained, but also that an early amplified azan is not unthinkable as long as the volume is below 80 decibels (which is always the case, also during the day).

In the meantime, the SGP has continued to protest the amplification of the azan during daytime. In Middelburg, the city where the party was founded in 1918, the Yildirim Beyazit Mosque—conveniently named after an Ottoman sultan who laid siege to Constantinople—decided to amplify the azan in 2015. This quickly led to protest from SGP and CU (Christian Union) municipal councillors, who said that hearing the azan "hurt" them.[15] The volume of the azan in Middelburg was, however, so low that one critic mocked the local orthodox Protestants as suffering from "phantom pain." Local members of other political parties, among them the Labor Party and Democrats 66, emphasized that equal religious liberty allowed the mosque to broadcast the azan, which it henceforth did.

"The azan violates secularism!"

So far, we have seen that proposals for banning the amplified azan, whether based on culturalist or on religious beliefs, have not been successful. Other grounds for rejecting the azan are based on "secularism," which in the Netherlands, as previously mentioned, is commonly interchanged with the phrase "separation of church and state" (*scheiding van kerk en staat*). The views of the Atheist Secular Party (ASP, *Atheïstisch Seculiere Partij*) are an excellent example of the objection that the azan would violate secularism. When the Center Mosque in Deventer, a town in the province of Overijssel, announced its intention to amplify the azan on a daily basis, the ASP was one of the small local organizations that called for action against it. "Dismayed" by the mosque's proposal to test the amplified azan for a week, the ASP, a group that promotes "reason" over "religion," had two complaints.[16] First, they believed that information and discussion meetings about the azan should not be held at the Center Mosque: "This procedure is hurtful for people with other convictions, including us as the Atheist Secular Party. People with other convictions, who have a different faith, people who have no interest in religion, do not feel called to go to a mosque." Instead, the evening should have been organized on a "neutral terrain . . . where every person feels [equally] free to express his or her opinion."

A second and more far-reaching objection of the ASP was that the state cannot allow daily calls to prayer without violating the principle of equality vested in article 1 of the constitution: "You are privileging one specific religion [by allowing it] to pollute the public space with calls to pray for their greatest god, while other religious people believe in other gods and for many others there is not even such a thing as god." Even worse was the fact that the azan could be heard in the private space of one's home. The ASP made its argument regarding the equality principle more robust by adding a point about context, namely that the azan does not fit in a "secular society such as the Dutch [one]," as well as a legal argument, namely that the "text of the call requires further analysis" because it is "discriminating towards the unfaithful."

Without revisiting teleological secularization theses of the past, which viewed secularization as a goal and inevitable consequence of modernity, one can indeed say that, roughly speaking, Dutch society has undergone significant secularization since the Second World War, particularly in the form of de-churching (*ontkerkelijking*). An assessment in 2006 suggested that about half the Dutch population believed in a god (Becker and Hart 2006: 93), following a general trend of people identifying increasingly as either atheist or agnostic. The ASP objected that religious individuals would be equally offended if the large group of atheists in the Netherlands would "ride with a sound wagon that proclaimed that God, Allah, Jahweh, Thor and so forth do not exist." And therefore, so their argument goes, the Netherlands requires implementation of the "*laïcité* principle," which the ASP interpreted as the prohibition of all religious expressions in public spaces. While SGP members may have lamented the fact that Dutch society had secularized, the ASP believed that this had not gone far enough. By distributing a pamphlet against the Center Mosque's azan, they actually objected to a constitutional secularism that facilitates public worship. Their ideal form of radical secularism appeared to be unconstitutional: a wish, not a reality.

A skeptical question needs to be asked here: Is the violation of secularism, of which the ASP warns Dutch society, the only motive behind the call for banning the amplification of the azan? In theory, the ASP agrees that sounds from Christian organizations should also be banned. However, the party has not protested against church bells. These complaints can be said therefore to be implicitly biased in favor of Christianity, despite their stated atheist or humanist underpinnings. Such contradictions have become generally apparent in the context of increasing religious diversity in European countries (sec. Bader 2007: 35–64, Bhargava 2010a: 81–102). As we saw earlier, in the section on orthodox Calvinist objections to the azan, Dutch constitutional secularism can correct an explicit bias in favor of Protestant ideas and practices. In resisting the claims of organizations such as the ASP, that religion does not belong in public life, secularism also protects against implicit religious biases in favor of Christianity in general and Dutch-Protestant sensibilities against noisy religion in particular.

Neither small organizations such as the ASP nor national political parties have been able to ban the amplification of the azan by invoking the principle of secularism. On the contrary, the Ministry of the Interior and Kingdom Relations has published a handbook (Overdijk-Francis et al. 2009) for all Dutch municipalities to help them deal with pragmatic management of religious diversity, and it emphasizes that the azan is permitted by the constitution. The handbook was published in 2009 and explains in detail that mosques do have a right to amplify the call to prayer, and that limitations placed on the call cannot lead to its silencing (Ibid.: 19–23). When Geert Wilders again asked parliamentary questions about a "daily imperialist mosque call" in 2013, the Minister of Social Affairs, Lodewijk Asscher, replied that "the principle of the separation of church and state" entails that the government does not discriminate against a religion or style of worship (*wijze van geloofsbelijdenis*), or give one rights which it denies the other.[17] Asscher referred to the handbook as definitively settling the manner and leaving no grounds for banning the azan, as Wilders had requested.

Even though the separation of church and state is often mentioned in debates and conflicts about mosque issues, the Dutch Constitution does not explicitly demand a "separation" of the two realms. The 2009 handbook does not use the words *secularism* or *secular*, and instead points out that "the principle of separation of church and state is not established by the Dutch Constitution or in international treaties" (Ibid.: 9). What matters in practice are constitutional rights that protect against religious discrimination and ensure a specific kind of state neutrality, namely by respecting the relative autonomy of religious organizations but without entirely prohibiting state-religion interactions. It would perhaps be illuminating to note then, as Veit Bader does, that it is the liberal democratic Dutch constitutional state and its specific characteristics that protect public expressions of religion. The use of the term *secularism* is not essential for the state to perform this function. Constitutional principles such as the prohibition on discrimination (article 1), the protection of religious liberty (article 6), and the freedom of speech (article 7) enable separation, but also interaction, between church and state. The Dutch word for secularism, *secularisme*, is not frequently used in debates about religion in the public sphere and I rarely came across it during my field research about the azan. At the end of this chapter, we will return to the question of whether "constitutional secularism" then can be said to successfully describe the modern Dutch state and whether or not we can abandon the term altogether.

If the state's implementation of constitutional secularism is in tension with Dutch secularists such as the ASP, then there is a form of cultural secularism operative in the Netherlands that requires more scrutiny. The ASP is an activist expression of a broader alliance in society between secularism and nativism. In this form of cultural secularism, nativism is not merely an issue that is to be located in extreme anti-Muslim parties but is rather a phenomenon that is widely distributed across Dutch society. It would be equally mistaken to think that the division between groups that oppose or permit the azan follows clear and rigid divides along political lines. Elements of nativism have been adopted by parties such as the Labor Party, which, especially since 9/11 and the murders of film director Theo van Gogh and politician Pim Fortuyn,[18] increasingly called on migrants to culturally "integrate" and to affirm "Dutch values." However, politicians of left-wing parties such as the social-liberal Labor Party and GreenLeft, the more radically egalitarian Socialist Party, the liberal center party Democrats 66, as well as the right-leaning Christian Democratic Appeal have rarely explicitly protested the azan, if at all. Right-wing parties such as the Liberal Party, the Party for Freedom, and the Reformed Political Party, on the other hand, have explicitly challenged Muslims' rights to amplify the azan.[19] That does not mean that leftist voters cannot and do not resist the azan. Thinking in facile political categories of left and right cannot explain why a Liberal Party politician would assist a mosque in Deventer (Chapter 4), nor does it offer an insight as to why, in the small town of Zutphen, members of the Socialist Party questioned a mosque's right to amplify the azan.[20] In other words, although one can say that right-wing or conservative parties tend to be more critical of public Muslim practices, we must be careful not to create a black and white image that distracts from a pervasive nativism and cultural secularism.

Oskar Verkaaik is one of the notable anthropologists who have examined the connections between secularism and nativism, or what he also simply calls "nationalism" (Verkaaik 2009). It is impossible to reproduce his analysis here, but it will be helpful to note three characteristics of nativist conceptions of Dutch culture and secularism that he identifies. These characteristics explain that cultural secularism tends toward nativism in the Netherlands.

1. The view that secularism is typically Dutch has strong cultural roots in the 1960s. There is no doubt that ideas about the separation of church and state run deep in the history of the Netherlands—for example, Hugo Grotius criticized their fusion in the early seventeenth century (Grotius 1945: 37). But the mass secularization of Dutch society began only after the Second World War, when rapid de-churching determined one of the greatest shifts in popular religiosity in European history— to such an extent that very basic knowledge of Christianity was lost among great swaths of the populace. While the 1950s were still characterized by Dutch domesticity and pillarization, a 1960s rebellion against all forms of authority, notably against Christianity, signified a major shift in what came to be regarded as typical Dutch culture. Despite the continuing presence of religious life, a disdain for organized and public religion, which of course also betrays an older Protestant heritage, came to be considered characteristic of the Netherlands.

Partly in reaction to Islam, being culturally secular has been defined as being "truly" Dutch. The presumption is that Muslims in the Netherlands should lose their religion, if not in their hearts, in *foro interno*, then at least by giving up the pursuit of organized forms of Islam, in *foro externo*. And if they are adamant about remaining Muslim, they should practice their religion very much like Catholics were required to do in the not-so-distant past, by refraining from manifesting their practices in the public. Groups such as the SGP, which is clearly Protestant in its outlook, are viewed as anachronisms by the majority of Dutch citizens for whom organized religion plays no decisive or comparably all-encompassing role in daily life.

2. Dutch cultural secularism is antireligious or postreligious. The memory of the 1960s rebellion against Christianity heightens the rejection of Islamic practices, which are seen as reminiscent of a Dutch religious past that has been overcome. One of the main components of being post-Christian is "sexularism" (Verkaaik 2009: 155, after Scott 2009), a secular emphasis on sexual liberty, gender equality, and individualism. For the Dutch, "Muslims stand for the theft of enjoyment. Their strict sexual morals remind the Dutch too much of what they have so recently left behind" (van der Veer 2006: 119). For example, when a Moroccan-Dutch woman opened a wine bar—a symbol of pleasure—in Rotterdam in 2014, this was hailed as "integration" with the Netherlands.[21] These ideas, imaginings, and memories are incorporated in everyday understandings of being "secular." Verkaaik argues that in an age of secularization in which the Catholic Church experienced a downfall, ceding social hegemony to the nation-state, this Dutch cultural secularism stands not for the separation of church and state, but for the "conviction that only freedom without faith is a true freedom" (2009: 166). In other words, Dutch cultural secularism functions as a "general and comprehensive doctrine" (Rawls 1987) with its own social practices and (anti)metaphysical beliefs. From such a perspective, the azan is experienced as old fashioned, as "out of time." This leads people, as we saw in Chapter 1, to constantly ask why Muslims cannot "act normal" and just use a pocket watch or smartphone application, or better yet, become enlightened and abandon their religion.

3. Dutch cultural secularism is a nativist reaction to globalization. While, in the anticlerical era of the past, Dutch secularism was oriented toward the future, today the separation of church and state is often seen as an unchanging or static accomplishment that must be preserved. This defies empirical data, which suggest that public, symbolic expressions of religion have become more "accepted" (in a minimalist sense) since the 1980s, a subtle example of which is the use of loudspeakers for the azan. Dutch secularism, as it is implemented by the state and practiced in society, has de facto never stopped changing. In Chapter 2 we saw that the notorious Procession Prohibition was lifted as late as 1988, while in this chapter and the next it becomes clear that shifts in the forms of public religion that are deemed acceptable are constantly under negotiation and alteration. However, cultural secularists tend to focus on preserving a Dutch status quo, in which the Netherlands is "imagined" (Anderson 2006) and fixed through the prism of folklore and nationalist history, with references to a so-called Judaeo-Christian past, Dutch humanism, and the Enlightenment. From such a perspective, the azan is experienced as not just misplaced in time but also "out of place" (Chapter 4).

This insight into Dutch secularism leads us to question the view that the secularist rejection of public expressions of Islam is solely rooted in the idea that secular freedoms are threatened, especially since the Muslim community accounts for roughly 5 percent of the population (and that figure holds only if we assume—erroneously, of course—that the entire population engages in religious practice). Anxieties about Muslims have roots in a fear that the Netherlands of the ancestral past, conceived in a one-dimensional way (Jong 2011; Mepschen 2016), is disappearing, which also accounts for Dutch Euroscepticism and repeated reassurances from politicians that they will protect the Netherlands's sovereignty in their negotiations with the European Union. Concepts such as globalization and identities such as European, however, are abstract in comparison with the actual sight of a mosque being constructed in one's backyard. The mosque, headscarves, and the sounding of the azan come to vividly and viscerally signal a disappearing Netherlands.

In sum, Dutch secularism—as a form of cultural identification that posits the secular against the religious—has been subject to nativism. The intertwining of cultural secularism and nativism is reflected in the Dutch distinction between native, "autochthonous" Protestants and nonnative, Muslim "allochthons." In other words, if cultural secularism is in this process turned into an ethnicity, calling for prayer and the resistance against it are then claims par excellence by rival ethnicities to constitute the Netherlands's contemporary and future identity. Whether the azan should be broadcast thus becomes part of a public debate about who the nation wants to be. And since culture is easily read from the body, such rivalries come to be characterized by subtle forms of everyday racism (Amin 2010; Tamimi Arab 2012; Essed and Hoving 2014).

Mobilizing Muslims: The PVV and the Islam Democrats

The political party that has most strongly identified itself with calls to ban the public presence of Islam in the Netherlands is Geert Wilders's Party for Freedom. Since its founding in 2005, after the murders of film director Theo van Gogh and politician Pim Fortuyn, the PVV has repeatedly described mosques as "palaces of hatred," whose construction should be banned from the Netherlands on cultural-nativist grounds. In 2013, for instance, the PVV started a campaign against mosque construction by launching the website mosknee.nl or "no mosque," which advised citizens on how to protest plans for mosque construction in their neighborhood. I do not intend to sum up the PVV's activities against mosques in general. Instead, I want to focus on a PVV protest against the "Islamization" of the Netherlands, this time concerning the azan. The consequence of this protest was that it has led to increased demand for the amplification of the azan. The PVV protest evidences how the demand for the azan is interwoven with Muslim experiences of cultural exclusion in the

Netherlands. In response to PVV protests, Muslim activists have mobilized to increase Muslims' awareness of their rights under the Dutch Constitution to amplify public calls to prayer.

The Hague has a relatively long history with the amplified azan, going back to the 1980s in the case of the Aksa Mosque (see Chapters 1 and 2). Interestingly, however, in 2013 the PVV chose the small and barely visible (Turkish Shi'ite) Ehli Beyt Mosque to draw attention to noise pollution associated with azan amplification. This mosque's azan volume is very low in comparison with the Aksa Mosque, which broadcasts the azan from its minarets in Chinatown in The Hague's city center. On behalf of the PVV, municipal councillor Daniëlle de Winter made a video of the Ehli Beyt Mosque's azan. Her complaint was then reported in the influential and populist *Telegraaf* newspaper and its website. This prompted a critical response on the paper's website by municipal councillor Hasan Küçük of the Islam Democrats, a small political party active in The Hague. He called on more mosques to amplify their call to prayer.

In the winter of 2013, I visited Küçük and his colleague Said Boulayoun at their City Hall office for a conversation. At the time, Küçük had already been involved with the issue of the azan for a few years.

> PTA: I got the impression that you first had to figure out what the rules surrounding the azan were, that there is a lot of uncertainty about the issue among Dutch Muslims.
>
> SB: Let me explain how this began. In the first instance, we wanted to support a mosque, and to help them submit a permit application for the call. So we went looking for the regulations. Does one need a permit? We couldn't find anything about a permit and wondered whether it actually existed. I then asked the mayor's advisor [Victor Dobbe, VVD] about the matter, and he replied that there was no need for a permit.[22] In principle, though there are some specific rules and exceptions, we could just do it. It dawned on us that we didn't have to apply for anything and that the right to call to prayer is anchored in the law.
>
> HK: And if people complain, the municipality is allowed to set a norm for the sound level, but never to ban the azan.
>
> SB: And in The Hague such limitations have never been enforced. Although the law allows for limitations of the azan, municipalities usually do not go so far as to enforce limitations.
>
> HK: The neighborhood should not be bothered, you understand? If the sound is audible at a distance of two or three hundred meters, then that can't be very bothersome because it can barely be heard. But if the sound had a

radius of two kilometers, and you lived close to the source, then that could be annoying for you. It also depends on the height from which the sound is broadcast. For mosques, that usually means from the rooftops because many mosques don't have tall minarets.

PTA: When did you begin to take an interest in this issue?

HK: It started two years ago, in 2011. Each year in the summer, we [Islam Democrats] come together and make a schedule for the whole year. We make a list of important points that we want to put on the political agenda, and to which we will commit ourselves. The azan was one of those topics. So after finding out what the law states exactly, we brought together different mosques to talk about the issue in May 2012. We informed them that it is possible to broadcast the call, even five times a day if they wanted to, and that there is absolutely no permit requirement. Many people looked astonished, saying that 'no, you have to have a permit, you have to ask for permission, because without bureaucratic permission, nothing can be done in this [over-organized] country, right? . . . So we then showed them a statement of the mayor's advisor, including what the law states about religious sounds in public spaces, and reassured them that they could begin. The only thing they needed were loudspeakers.

It was not the first time that mosque organizations realized that a permit was not required. We may recall, for example, that in 1993 when a newly built mosque in the city of Leiden wanted to amplify the call once a week, the municipality came to the conclusion that the mosque "does not need a permit" to use loudspeakers (Chapter 2).[23] However, this news remained local at the time because many purpose-built mosques were still to be constructed and, more importantly, because second- and third-generation Muslims (who are better educated than their parents) had not yet begun to demand their right to full and equal Dutch citizenship with the fervor that they would display a decade later. And of course, the rise of the internet allowed the quick spreading of such news among Dutch Muslims. The demand for the azan, therefore, is not new but it has become a more significant channel for activism than in the past:

HK: If the churches are allowed to produce sounds, then we are as well. There is often a commotion about churches in the big cities, because they are empty and often not used as churches any more, but you can hear them all day, five times at five, pounding twelve times at twelve. I have always lived close to a church and think it's beautiful, but there are also people who have complained about the churches. Why should the church be allowed to make so many sounds [besides the clock function of bells] if it is not used as a house of worship? So there have been incidents where people protested against church bells, but I think the churches should be allowed to continue as they are, because churches are a part of the Netherlands. And mosques are a part of the Netherlands, too. And synagogues. If you look carefully, you can see that the old Dutch synagogues are not very visible. I think this shows that they did not feel so safe in the past, to have built synagogues like that. That is sad, because no one should have to hide. The same goes for temples, for anything, namely that people should not be afraid to be what they are. The same goes for mosques. They should not be invisible. They are there, but sometimes they try hard to be invisible to the non-Muslims. To be honest, I don't think we have religious liberty for that! Despite the freedom to practice a religion, we see that mosques don't always want to exercise their rights, out of fear, ignorance, because they don't want to attract negative publicity and because they don't know how to deal with such attention. The board members of Dutch mosques, [who are] unfortunately too often still from the first generation of migrants, don't know what to do. But come on! An azan is just part of a mosque. And in the Netherlands we are free. That's why we have tried to remove these barriers. [Since our information session] a few mosques have started to sound the azan, and a few are considering doing so in the near future.

PTA: So the mosque in The Hague that was in the news recently, the Ehli Beyt Mosque, began to use speakers thanks to your advice?

HK: Yes, the only thing we did was to inform them. We explained that they do not need a permit. A year later, the PVV has tried to make an issue out of it. But in the months before, there was no problem. After the PVV's campaign against the azan, two people sent a letter of complaint. But [the azan] was only [amplified] once in the afternoon on Friday! And the volume was really low! You could only hear it within 100 meters. One of the people who had complained lived 200 meters away, and another 500 meters. So they couldn't have even heard it. The mosque had also sent flowers and letters to the neighborhood to announce that they would use speakers for the call each Friday, but even months after they had done so, many residents did not know that the mosque was amplifying the call because the volume was so low and only once a week. It's just a symbolic sound that one can barely hear.

Muslim debate over the amplified azan

Not all Muslims shared Küçük's activist stance, and not merely because of ignorance or old-fashioned ways. For example, the Fatih Mosque in Amsterdam did not at the time seriously consider amplifying the azan. Mehmet Yamali, the mosque's spokesman, joked about having the azan in the center of Amsterdam in the Jordaan district: "The azaan in the Jordaan," he rhymed, as if he had just uttered a paradox. The streets and canals of the Jordaan are widely thought to constitute Amsterdam's historic heart, attracting tourists to its many art galleries, shops, and restaurants, the Anne Frank House, the Western Church, and the Homomonument that commemorates the persecution of gay men and lesbians. The Fatih Mosque is located nearby, on the Rozengracht where Rembrandt once lived. But because it is housed in a former Catholic church, people passing through the street do not realize that it is a mosque (Beekers and Tamimi Arab 2016). Yamali told me that concerns about securing permits to renovate the entrance led to them setting aside the question of the azan. Besides, he said, "It is not necessary for us to call to prayer, since most attendees don't live near the mosque anyway, so they wouldn't hear it." On the other hand, to have the "azaan in the Jordaan" would mean that the azan could be heard in a space that is usually categorized as typical of Amsterdam and therefore non-Islamic in nature. To sound the azan there required a greater acceptance of Islam in the capital, Yamali believed. "Now is not the right moment to demand such things." He was more interested in other issues such as dogmatic interpretations of Islam, which he believed should be addressed first. Rather than pushing for recognition in an activist way, Yamali thought that Muslims should first focus on emancipating themselves from within, through meditations on Islam and by being open to compromise with people of other persuasions. "When I was young, I was more aggressive in pushing for Muslim rights, but now I think we need to calm down," he once said. In short, Yamali hoped for a peaceful transition, at the grassroots level, to the possibility of broadcasting the azan in the Jordaan.

In contrast to Yamali, Küçük believed that the emancipation of Muslims hinged on actively demanding the right to amplify the azan. Thanks to the attention drawn by the PVV to the azan in The Hague, he said, more mosques began to consider broadcasting the azan because many had not realized that a permit was not required. As a politician, Küçük disagreed with the strong emphasis some mosques placed on seeking compromise and reconciliation.

> PTA: What do you think about mosques that do their best to get the neighborhood to accept the azan, or that don't broadcast the azan out of respect for others?
>
> HK: I think that they behave as if they don't have equal rights. And I think that the municipality should not be involved in deciding whether an azan will be broadcast or not.

PTA: The Center Mosque in Deventer, for example, wanted not only to exercise its rights, but also to get the neighborhood and non-Muslims to recognize their right to the azan.

HK: But they will never do that. . . . Not all non-Muslims have a problem with the azan. [Those who complain do so] for ideological reasons. [Conducting a poll] to find out whether or not to broadcast the azan [which happened in Deventer; Chapter 4] is not the answer. I think that's the same as classifying yourself as a second-class citizen. Look, for example, if all the Muslims in The Hague would vote for an Islamic political party and it became really big, should the Muslims do a poll next time to see whether they are allowed to vote? So we have this right. The others who complain know we do, but they don't agree with that right. That's the issue. They simply don't agree with the fact that we have the right to amplify the azan. But I didn't make that law. It was already there, so to say now that it does not fit Dutch culture is ridiculous.

PTA: Do you think that it is a good idea to organize dinners and events to reconcile those people with the mosque?

HK: I really think that's nonsense, just utter nonsense. If those people are really against the azan, that has nothing to do with the call to prayer. If they are against the azan, what they are expressing in fact is that they are against the Muslims who live in the same neighborhood. To protest so much against the azan means that one does not truly accept the other, who may have a different life style. And the azan is then one excuse to show this hostility. For example, when people living in other cities complain about the azan somewhere else they are simply against the azan [i.e., against Muslims]. . . . A mosque that organizes dinners looks at it from a social cohesion perspective; I mean a moral, Islamic, perspective. But I think that communicating with the neighbors does not mean that we should ask permission for the azan. I look at the issue as a politician, and as a matter of duties and rights.

PTA: The discussion is indeed often reduced to a legal and political debate about the azan. What about the social and moral issues?

HK: I think that people know very well what this is about. But they simply don't want it. I often look at things from the perspective of Islamophobes, because I think it often boils down to Islamophobia. How would they feel? [They might respond,] for example, that in some places in Turkey, it is not likely that a church could be built without starting a war. I am really upset about such things. I am Kurdish myself [i.e., familiar with Turkish discrimination against minorities], and I think that it's very important that everyone can be whoever they are, wherever they are.

If someone does not accept you to begin with, what can you talk about? Is
it really worth the trouble to change a small portion of those people through
dialogue? Continuously tiring yourself with that? I think that if Muslims want
to be accepted, they should simply be really good Muslims. If you are someone
who is honest, does not steal, is just, and so forth, that is more important. I
think that we are too often not good enough, and that has been a source of
prejudice and stigmatization against us.

In 2012 and 2013, debates between Muslims about the azan became more public
as the Center Mosque in Deventer decided to amplify the azan on a daily basis.
These occurred mostly online, indicating that it was a public debate between
young or middle-aged Muslims, rather than the elders who shared similar
concerns but engaged less in Dutch public debates. Active blogger Badr Youyou
wrote a column entitled "That the call to prayer is a right, does not mean that you
have to exercise it" in the Dutch-Muslim blog "We are staying here" (*Wij blijven
hier*).[24] Youyou called on fellow Muslims to "avoid conflicts," which he believed
had a higher priority in Islam than exercising the right to call to prayer. These
requests to "avoid *fitna* [here: civil strife]" often fell on deaf ears. Though Youyou
received positive as well as negative comments, the latter were particularly
striking. On Facebook, user Adam Mohammad wrote: "Badr Youyou strives
for an Islam that must keep quiet and not be visible to the public, a shadow of
itself. In so far as I know, a free democracy does not work that way. We don't
live in a time of master and slave mentalities." Nial Marmouch connected the
issue to racism: "Apparently, my appearance is also sometimes experienced
as provocative. I think I need to look more Dutch." Abdel Hadi thought that
taking a step back for the sake of compromise was "against human rights" and
would lead to "doing away with Islam." In short, the genie was out of the bottle.
Among Dutch Muslims, the azan had become one of the topics of public debate.
It was not long before Nourdeen Wildeman, an activist Dutch convert who is
well known among Muslim youth, published a critical response to Youyou:
"Use the right to call to prayer!"[25] Wildeman's reply revolved not only around
the question of political rights and duties, but also on the status of the azan
in Islam from a religious perspective. Youyou had said that the azan was only
mandatory inside mosques, and that loudspeakers were therefore not required,
but Wildeman's interpretation was that the azan was a "broader form of worship"
that has meaning, even when the worshiper was all alone. He cited a prophetic
saying from the canonical Hadith collection of Bukhari (translation by Muhsin
Khan, Nr. 583) to justify his interpretation of the Dutch case: "So, whenever

you are with your sheep or in the wilderness and you want to pronounce azan for the prayer raise your voice in doing so, for whoever hears the azan, whether a human being, a jinn [daemon, genie, spirit] or any other creature, will be a witness for you on the Day of Resurrection." Wildeman, like Youyou, laid emphasis on avoiding conflicts over the azan with nonbelievers. However, referring to the "constitutional freedoms" that Muslims enjoy in the Netherlands, he said that Muslims should not "hide in their homes so that no one can see us." Not calling for prayer, for Wildeman, was no different from not wearing the veil or not constructing mosques. If mosques do their best to be friendly toward their neighbors and call to prayer after having contacted their municipality and neighborhood to agree on a time span and a volume, and a resident is still not satisfied, then that person "is upset about the Constitution and local government: you can't blame Muslims for that." Not surprisingly, Wildeman's activist stance received positive reactions on the blog and on Facebook. And yet, "a call to prayer is more than merely a technical and bureaucratic matter," more than a matter of rights and duties, wrote anthropologist Martijn de Koning in the newspaper Muslim Today (*Moslim Vandaag*).[26] In other words, the issue of what kind of toleration and ethics of cohabitation should be practiced remained unresolved.

The right to feel at home

Disagreements about the azan have continued to be passionately discussed between Dutch Muslims. When I asked two young Turkish-Dutch men about the azan, in the hookah or shisha bars that are nowadays popular in Amsterdam, their differing views quickly led to a quarrel. One of them connected the azan to the functioning of a just, democratic state and society, and described the azan as a right. The other was less interested in the debate about rights and democracy, and said that Muslims should simply not force others to hear the azan against their will. "This is not Turkey," he said, to which his interlocutor reacted furiously. The latter's mother was Dutch and his father Turkish, and he himself did not want to choose between the Netherlands and Turkey when it came to religion or culture: "It's our right to amplify the azan, we live in a democracy!" But whether they agree with an activist politician like Hasan Küçük or support the position of compromise held by mosque spokesperson Mehmet Yamali, for many Dutch Muslims the azan is relevant for feeling at home. Despite their differences, the two Turkish-Dutch youths agreed on this broader implication of the azan.

The desire to feel at home, which I will discuss in greater detail in Chapter 4, is strongly influenced by national Dutch identity politics and debates. Important for our discussion on constitutional secularism is that the legal right to the azan makes it unnecessary for Muslims to compare their situation with that in other countries, although news that a mosque in Sweden or the United States is allowed to broadcast the azan may be picked up. In Chapter 1, I described a cosmopolitan, European ecumene for Islamic architecture. However, the discussion was primarily focused on the Netherlands. Comparisons were made mostly between and within various Dutch cities. In a similar vein, Verkaaik has noted that Dutch Muslims look to other mosques in the Netherlands for architectural inspiration (Verkaaik 2012: 169). Similarly, some mosques had amplified the azan for years, and others had not. To create a sense of belonging and to have what other mosques already have, people often demand the azan. In response, groups like the Islam Democrats receive hate mail and threats, often expressing the sentiment that "if they don't like it here, they should go back to their country." The "native" position is not considered debatable by nativists (Duyvendak 2011: 100). In this context, Muslims experience rejections of the azan as direct attacks on their right to feel at home in the Netherlands. Hasan Küçük made this clear by appropriating the term *integration*:

> When you go to the mosque, there are often people relaxing in front of the door, usually when it's warm in the summer. When they hear the sound of the mosque [the call to prayer], they go inside. That's very pleasant for them. And it's better for the neighborhood, because they feel more at home. I think it furthers their integration, because being accepted results in greater participation. That is something natural: if you accept me, and I feel at home in my environment, then I will feel more committed. And the azan is a part of that, because many Muslims say that it makes them feel good. My father, for example, once said that he had heard the azan when passing by a mosque. He said that that made him feel at home, that it was as if he was back in Turkey. If that sound can let such feelings emerge, then that is very positive. . . . The people [Muslims] don't consider themselves as guests any longer. We are a part of society, Dutch citizens, and it is our country. . . . It's exactly like princess Maxima said [that there is no such thing as "the" Dutch identity]. . . . The azan is like voting. One doesn't need permission to vote. If you are a citizen, then you can vote. Period. End of discussion!

As in other cases, the municipal office of The Hague affirmed mosques' right to broadcast the azan. According to the *Telegraaf* newspaper, a municipality spokesman confirmed that the mosque did not need a special permit to broadcast the azan and that, in case of disagreements, rather than solving the matter by going to court, the municipality was willing to appoint a negotiator for informal conversations between residents and the mosque board.[27] Küçük hoped that this message would motivate more Dutch mosques to sound the azan in the future. For him and others, the legal right to sound the azan promised the ability to fully feel at home in the future:

> Thanks to the PVV['s complaints] everyone in the Netherlands now knows that we are allowed to amplify the azan. It's Dutch! [laughs] We, the Islam Democrats, had done our best, but many didn't listen. So sometimes, one needs the PVV, because people don't know what their rights are. . . . Our goal is to make mosques aware of their rights. For now, we are already happy if mosques amplify the azan for the Friday prayers. During Ramadan, we would [also] like to hear the call for the evening prayers. Eventually we would like to hear the azan four times a day, so not for the morning prayers yet. And *inshallah* (God willing), in ten or twenty years we can hear the azan five times a day [laughs]. Five times a day! If that happens in the Netherlands, then we [will] know that we are recognized and belong to this society.

Have liberalism and secularism silenced the azan?

After decades of constructing mosques in the Netherlands, Dutch Muslims have addressed the right to amplify the azan as the next step in their demand for equal rights. Despite persistent nativist resistance, thanks to legal equality, historical precedents, and increased practical experience by municipalities with mosque building issues, the right to purpose-built mosques has been strengthened (cf. Verkaaik and Tamimi Arab 2016). In the case of the azan, we have so far seen how constitutional secularism enabled the increasing demand to amplify the azan. How this constitutional secularism will maintain itself against the bottom-up pressure from nativist secularists in society and the top-down influence of xenophobic political parties remains to be seen. Despite skepticism in Dutch society against the azan, the Netherlands has not allowed referenda on such matters, unlike Switzerland where a majority of the populace voted in favor of a minaret ban in 2009. In other words, when it comes to constructing mosques or amplifying the azan, Muslims do not need a radical alternative to constitutional secularism. It would be more accurate to say that what is required for the societal emancipation of Muslims is an alternative culture of secularism, one that promises greater toleration of public worship.

Isaac Weiner has observed a similar unfolding of events in the United States. In his book *Religion Out Loud*, he ends with the positive account of an American Muslim community's azan being "able to be broadcast freely without censure" (2014: 191). In the introduction, however, he writes: "Liberal theory and legal regulation have not always been able to keep religion quiet" (2014: 7). To prove the latter claim, he discusses the struggles of various religious groups throughout American history. This does not sit well with the positive side of the story of the governance of religious plurality, namely that American liberal governance has granted different religions the right to create religious soundscapes but without totally ignoring the rights of others to be left alone. Contrary to Talal Asad's (2003) sweeping critique of secularism and liberalism, which Weiner cites without specific discussion, Weiner shows that a trend toward constitutional secularization enabled US courts to reject religious arguments against religions that did not subscribe to a dominant Protestant morality. Hence, only secular or profane arguments could be made to prohibit a religious group's sounds, such as Catholic bell ringing or Jehovah's Witnesses who used megaphones in public parks. However, Weiner also shows that, despite constitutional disestablishment, "numerous state laws continued [in the nineteenth and twentieth centuries] to privilege and promote Protestant moral precepts on expressly religious grounds, and several state courts explicitly affirmed that Christianity was part of the common law" (2014: 28). He further describes how principles of secularism have been employed to the theological advantage of certain groups against others, and argues nevertheless that it was the "broader secularizing trend in US law" that enabled the limiting of Protestant bias, in particular against Catholics (2014: 35). A secular government treats religion, as much as possible, "like anything else, entitled to a robust public presence as long as it remained subject to otherwise valid content-neutral nondiscriminatory regulations" (2014: 152). Since a (relatively) similar kind of constitutional secularism is also implemented in the Netherlands, we can say that political liberalism in a Rawlsian sense (2005), that is, that promotes equal rights regardless of substantial cultural and religious claims, has enabled the azan in a social context in which cultural secularism dominates.

We could go one step further in our argument by saying that the data offered in this chapter shows that what matters perhaps more than "secularism" in actual practices of governance are practices of constitutionalism (sec. Bader 2007), that is, not only the law but also the willingness by involved actors to implement it in practice. Concepts such as "constitutional secularism" and "cultural secularism" are useful for exploring the complexity of secularism in the case of the azan, but can also simplify the same empirical complexity. One objection would be, for instance, that what I have called *cultural* and *constitutional secularism* overlap. This overlapping can be shown to be part of "a Secular Age," in which religion has become "one option among others" (Taylor 2007: 3) for majorities in countries such as the Netherlands, rather than the unquestionable background of all citizens. The term *secular*, then, does not mean a simple privatization of religion that is now overturned because of Islamic public worship. In a culturally secular age, the ways secular states regulate (minority) religions function as incentives to respond to state definitions of religion and of the boundary between the religious and the nonreligious. This secular regulation and governance of religions has no (explicit) divine goals, but is geared toward the profane problems of order, stability, and cohesion. Isaac Weiner's understanding of constitutional secularization as treating religion like "anything else" resonates with this view of the secular age as an era in which religion is culturally one option among many.

Because of the possible vagueness of the term *secularism*, we could also tell the story of the azan without "translating everything into the language of *secularism*" (Bader 2012: 22), and instead opt for precise descriptions of institutions, laws, policies, and implementations in practice. Such an approach would not avoid the term *secularism* because the Dutch state is not a secular state or because the constitution is not a secular one, but because in calling state and constitution *secular*, we have not yet explained how the Dutch system may contrast with others. To do that, we need to explain in detail how the state functions in practice. The absence of an explicit mention of the "separation of church and state" in the Dutch Constitution already suggests that priority lies with codified rights and principles rather than "secularism." Philosopher Veit Bader interprets this as a priority for *liberal democratic constitutionalism*. Bader's term may be preferred over "constitutional secularism," since there are authoritarian secular regimes, with secular constitutions, who discriminate against religious minorities. Obviously, his use of the terms *liberal* and *democratic* cannot mean random majoritarianism; rather, they refer to countries that uphold democratic principles such as equality to manage and allow the production of religious pluralism. Therefore, if we base our argument on states that actually exist and not on imagined alternatives that are nonexistent at present, the divide between non-liberal, nondemocratic states and liberal democratic states becomes more decisive than the divide between the secular and the religious. In that sense, we can avoid the confusing term *secularism* altogether. Instead, we can talk for instance about the twin autonomies of the state from the mosque and the mosque from the state (cf. Bader 2012: 21). In the Netherlands, the (relative) autonomy of religions from the state has the consequence that the state may not disallow sounds on religious grounds, whether they be church bells, the azan, or the sounds of other groups like the chanting of Dutch Hare Krishna. Collecting such aspects within the scope of a single concept—"secularism"—can be very imprecise when we are spelling out the empirical characteristics of national models of governance such as French republicanism versus Dutch liberal democratic constitutionalism.

Despite these precautions, I also think that we cannot avoid the concept of secularism altogether. This is because constitutional secularism is an institutional arrangement that enables stakeholders to challenge religious bias or bias against religions in society as well as government. As Akeel Bilgrami puts it, secularism, when required, can take an "adversarial" stance against religion (2014: 4, 12–13), but also against secularists who discriminate religious minorities. Ultimately, constitutional secularism is an oppositional concept that "knows itself" primarily through opposition to political (and constitutional) theocracy. At the start of this chapter, I wrote that we do not need to delve into the question of theocracy to show the merits of constitutional secularism in the Netherlands. There is simply no realistic prospect of the strong establishment of any religion in this context. Political theocracy exists mainly in Dutch imaginings of the European past, or in theocratic countries that are perceived as distant and non-Western. In Dutch public debates, theocracy is often invoked selectively to resist the public presence of Islam in the Netherlands and to justify anti-Muslim racism. The concept of theocracy, a critic can persuasively argue, is therefore not helpful in explaining the nature of secularism in the Netherlands today. Such a critique, however, does not take away the fact that the term *constitutional secularism* implies a power that is geared toward disciplining and regulating not only religious bias, but also secularist bias against religious minorities as is the case in the Netherlands today. To use the word *secularism* here is to acknowledge this power relation that is obscured in the more neutral sounding "nonreligious" liberal democratic state.

Also, many scholars from various backgrounds succumb to the platitude that, because secular regimes have committed crimes against humanity, constitutional secularism is not necessarily the answer to resolving one (religious) group's bias against another (e.g., van der Veer 2001: 20; Asad 2003: 10; Bader 2007: 97). This misses the point, for we have still not done away with the normative rejection of the strong establishment of a religion (sec. Bhargava 2010a: 92).[28] While theocracy is a generalizing concept and there can be many different institutional arrangements that are theocratic or have theocratic elements, and even though these can differ substantially in degrees of equality and liberty actually achieved, the point of constitutional secularism is that religious regimes of governance are prone to be biased to an unacceptable degree. Theocracy is fundamentally incompatible with liberal notions of fairness toward different religions and especially (religious) individuals, whether these regimes exist in contemporary reality or back in history, and whether they are strongly or weakly established.

Weak establishments of churches still in existence in European countries clearly show "signs of earlier strong establishment," as we saw in Chapter 2; disestablishment is therefore required for full equality. In countries like the Netherlands, "Existing legal rules and practices should be scrutinized for morally intolerable ethno-religious bias and we can expect many instances of outdated ethno-centrist and denominationalist bias" (Bader 2007: 153). This prescription can be nuanced by arguing that the weak establishment of a religion does not necessarily result in grossly biased connections between the state and religion(s) (Modood 2014). But, while the weak or moderate establishment of a church is not problematic per se or will not automatically lead to a bias against the principles of the liberal democratic constitutional state, we have seen that in the Netherlands the long path toward weak establishment and even constitutional disestablishment, though the monarch remains a Protestant (with a Roman Catholic queen), has coincided with treating different religious groups more fairly. This need not always be the empirical case, but the suspicion of the establishment of an organized church or a religion remains justified, thanks to successful historic precedents of legally overturning Protestant bias in, for example, the United States and the Netherlands (Weiner 2014; Chapter 2).

To conclude, the case study of the azan shows that the 1983 disestablishment of the church in the Netherlands is being tested in the twenty-first century by Islamic claims to implement equal rights. This has prompted the "counter-mobilisation of old religions, nativists and aggressive secularists" (Bader 2007: 224). It is important to recall that the voices in society that wish to silence the azan are not themselves "secularist" per se. The case of the SGP's orthodox Protestant resistance to the azan demonstrates that the fundamental issue in such conflicts does not have to be secularism, and that one does not need to be a secularist to be against the azan. A biased culturalist nativism, tied to old Protestant notions of the nation, underlies the thinking of various groups that are against allowing the use of loudspeakers for the azan. By moderately disciplining these biased voices through legal limits, Dutch constitutional secularism enables the amplification of Islam. In the next chapter, we will observe this further at the micro level of mosque-municipality-neighborhood negotiations.

Regulating Nostalgias: Azan Negotiations in a Dutch Town

A better environment begins with oneself. Many Dutchmen are irritated by the pollution of public space by Islam. In some places our streets increasingly resemble the streetscapes of Mecca and Tehran: headscarves, hate-beards, burqas, men in weird white dresses. Madame President, let us for once do something about this. Let us reconquer our streets. Let us make sure that the Netherlands will finally again look like the Netherlands.

Geert Wilders in the Dutch Parliament, 2009

***

In the winter of 2013, I attended a dinner in the dreamy town of Delft. The hosts and friends were a mixture of so-called hipsters, industrial design graduates, and one left-leaning economist—not the kind of people that support conservative Dutch political parties. I was asked about my research and mentioned the example of using loudspeakers for a daily azan in Deventer, a small town in the province of Overijssel. One of the guests, Julie, knew all about it because her sister lived a block behind Deventer's Center Mosque. "They were really pushy and insensitive to the neighborhood," she said indignantly, speaking of the Turkish-Dutch Muslims in the town. The others politely refrained from commenting. On another occasion, I spoke about the Deventer azan case with Marieke, a young interior designer working in Amsterdam. "I think you have to see it as driving a car," she said. "It's common sense to drive on the right side of the road. If anyone changes the driving direction, that will lead to a crash. I don't understand why people [the Turkish Muslims] can't see that." I nodded and Marieke appeared at ease and calm. For her it was common sense, or at least the first thing that came into her mind, that the daily afternoon amplification of the azan would be a step too far. In anthropological parlance: Muslims should refrain from such demands because they violate an existing cultural consensus.

In her immediate reaction, whether or not the law or local government affirmed the right to amplify the call did not play any role.

Julie and Marieke are progressives with cultural roots in the Dutch 1960s, with the "live and let live" attitudes of their parents' generation. According to sociologist Jan Willem Duyvendak, such examples of indignation or hesitance to affirm Muslims' rights to public worship may seem surprising, due to an often exaggerated notion of the Netherlands as a highly pluralist and tolerant society. In fact, on the basis of several corroborating surveys, he argues that in terms of shared values, the Netherlands today is one of the most homogenous countries in Europe (2011: 88). Its citizens see themselves as agreeing on many basic, progressive values, while the presence of especially conservative Muslims is seen as spoiling cultural unity. In other words, the unwanted presence of Muslims actually undermines the self-conception of the Dutch as essentially progressive, and the idea of religious tolerance—for which the Dutch are famous—has been repeatedly questioned and examined, not only by scholars but also more broadly in Dutch civil society and beyond, in light of the irritating presence of public Islam. Marieke did not appear to think that describing Muslims as individuals who are driving on the wrong side of the road betrays a nativist bias or intolerance. That was simply how things were. It cannot be sufficiently emphasized that ordinary citizens like Julie and Marieke, who are not at all conservative or extreme, usually prefer not to hear the azan in their backyards. They do not, however, impolitely dwell on such matters. Likewise, Dutch Muslims of all backgrounds have told me, on many occasions, that it would be an unwise provocation to amplify the call to prayer because Dutch non-Muslims are not used to the azan. This argument is possible because of the view that Islam does not absolutely require a loud azan. Muslims can practice their religion, therefore, without attracting too much negative attention with the call to prayer. Since only 5 percent of the Netherlands is Muslim, and an even smaller portion actually practices Islam in a mosque, many nonpracticing and less than strictly observant Muslims told me that the whole issue should not be blown out of proportion. None of these everyday conversations with Muslims and non-Muslims, however, ever led to someone claiming that the azan should be explicitly banned by law.

In the previous chapter, we saw that political parties ordinarily categorized as right-wing or conservative have been rather active in trying to limit or ban the azan, though without any serious proposals or amendments to the constitution. We should also take into account that, at the local level, members of those same parties can assist mosques to amplify their call to prayer. While a member of parliament engaged in noisy media politics may apply a culturalist notion of secularism and propose a ban on the Muslim call to prayer, an alderman or *wethouder*, literally an "upholder of the law" who works at the local level, may employ a constitutional notion of secularism that facilitates amplifying Islam in the Netherlands. The logic of a negotiation for the azan in a small town, and the task of an involved alderman looking for a practical and lawful solution, is very different from the language and interests of culturalist critics of the public presence of Islam. Faced with demands by mosque leaders, local bureaucrats (*ambtenaren*) and politicians try to balance competing demands without stepping outside the rules set by the Public Manifestations Act. Following John Bowen et al. (2014), we could say that different actors engaged at different sociological levels employ different "practical schemas" with respect to the azan.[1] My empirical data suggests that it is inaccurate to conceptualize the state and Muslims as two homogenous blocs in a face-off (compare Bowen et al. 2014: 4), nor are secularism or liberalism in a face-off with Islam. Instead, what we find on the ground is a multilayered Dutch state that calls for a qualitative ethnographic approach that does justice to its internal contradictions and contingencies. As indicated in the previous chapter, the facile political categories of left and right are also not helpful here. It is not my intention in this chapter to set up Muslims and non-Muslims, natives and nonnatives, as monolithic, opposing categories either. Divisions around the azan are, however, de facto centered around thick, commonsensical notions of the idea of home (e.g., Ghorashi 2003), a form of nativism that makes it difficult for "allochthons" to feel at home in the imagined community that is the Netherlands. At the same time, pressure from Muslim citizens to change definitions of what *home* means in Dutch streets, particularly in the case of the azan, is experienced by the majority of the "autochthonous" population as insensitive and as environmental pollution. Therefore, since this chapter is about a group conflict shaped by stereotypes, I conclude with a reflection on the possibility of undoing "us versus them" thinking in relation to the praxis of constitutional secularism in the Netherlands.

The main goal of this chapter is to document local azan negotiations and describe how they slowly shifted aural boundaries in a small Dutch town. In Chapter 3, the emphasis was on theoretical debates regarding constitutional secularism and Dutch laws and policies that enable Dutch Muslims to amplify the azan, despite various complaints. My claim about the positive value of secularism as correcting bias against religious minorities now needs to be further corroborated by a specific ethnography of azan negotiations. How do state actors, mosques, and neighborhoods actually interact to come to an agreement on the use of loudspeakers? In other words, how does constitutional secularism, defined as the separation of church and state in Dutch public discourses, actually function on the ground?

Before moving on to the case study, I start with an explanation of how the azan, perceived as both noise pollution and as a way of realizing home in a small Dutch town, can be productively interpreted through the concept of nostalgia. Rather than any notion of secularism, the complaints and demands in actual negotiations revolved much more around sentiments of feeling at home or feeling alienated. Turkish-Dutch Muslims in particular often explicitly used the word nostalgia (*nostalgie*), claiming that the azan reminds them or their parents of Turkey but also that broadcasting it can help them to feel at home in the Netherlands. My analysis of the soundscape dispute in a small town like Deventer builds on two books that analyze home feelings in the Netherlands more broadly, *The Perils of Belonging* (Geschiere 2009) and *The Politics of Home* (Duyvendak 2011). The documentation of Deventer's azan negotiations begins with the first informational meeting that was held one evening in the summer of 2012 with irritated neighborhood residents, followed by a history of Turkish guest workers and the construction of the Center Mosque. We then turn to negotiations in the autumn of 2012 and the views of the mosque's chairman, Orkan Yücel. A poll was finally conducted in January 2013 to assess how many residents objected to the azan and whether an agreement on a daily azan could be reached.

Nostalgia and pollution in a small Dutch town

To develop a more complete understanding of how the Netherlands is dealing with religious diversity, ethnographic data from the major cities of the South and North provinces of Holland, Amsterdam, The Hague, and Rotterdam, need to be balanced with developments in small towns and cities in other provinces. It is precisely in small towns that the globalization of the local is experienced as very intrusive, and also where residents with not-in-my-backyard sentiments often express feelings of "white powerlessness" (e.g., Maly et al. 2013; Byrne 2007) in the face of powerful economic and political institutions and encroaching globalized Islam. Such feelings are mobilized and provoked by Party for Freedom leader Geert Wilders. In 2013, for instance, he spoke about the threat of economic downfall at the hands of a "Brussels elite." It was not the economy, however, but Islam that was "the greatest problem that faces our nation." Such political parties feed the "old demon" of racism, which, contrary to popular Dutch belief, never disappeared (Gray cited in Essed and Hoving 2014: 13–14). That is why Philomena Essed and Isabel Hoving chose an image of an endangered, typical Dutch landscape for the cover of their volume *Dutch Racism*. As black clouds gather, ecological disaster is impending (Figure 8). The toxic politics of racism are endangering the Netherlands in a time of European economic and political crisis.

But contrary to the volume editors' perception of racism as quintessentially polluting, the image can also be interpreted as depicting how alien environmental pollution threatens an "autochthonous" conception of the Netherlands. The black clouds would then symbolize the immigrants whose kids will go to "black schools" (*zwarte scholen*), as they are called in the Netherlands (this includes schools with many Muslim citizens of Turkish and Moroccan descent). Immigrants are coming to change a nostalgic Dutch landscape comprising an open field, grazing cows, and a beautiful array of white clouds: a landscape and a skyscape that can still be seen throughout the Netherlands, but also in paintings from the "Golden Age" (*de Gouden Eeuw*; the seventeenth century) engrained in the cultural self-understanding of the Dutch. In response to such a danger of pollution, the function of defending what is perceived as local and nostalgia

Figure 8 Cover image of *Dutch Racism*. Frits Weeda. Diemerzeedijk, 1962.

for a homogenous nation is to affirm a conception of the self under threat (cf. Duyvendak 2011; Boym 2001). Indeed, psychologists have consistently described nostalgia as a resource for the self: "Nostalgia serves a diverse array of functions, ranging from its buffering effects on loneliness to its enhancing effects on explicit self esteem. The breadth of these functions suggests that nostalgic reverie serves to affirm the self, protecting it from threat" (Vess et al. 2012, see also Sedikides et al. 2009; Wildschut et al. 2006). In social psychology, nostalgia is linked to the individual's experience of crisis in a society where one may not feel at home, and in some cases to clinical depression and psychosomatic symptoms. Feelings of nostalgia are also frequently associated with sound, especially music, by psychologists, sociologists, and anthropologists, and can be understood as coping strategies (e.g., Khorsandi and Saarikallio 2013; Gazzah 2008; Zentner et al. 2008; Jäncke 2008; Juslin and Sloboda 2001). For Dutch natives, nostalgia for a past home can provide a sense of group identity, and can counter feelings of being alienated in one's own neighborhood. At the same time, nostalgia functions as a coping strategy for immigrants in their new home to construct and recall memories, to fantasize, and often to undergo bittersweet processes of coping (cf. Akhtar 1999). For immigrants, refugees, and their children, nostalgic sentiments can dominate everyday life even decades later, and help to preserve and (re)construct ancestral identities. As a response to (perceived) loss, nostalgia makes the present meaningful by functioning as an existential resource (Routledge et al. 2011; Duyvendak 2011: 28).[2]

In Chapter 1 we saw that avant-garde solutions to the azan are rarely backed by the ordinary everyday worshiper who does support the use of loudspeakers. He—they are usually men—is much more interested in retrieving the familiar azan, which challenges Dutch ideas about the local with a transnational Turkish Muslim presence (cf. Kendall 2009: 305). The Center Mosque in Deventer too reproduces the familiar forms of typical "Ottoman" mosques: its minaret and accompanying amplified azan are based on what can be seen and heard in the streets of Istanbul. Both the Turkish-Dutch citizens, who feel that they are represented by a mosque, and the Dutch population that recognizes itself in the windmill next door appeal to primal forms of belonging (cf. Geschiere 2009: 223), which are experienced as natural and needing no explanation because they are connections of blood and soil, *Blut und Boden*. Nostalgic feelings of home are at the same time future oriented: they project an ideal from the past for a future home, spelling out rules of homemaking in the here and now. When such nostalgias compete, the matter quickly becomes one of making or breaking home feelings by appropriating territory (Maly et al. 2012;

Weiner 2014: 163). In the Netherlands, migrants who express their feelings of nostalgia or homesickness for their or their parents' country of birth in a way that is critical of the Dutch situation frequently receive the angry response that if they do not "feel at home" they should "go home." Duyvendak sums this up as that "The native position is not in question, along with their views on what is required to feel at home in the Netherlands" (Duyvendak 2011: 100).

Echoing Mary Douglas (2002 [1966]), Duyvendak also writes that Muslims "spoil" (2011: 101) the home feelings of Dutch natives, and that mosques, headscarves, and the call to prayer are symbols that are perceived as being "out of place" (2011: 85). The concept of autochthony, used in all layers of society, helps to create the strong feeling that "natives" (*autochtonen*) have the right to prescribe which religious aesthetics are out of place and which are not. The realization that little can be done to stop the construction of a mosque or the use of loudspeakers for the azan is then met with great indignation, frustration, and a sense of not being heard. These emotions are expressed by describing the azan as a kind of noise pollution (*geluidsoverlast, geluidshinder, herrie*). The Dutch words for noise pollution indicate a transgression of commonly accepted sonic boundaries and have the benefit that noise pollution can be rather easily interpreted as a neutral concept, so that it does not appear biased against a specific religion. However, when Muslims invoked the parallel with noise caused by cars, trains, and so forth, the response was a rejection of an equation of the azan with ordinary secular sounds. This comes as no surprise, recalling Douglas's analysis of noise pollution as cultural, symbolic, and political.

Therefore, in the Netherlands, the association of the azan with noise pollution cannot be disconnected from more general negative evaluations of Islam as a religion, fear of violence, and pejorative imaginings of Muslims across Europe. The religious aspect of the azan is experienced as transgressing the hygienic distance between non-Muslims and Muslims as an impure sacred. Douglas stresses that relations with the sacred "are bound to be expressed by rituals of separation and demarcation and by beliefs in the danger of crossing forbidden boundaries" (2002: 27). "Pollution behavior" (2002: 43), such as setting clear boundaries of private and public, may help to ameliorate the threat, but amplified sounds can partially undo the distinction. Isaac Weiner aptly describes this for the American context as sound "spilling over and across imagined boundaries between public and private, between self and other," and "in ways that have often felt uncontrollable and uncontainable" (2014: 2). Sound easily transgresses pollution boundaries, which is why it is so often described as testing the limits of tolerance. As one elderly lady, sitting in her home in the town of Amersfoort, told a television crew: "I feel vomited out [*ik voel me uitgekotst*] of the neighborhood!" The proximity of a mosque and the intrusion of the azan had made her feel sick, emphasizing her loneliness in a neighborhood where she had little meaningful encounters with the Muslim others.

For those who are strongly agitated by the azan, it is not merely an annoying but an unwanted sound that turns the listener into an unwilling object of sacred Islamic attention. Their irritation suggests that the sound of the azan is associated with the sensation of touch, turning the Islamic soundscape into a type of physical threat, albeit a very soft one.[3] Nevertheless, because touch is the "most personal of the senses," according to musicologist Raymond Murray Schafer, and because hearing is "a way of touching at a distance" (1994: 11), sound can be experienced as intimate and, when disliked, intrusive. Similarly, the simple definition of dirt as matter out of place and hygiene as a matter of aesthetics (Douglas 2002: 44) fits well with the rejections of the azan in Deventer as noise pollution. The transgression of common sense, as in driving on the wrong side of the road, is associated with impurity and danger, provoking anxiety and fear.

The first informational evening on the amplified azan

The dispute about Deventer's Center Mosque began in the summer of 2012, after the mosque had mailed a letter to neighborhood residents in which it announced that the call would soon be amplified on a daily basis:

> Dear neighbors,
>
> We want to inform you about our intention to amplify the azan (the call to prayer). . . . Depending on the period in the year, it will be once or twice a day. The azan lasts for about 2 or 3 minutes (with a maximum of 5 minutes). Our equipment is, in terms of volume, in accordance with existing agreements with the municipality of Deventer.

Mosque chairman Yücel anticipated negative reactions and told the local newspaper *de Stentor* that "We don't want to engage in a battle with the neighborhood to sound the azan at all costs." Neighbors likewise emphasized that they were not looking for trouble. One woman said to the paper: "I am not against the mosque, not at all. . . . That they want to broadcast the call to prayer every Friday is fine, but to have to hear that every day goes a bit far, I think."[4] In a critical article, one of the newspapers' editors, Berend van de Sande, agreed that the "Friday azan by now belongs to the neighborhood, just like the church bells on the Sunday morning" but that a daily azan would be "a step too far."[5] These initial moments in the azan negotiations later proved to be crucial. Scholars of noise annoyance have repeatedly concluded that the nature of relations between neighbors, good or bad, and the perception of noise avoidability determine the experience of annoyance (Bröer 2006: 27–29; Bosnak 1998). Residents respond better to policies of noise annoyance management when they appreciate prior procedures in which they were allowed to express an opinion (Schuemer and Schreckenberg 2000). On the other hand, resistance to the azan existed prior to any negotiations—its undesirability had been a topic of discussion when the mosque construction was planned.

Non-Muslim residents I spoke with frequently expressed dismay at the letter's religious content. It was important for azan opponents to preserve a right to indifference toward Islam, and they wanted to discuss the matter without going into the specific content of the call. One man joked: "For all I care they can call to prayer for the flying spaghetti monster. To me, it doesn't matter what their religion is." Despite the fact that parts of the neighborhood were on summer vacation at the time and had not seen the letter, the mosque received around seventy e-mail replies, many of which were negative. In response, those who had complained were invited to an "informational evening" so that the mosque chairman could explain the intention and desire of the mosque. My first visit to the mosque was for this meeting in July. Visitors were greeted warmly and offered something to eat and drink. It was obvious that the event organizers were doing their best to appease their guests. They had refrained from inviting the mosque's members, and limited the Turkish presence to just a few people who were interested and had helped organize the evening. As the visitors gradually arrived, the mosque chairman and an assistant started up their PowerPoint presentation. Around forty neighborhood residents were present. Most of them seemed calm, but I was astonished to see an elderly man entering the room with an angry look on his face. It began to dawn on me just how upset some neighbors were.

Orkan Yücel, the middle-aged chairman of the mosque, explained the program for the evening. He wanted to talk about the basics of the Islamic call to prayer, the desire to amplify the call, and how often the mosque would like to do so. The chairman spoke in a soft and calm tone, but his message that the mosque would amplify the call on a daily basis irritated the audience. They had basically come to the informational evening to protest that decision. The old man who was visibly angry stood up and objected in a loud voice. It was not long before I found myself in a tense atmosphere in which the chairman was repeatedly and harshly criticized for "deciding without discussing the matter with the neighborhood" and for "not respecting agreements made earlier." The residents were angry that the letter that had been sent to them suggested that the matter was already decided, and the evening was intended to be informational rather than dialogical (Figure 9).

The chairman explained that the mosque had decided on a compromise, namely to limit the daily azan to once instead of twice a day. By doing so, Yücel felt that he respected both the non-Muslim as well as the Muslim residents' demands. Two young men stood up and asked the chairman whether this meeting would affect the decision to amplify on a daily basis at all. The chairman answered that residents should be informed, but that ultimately it was the mosque community's right to decide since it was their property and the azan would not exceed the volume for which a permit is required (in fact, a permit is not required for religious sounds). "If you have already decided, then this meeting is useless," the young men countered and left the building. A moment later, another man who had been silent so far stood up and said in a loud voice that the evening was pointless because there was no real interaction between the opposing parties. As he left, he shouted, "You Muslims are always like this!" At this point some in the crowd tried to hush him. A few residents clearly wanted to avoid talk of Muslims being "good" or "bad." They simply repeatedly stated their desire not to hear the call to prayer as neutrally as possible: "Everyone has a right to their religion . . . [but] we don't want to hear it when we are sitting in

Figure 9 First informational evening on the azan in Deventer (author on the right). Photograph by Ronald Hissink, Summer 2012.

our backyard. That's all." Rather than criticizing religion, they tried to debate the azan merely as noise rather than as sacred sound. The azan opponents wanted to avoid being perceived as bigoted against a religious minority, and understood that anti-Muslim statements would not be accepted in public debates.

Weiner has made a similar observation in the United States, where Christian exclusivity was not defended in public debates around the azan in Hamtramck. In his fieldwork, he found that "even the most extreme advocates of Christian exclusivism recognized that those arguments would not be welcomed by Hamtramck's council. . . . Secular modes of governance required an alternative set of public arguments" (Weiner 2014: 175–76). This was even more the case in secularized Deventer than in Hamtramck (a town connected to Detroit), where Christians could not resist delving into the azan's religious significance and debating theological differences with Muslims (2014: 181). None of the azan opponents in Deventer made references to Christianity in order to reject the azan. The right to be free from religion was clearly more important to them than defining Islam as a threat to Christianity. The mosque chairman joked a few times that maybe one day opponents would find the azan beautiful, which made people smile or laugh, but they remained steadfast in their refusal to engage in any kind of *verstehen* of Islam. The result of the residents' performance of supposed indifference toward the meaning of the azan, both from a religious perspective and from the perspective of the former guest workers, was that much of the evening was about coming to a formal agreement.

The chairman also said that, from a religious perspective, the amplified azan was not mandatory. This too is worthwhile to compare with Weiner's research, in particular his description of American Jehovah's Witnesses who refused to differentiate between aesthetic religious forms and essential beliefs. They could not, in Weiner's description, distinguish the practice of proselytizing with megaphones in public parks from their inner beliefs. This contradicts the fact that Jehovah's Witnesses were happy to stop using megaphones after they felt vindicated by the Supreme Court and found that it was not an effective way of proselytizing (*Saia v. New York*, 1948; Weiner 2014: 135). The particular form of the practice of using megaphones attached to cars to spread their message was, in hindsight, not so essential after all. The same can be said of the Turkish-Dutch Muslims in Deventer, who insisted on the right to amplify the azan, but never claimed that using loudspeakers was essential from a religious perspective. Departing from a strictly Islamic perspective, mosque goers in Deventer differentiated between the amplified azan and the ultimate inner content of their religion.[6] The desire to amplify the azan had more to do with the Turkish-Dutch residents' right to public religion and with nostalgic feelings about Turkey, but it was also linked to the wish to continue a religious practice which they saw as important—though not essential in an absolute sense—in Islam. The chairman also resorted to defending the desire to amplify the azan with a nativist argument, rather than one based exclusively on civil rights: "We have been here for fifty years and it is therefore our right to publicly practice our religion." The fact that the use of loudspeakers was not mandatory from a religious perspective, however, was seen as an opportunity by opponents to convince the mosque not to broadcast the azan. The non-Muslim Dutch residents were careful to steer the discussion away from ethical topics such as the sense of feeling at home, nostalgia, and cultural recognition. They repeatedly asked why the call had to be broadcast if it was not absolutely necessary for the religion. Some openly wondered if, given this theological fact, it fell under the rubric of religious liberty.

Accustomed as they were to the Dutch *poldermodel*, a culture of pragmatic and inclusive negotiation that is the basis for what political scientist Arend Lijphart (1999) described as the consensus model of governance, the residents felt that the Turkish-Dutch chairman did not understand their way of doing things and used language that was too authoritarian. He spoke as if he was "commanding," something that does not belong in a "democracy" and causes a great sense of "anxiety."[7] When the disagreements began to escalate, a former chairman of the mosque who was also seated in the audience jumped in to ease the situation. Orhan Arslan spoke in a tone that gave the residents more confidence that the mosque would indeed listen to their wishes. The former chairman, who was a municipal councillor affiliated to the progressive GreenLeft party, had more experience in dealing with such situations than the new chairman, who worked in Information Technology. Finally, an agreement was reached that, as a test, the mosque would broadcast the daily call only for a week, and that neighborhood residents would come together again after the summer vacation for another negotiation. A few days later Lenie, one of the Dutch neighbors, said:

> The event, the way everything went, the communication style, has caused much unrest. That includes people who did not attend the event. What I noticed at the informational evening is that some said that they are integrated and speak the language, but that again communicating was the main obstacle. The fact that one speaks the language does not mean that one can communicate. For that one needs a basic understanding of the culture and I believe the chairman lacked such an understanding. It was thanks to the former chairman jumping in that

a real conflict was averted. What I personally think is that we, as neighborhood residents, are not taken seriously. That feeling still exists.

Another issue was that the residents complained that, when the mosque had sought a construction permit for the building more than a decade ago, it had agreed not to amplify the call more than once a week on Fridays. This point turned the discussion at the informational evening into a dispute over the legal standing of oral agreements made in the past; were they binding or not? According to Daaf Ledeboer, a municipal councillor from the Liberal Party, the chairman could not demand to amplify the call on a daily basis because of these former agreements. The chairman was unprepared for such an argument, since he did not know about earlier agreements or about the specifics of Dutch law. Ledeboer's argument was flawed, since the azan is constitutionally guaranteed, but created an opportunity to argue against the azan in the heat of the moment. The discussion was thus pushed further toward a legal debate, rather than a moral one. Before coming to the meeting, Ledeboer, who lives in the neighborhood, had already written to the municipality with questions about the mosque's demand for the azan. Mayor Heidema (Christian Union, a conservative, centrist party) had responded that it was "wise to start a dialogue with the neighborhood" and that "currently the sound volume does not exceed what is legally allowed."[8]

Turkish guest workers and the construction of the Center Mosque Deventer

A few days after the informational evening, the mosque chairman sent an invitation to the neighborhood for an *iftar* meal, an attempt to make peace with the neighborhood, and the holy month of Ramadan provided the opportunity. At the same time, he felt hurt and later confided to me that he had avoided making sharp statements at the first informational evening, but that he could have. He mentioned the neighborhood residents' proposal that the mosque be built away from the city on a "deserted field, where no one would be disturbed by the building or the azan. . . . I could have used these things also to criticize them, but I didn't." Although Yücel said he preferred to leave such memories behind, they influenced his determination to demand the daily broadcasting of the azan. He furthermore connected these feelings to the history of Turkish guest workers in Deventer. The chairman's argument about the nostalgic longings of his parent's generation did not, however, impress his opponents. Moreover, the old guest workers did not speak out in favor of the azan themselves, nor had they previously pushed the neighborhood to accept a daily azan. As in many mosques across the Netherlands, second- and third-generation immigrant Muslims are more vocal than their parents. Since Muslim communities today do not consider themselves to be guests or foreigners, the elders' wish for a nostalgic azan becomes mixed with a struggle to belong. The younger chairman thus spoke on behalf of his father, but also on behalf of his own generation and that of his children; the demand for the azan found itself, as is often the case with nostalgia, between the past and the future (cf. Pickering and Keightley 2006). The desire of those who would rather silence the azan, on the other hand, is motivated by an aggressive desire to forget: to see the Turkish-Dutch "integrate"—or better yet "assimilate"—and forget about their past, be it religious, cultural or linguistic.

It is easy to forget the sober conditions of life, even poverty, in which the Dutch working classes lived shortly after the Second World War. Fascinating film footage collected by Paul Scheffer and René Roelofs in their 2013 documentary *Land of Promise* shows the poor living conditions of migrant workers in the Netherlands, Germany, the United Kingdom, France, and Sweden, who had left behind even more abominable situations in Turkey, Spain, Italy, Greece, and Morocco, among others.[9] The film's power lies in the shocking footage of small and dirty guest worker pensions as well as examples of explicit racism and abuse. Images of the denigrating hiring experiences of guest workers from Morocco bound for the Netherlands, being treated like cattle by Dutch contractors and local bureaucrats, speak for themselves and stand against Scheffer's narrative which attempts to somewhat relieve feelings of historic guilt in the contemporary Netherlands. By portraying migration as essentially painful and diversity as a natural cause of social melancholy, resulting from a sense of loss both on the part of migrants longing for home and the people of the host nation longing for a simpler past, the film aims to take into account multiple sides of the story of migration. Scheffer thus prepares the shocking images of blatant racism and violence to make them palatable to a general Dutch public that finds it hard to swallow the word racism (Tamimi Arab 2012; Essed and Hoving 2014). He does not criticize the European obsession with national culture or the idea that postcolonial migrants are viewed as the cause of an imperiled "Englishness," "Dutchness," "Frenchness" and so on (cf. Gilroy 2005: 115, 118). Nonetheless, his collected footage is a sober reminder that guest workers encountered unabashed racism in their land of promise during the "live and let live" 1960s and 1970s.

The story of the guest workers actually begins with towns like Deventer. Turkish workers were brought to the town in the 1960s by pioneering companies such as Thomassen & Drijver-Verblifa, a manufacturer of cans. Before hiring Turkish men for its factories, the company had employed people from Spain and Italy. In 1953 it had also hired former Moluccan soldiers who fled during the Dutch war against Indonesian independence. Fleeing from the Russian Red Army in 1956, Hungarian refugees ended up in the Netherlands by chance and worked for the company as well, but many of them later migrated to Canada. These were temporary solutions. The company grew significantly in the 1960s and needed cheap labor from abroad. Spanish workers were appreciated, also for being "culturally closer" to the Dutch (Muus 1986: 2). Because of the authoritarian Franco regime, however, the company soon lost interest in Spain. Another argument in favor of expanding the pool of guest workers was that the company would be vulnerable if it was dependent on a single nationality of workers. In 1964, preparations were made; recruitment in Turkey began in 1965 and continued until 1973.

We get an impression of the circumstances from a study by Philip Muus in which he examined Turkish employees' wish to either stay in the Netherlands or return to Turkey (1986). Muus interviewed the personnel chief of Thomassen & Drijver-Verblifa, who had been personally responsible for hiring workers from Spain, and subsequently from Turkey. Excerpts from Muus's interview reveal how the concept of the guest worker came into existence:

Then we said [in the 1960s], and I think that T&D [the company] can in general be proud [of this], that if we begin such a phenomenon, we must do so with a policy. Even though at that moment we did not know exactly what fish we were going to catch. We spoke in terms of short contracts, it was an idea of a year or two and then something would happen, but what that was we did not know. . . . Then we said, if we bring these people here, we should draft a policy for the manner in which we will do so. That policy can be summed up by saying: they are the guest workers. If we are the host, then we want to house these people in company pensions, in fact, to ensure hygiene, medical assistance . . . so that we have the feeling that we are doing this in a responsible manner.

Then we began hiring in Turkey, those were indescribable scenes. One would be notified that you had to be somewhere in Turkey. The attaché was in Ankara, and in Trabzon, those were the two places where the hiring effectively took place. But that meant that there, somewhere in Ankara, they had gathered a hundred people there, while we usually talked of hiring a group of fifty to sixty men. These people had often traveled two or three days; they would arrive in Ankara two days earlier; yes, it was terrible. One does not need to be very sentimental or emotional to think so; in a small space . . . a hundred people were crammed, standing stiff against each other, with a bundle or a package or a small plastic bag, with god knows what . . .; almost all of them from the countryside, the territories for scouting and recruiting. Then you would select from this group. It was a given that you should not be impressed by the medical check, which proceeded like assembly line work; . . . . Anyway, the people came in, a sad bunch. We would select with the help of our translator. They would be given a piece of newspaper that they had to read. One would get the impression that the majority were illiterate. On top of that there was the insane situation that selectors from other companies said that in Turkey many people suffer from varicose veins, and those selectors said: you have to have their trousers lifted to see if they have varicose veins. . . . It was really beastly, it was a kind of slave trade. Once we had seen them, those people were driven back into that small space and at the end of the day you had to select sixty of those guys. In itself that would lead to the most horrible scenes: guys who wanted to thank you, offer gifts or whatnot, others who would come in crying and asking whether they could not try to join us. Three weeks later they would arrive at Schiphol airport, totally alienated people who had no clue; documents in the Turkish language; when you would see them on the escalator . . . those people entered a different world. (my translation, Muus 1986: 12–14)

The original idea of the worker as a guest was that he should ultimately return to his country of origin. The leftist government of the 1970s held to the idea that the Netherlands was "definitely not an immigration country" (Maussen 2009: 126). It was only in the 1980s that Dutch governments began to shift toward the idea that the Netherlands had de facto become an immigrant country.[10] During this period, the government replaced the term guest worker with the category of ethnic minority (Penninx 1979). According to Muus, though some Turkish workers did eventually return to Turkey when the company offered a sum for their departure, most stayed and brought their families over through a reunification program. Sometimes they were united with their families after more than ten years of living in the Netherlands. We can gauge how difficult the workers' situation was from the personnel director's description of their yearning for home:

Those people lived separated from their families for years. [But] they had an idea that they could enjoy a higher living standard in the Netherlands, better opportunities than in Turkey. I repeatedly had the feeling that their separation from their families led to continuous negotiations [with their employers] about whether they could . . . go on vacation for a second time, or whether the vacation could . . . be extended. And furthermore there was the phenomenon of weekly telegrams: child in hospital, father was ill, come immediately. There was a general need to be with the family. (Muus 1986: 15)

Only rarely do the old men of the mosques talk publicly about their emotions surrounding their migrations. An exhibition at the Fatih Mosque in Amsterdam, whose members share a history similar to that of Deventer's former guest workers, gave a glimpse of this past. Photographer Mary Schermer asked the mosque elders whether she could make and exhibit their portraits, holding in their hands a photograph from the time of their arrival in the Netherlands, and accompanied in the present by one of their grown children. After careful consideration—some of the men did not understand the request, or mistrusted the artist's intention of putting them under the spotlight of an art exhibition, while others dismissed the very idea of a photographic exhibition in the mosque's entrance hall—Schermer was given the opportunity to visually document their stories.

Her pictures, exhibited in the mosque in 2012, evoke nostalgia or even melancholy. The minimalist captions betray difficult times and loneliness, stories like that of Osman Üre and Mevlut Erarslan (Figures 10 and 11). Üre arrived in the Netherlands in 1971 at the age of thirty and worked for a sugar factory and then a Ford factory.

Figure 10 Osman Üre, the father, and Aydin Üre, his son. Mary Schermer, Fatih Mosque Amsterdam, 2012.

Figure 11 Mevlut Erarslan, the father, and Huseyn Erarslan, his son. Mary Schermer, Fatih Mosque Amsterdam, 2012.

He was reunited with his family in 1976. Erarslan also arrived in 1971 when he was thirty-four to work at the same Ford factory, but his family settled in the Netherlands as late as 1987. Standing next to the old men in Schermer's portraits are their son or daughter, symbols of their success and future prosperity, who are portrayed as supporting their fathers. The images invoke both loss and prosperity, a longing for the past but also a sense of being established in the present, displayed in the very building that the elders acquired three decades ago. While Scheffer's exhibition is only very modestly positive about contemporary European immigration societies, about the value of migration and, on a deeper level, diversity itself, Schermer's photo project tells an alternative story of both nostalgia and establishment. The children in the portraits represent a deeper embeddedness of the former guest workers in the Netherlands. It is these offspring of the former guest workers, who are better educated and well versed in "Dutch" ways, who decide to actively push for the right to construct a mosque or to demand the azan on their parents' behalf. Though the second and third generations may also criticize and expose their parents' shortcomings in art, literature, public debates, and so forth, they also often describe their fathers as pioneers who laid the foundations for a future in the Netherlands despite the meager resources at their disposal.

Notwithstanding the common narrative that guest workers became more pious as they aged, or that they did so under the influence of the Dutch society, workers practiced Islam in modest prayer spaces in their work environments from the moment of their arrival, for instance in the Deventer factory. Landman (1992) has documented how, as the decades passed, Muslims in the Netherlands felt a growing need to have more than just a prayer mat in a factory, to own a mosque of their own: "From mat to minaret." Guest workers had often settled for so-called garage mosques in the early years, small spaces that they creatively converted into mosques. Sometimes an old school or a church was given or sold to a mosque community. Also, modest buildings were constructed for practical religious purposes but without significant references to Islam on the exterior. In the meantime, small communities of former Turkish guest workers have cooperated for years to construct visible houses of worship. The Center Mosque in Deventer is one such mosque. It is built in a neo-Ottoman style, includes a minaret, and has a colorfully painted prayer space. It was realized thanks to the efforts of the local Turkish-Muslim community, which had to pay 750,000 guilders (340,000 euros) in the late 1990s to buy the 5,000 square meters of land on which the mosque was to be built.

The neighborhood, however, was angered by plans to erect a mosque on the Smyrnastraat in Deventer and initiated legal procedures (Landman and Wessels 2005). When the location for a new mosque building was determined in 1997, residents immediately organized to protest the decision. The municipality tried to accommodate complaints by hosting public hearings, but this only led to an increase in parking spaces on the mosque's property (to minimize mosque goers using street parking). A spokesman for the mosque association conceded that the mosque would not amplify the azan, which surprised an alderwoman on behalf of the Labor Party and "led her to object that this was a rather far-reaching concession by the Muslims" (Landman and Wessels 2005: 1129). In 1999, the municipality finally expressed its intention to agree to the zoning plans for the mosque. It received almost five hundred written complaints from the neighborhood.[11] Among these were that the mosque did not fit its surroundings, that the mosque would encourage "ghettoization" of the neighborhood by attracting more Turkish residents, and that the value of homes would decrease. However, the College of Mayor and Aldermen of Deventer concluded that the objections against the mosque were unfounded.[12]

The local newspaper reported at the time that there was a "fear that the mosque will attract even more allochthonous [non-native] residents and that the balance between 'white' [*blank*] and 'dark' [*donker*] will be lost."[13] In addition to protesting against the mosque, neighborhood residents worried that the mosque would amplify the azan. Anxious that mosque construction could be jeopardized, mosque chairman Kasem Akdemir responded by explicitly stating to the NRC newspaper that there would be no amplified call to prayer.[14] An informal agreement was made, however, that the call to prayer would only be amplified on special occasions or on Friday afternoons. The non-Muslim neighborhood residents later remembered this promise as significant in their acceptance of the mosque. However, construction could begin only in 2001 when a regional court decided in favor of the municipality and ruled that the objections against construction were spurious. The mosque finally opened in 2003. Landman and Wessels show some of the complexity of the situation when they mention that the organizers of the opposition "accepted their loss sportingly. After the judge had rejected their appeal, they sent their congratulations . . . and stressed that their fight had not been against the mosque itself, but against the location and what they saw as manipulations by the authorities" (2005: 1130). However, a decade later the new mosque chairman, Orkan Yücel, did not mention anything about a fair acceptance of the mosque. He remembered the opposition to construction as opposition to the mosque and to Muslims.

The second informational evening

A few months after the first (but before the second) informational evening about the azan, I interviewed the mosque chairman again. The mosque had broadcast the azan for a week as a test, but because many residents were on summer vacation, another test week was held in the fall. According to Yücel, especially the older men's desire to amplify the azan had much to do with a nostalgia for home, namely Turkey. The chairman also repeatedly emphasized in private and public conversations that "a feeling of 'home' is good for the contact with the city."[15] The young did not express the same need, the same intensity of longing for a lost home, as did their elders for the azan. But because of the conflict that ensued from the wish to amplify the call, young Turks in the neighborhood came out to defend their right to publically call to prayer.

> OY: So it's not just a matter of nostalgia, but also a matter of "The Netherlands
> is also my country." I myself have an azan application on my iPhone that
> I use as a practical tool. I use the free version because I don't need to
> necessarily listen to the entire azan. . . . The iPhone application is one of the
> fine instruments to use for the practical, religious, function of the call. But

the amplified azan that we want for our mosque is much more a matter of feeling at home. There is no desire at all to amplify the azan five times a day, and I don't think this will change in the future. We would however like to broadcast the call louder than we are doing now, but for now this is as far as we can go. The speaker volume can be set much louder. In theory we could broadcast the call so loud that the whole town would hear it. We don't need to do that, but it could be just a little louder.

PTA: Why do you want to broadcast the azan every day and not just on a Friday?

OY: Initially, I intended to realize the amplified azan, to broadcast it with a higher volume, only on Fridays. I thought that if I would demand a daily azan, the end goal of just the Fridays would be reached. But now I have changed my mind. I fear that if I just do this for Fridays, my successor will have a hard time if he wants to amplify the azan on a daily basis.

PTA: And what if the municipality does not cooperate with the mosque because of complaints by the neighborhood?

OY: I really don't want to mobilize our members to get the right to the azan. That would cause problems and conflicts, especially among the youngsters. I do have a community of a few thousand people backing my efforts. . . . In an extreme case, [if the azan was banned,] we would demonstrate in the city for our rights, but I don't think and don't want it to go that far.

Yücel hoped that the neighborhood would get used to the azan, that their irritations and fears would lessen and that he would slowly be able to increase the volume in time. To the public he insisted, however, that the volume would not be turned up, which they had a hard time believing. The chairman said that the current sound level was around 50 decibels, comparable with everyday speech and far under the 70 to 80-decibel noise pollution limit that requires permission from the municipality. Since he did not need a permit for broadcasting the call, he thought that neighborhood residents should not have too much to say in the decision-making process. It was, after all, the mosque's property and not theirs.

Such confidence is tied to Yücel's social position in the Netherlands. Thirty-nine years old and a father of four, he came to the Netherlands when he was sixteen years old and witnessed the construction of the Center Mosque in Deventer in his twenties. In 2011, he was appointed chairman of the mosque. When I asked why he became chairman, he answered that he had "worked twenty years for the Netherlands; now I want to work for Islam for two years." He intended to visit Mecca when his term was completed and dreamed of repatriating to Turkey, to a town close to Ankara where his brothers still live. Compared to the previous generation, he had clearly climbed the socioeconomic ladder. The difference in education, his experience in the Netherlands, and a general feeling of being in control—Yücel owned his own company—made him more capable than the elders to claim the mosque's right to the city. He believed, for instance, that the old men of the mosque were too soft on the municipality when it did not respect their wishes. Rather than asking for permission from local government officials in a passive manner to amplify the azan, he thought Muslims in the Netherlands should pursue and demand rights actively. This was also easier for him because, thanks to the pioneering guest workers, the mosque had already been constructed with hard-earned savings. This is significant, because it shows that even though Muslim emancipation is enabled by constitutional guarantees, this does not mean that political rights are automatically activated in practice: public religious presence is directly tied to socioeconomic emancipation. In addition, the mosque belonged to Diyanet, the Turkish Religious Affairs Directorate, and was thus linked to the Turkish state as well as connected to the many other member mosques in the Netherlands and Germany (on Diyanet see Sunier and Landman 2015; Laurence 2012).

In the meantime, Marco Swart, an alderman of Deventer affiliated with the Liberal Party, visited neighborhood residents and the mosque to talk about the azan. The municipality preferred not to intervene and emphasized the need for negotiating with the neighborhood.[16] The leader of the Labor Party, Diederik Samsom, also visited the neighborhood during his election campaign, and advised a cautious approach: "In my personal opinion, the Center Mosque does not need to sound the azan every day. But I do think that such a matter should be taken care of harmoniously. Not with a judge and a sound level meter in the hand."[17] Samsom did not want to get too involved and did not explicitly defend the right to religious calls to prayer. This is related to the fact that media attention pushes Dutch politicians toward more nativist positions (Verkaaik and Tamimi Arab 2016). Samsom provides a good example of this behavior: the national Labor Party leader went so far as to express a personal opinion that the mosque "does not need to sound the azan every day," while a local Liberal Party alderman actually helped the mosque to achieve its wishes, illustrating the complexity of Dutch politics and governance on the ground.

That a different political stance is possible was exemplified by President Barack Obama and New York City's mayor, Michael Bloomberg, during the 2010 controversy regarding a prayer space in an Islamic community center near Ground Zero. Bloomberg stated unequivocally that "There is nowhere in the five boroughs [of New York City] that is off limits to any religion."[18] In contrast to Samsom, and under far greater political pressure, Obama spoke out against anti-Muslim rhetoric:

> This is America, and our commitment to religious freedom must be unshakable. The principle that people of all faiths are welcome in this country, and will not be treated differently by their government, is essential to who we are.[19]

However, Obama too qualified his strong support for the so-called Ground Zero Mosque by questioning the "wisdom" of planning to erect a mosque on a location that could ignite fear and polarization. Unlike Obama, Samsom tried to circumvent the issue by speaking about harmony but not defending the azan's constitutional protection in the Netherlands. By saying that the mosque did not need to call to prayer on a daily basis, Samsom subtly suggested that harmony required Muslims to refrain from too public a presence.

Despite some politicians' calls against the azan and responses from ministers, including Labor Party Minister Lodewijk Asscher who stated that the Dutch Constitution allows the amplification of the azan (Chapter 3), azan negotiations happen mainly on the local level without interference from state actors at the national level. This is in contrast, for example, with aviation policies regarding noise nuisance, which are very actively debated by macro-actors, including the President of Schiphol Airport (Bröer 2006: 80). Also, while there are general constitutional laws in the Netherlands, Dutch society does not share a tradition of constitutionalism on par with countries such as the United States. It is therefore not surprising that Samsom insisted on building consensus in the neighborhood rather than looking immediately at what constitutional norms dictate. In practice, a decentralized approach in the Netherlands means that municipalities negotiate about the azan on the ground. This allows pragmatism to prevail, though the constitution (*de Grondwet*) looms silently but effectively in the background.

In preparation for the second informational evening on the azan in Deventer, alderman Swart decided to intervene by first talking with the mosque's chairman. Yücel said that he "was not sure if he could trust him, though he seemed a flexible, experienced, person." He was worried that the alderman would push toward reducing the azan's frequency or setting an upper limit on its volume. His mistrust of the alderman was caused partly by the fact that Swart had once said on television that the Turkish-Dutch should speak Dutch at home—most migrants of the first-, second-, and even post-migration generations viewed this as intrusive and incompatible with their sentiments toward their ancestral past, even if they did speak Dutch at home. After meeting with Swart, Yücel was nevertheless positive about the alderman's advice on managing the main groups that he needed to satisfy, mosque members who insisted on amplification as well as azan opponents.

The second informational evening was held in November 2012 at the Center Mosque Deventer.[20] The local television channel RTV Oost covered the meeting on television that night, beginning a news report by comparing the sound of the Deventer church bells with the sound of the azan, and with a reporter asking one of the mosque's neighbors why he does not want the azan. "I remember that we had agreed that the call would only be broadcasted on Fridays. . . . Now they want to turn up the volume too high. . . . If I wanted to hear something like that, I would go to Turkey," the neighbor answered. The chairman of the mosque is then interviewed to find out why the mosque wants to broadcast the call on a daily basis. "I have heard that some people have tears in their eyes when they hear the call," the chairman explained (whether this really happened could not be confirmed).

> It is their homesickness of more than fifty years that is at play here. It is the request of these elderly, and as the chairman of the Center Mosque I have to also listen to the people who have lived and worked here for fifty years, who have done something for this society. I have to give them something back in return. It's just two minutes per day that we are asking for, purely for the older generation.

The reporter ends his video with the chairman's statement that he does not want to turn the matter into a legal battle, even though the mosque has a legal right to broadcast the azan even multiple times a day.

In total, around 120 people came to the second informational evening. The atmosphere at the entry was tense. People entering the room were asked by a reporter accompanied by a television cameraman if they were "for or against the azan?" Everybody was welcomed by Swart, who chaired the gathering. The alderman began by emphasizing that he himself lived in the neighborhood and that his role was to solve misunderstandings between the residents. He spoke about the history of the mosque and the mosque board, and shared what he had learned, namely that at the time of construction an agreement had been made about the azan: to broadcast it once a week, not too loud, and also on special occasions. This had been an important condition for the neighborhood's acceptance of the new building. However, Swart explained, the elders now wished to hear the azan more often.

He received a host of different reactions. One resident complained that the alderman had not answered the phone. Another asked what the "real cause" of the wish for the daily azan was. A third said that she enjoyed the many religions and cultures in her neighborhood, but that she experienced the daily azan as an unnecessary provocation. In response, the alderman referred to his own Indonesian background and familiarity with an Islamic country. Though he was not a Muslim himself, he could empathize with the elders' need for the azan. At one point, Swart also described the Center Mosque as "moderate" and added that because of his perception of the mosque as moderate rather than "radical," he had chosen of his own free will to assist the mosque.[21] Swart was a representative of the state, but also wanted to participate in the negotiations for the azan. He was a neighbor of the mosque like the others, but his position gave him more influence to shape the outcome of the negotiations (Figure 12).

Despite efforts by the audience as well as by Swart and Yücel to foster a harmonious atmosphere, a commotion started when a few in the audience spoke in Turkish. Non-Turkish speakers criticized this as being "threatening." As chairman of the evening, Swart responded by asking for respect toward the elders who could express themselves better in their mother tongue. Because of such incidents and simmering emotions, the general atmosphere remained tense, as it had during the first informational evening. The mosque chairman emphasized that Dutch law allows the mosque to amplify the azan on a daily basis. "However, we think it is important that the neighborhood can live with

Figure 12 Second informational evening about the azan. Photograph by Ronny te Wechel, Fall 2012.

the azan. In fact, without the support of the neighborhood there will be no daily azan." This seemed to create a feeling of trust among the residents who felt that they had been wronged by not being included in the decision-making process. Both Swart and Yücel emphasized that it was necessary to include the whole neighborhood for better "social cohesion and acceptance." They stated that a decision by the municipality or a judge would, in the long term, harm the social cohesion of the neighborhood, and that the mosque wanted good relations with its neighbors.

Overall, the audience seemed confused and continued to ask each other and the organizers many questions, such as, "Are we going to make the rules [for the future] tonight?" "Why doesn't the municipality just decide? It was chosen democratically and could spare us this trouble." "How loud will the azan be? Sometimes [it was quite loud], and sometimes I heard nothing." "Why do you want the azan seven days a week?" "I am annoyed by the ruckus caused by Go Ahead [the local football team]. I have learned to live with that as well. Why can't you live with the azan?" "Can the azan be in Dutch?" "Can you imagine that the call to prayer for a faith that is not yours is disturbing to hear in one's own home?" to which someone responded: "Yes. I feel like that when I hear the church bells." Both sides spoke of "tolerance," being "fair," "us and them," "trust," "the unknown," "separation of church and state," and "sound in one's living room." Alderman Swart reacted to the "us versus them" rhetoric by repeating that it is "important to listen and not immediately think for the other." At the end of the meeting Yücel thanked everyone for their attendance and, despite some objections from the crowd, the tense atmosphere had somewhat lessened; there was even applause for comments about "respect" and "living together."

Polling for an outcome

After eight months, two informational meetings, and a two-week trial run, the neighborhood and mosque had not yet come to a consensus. The conflict attracted the attention of professional "mediators," who visited the mosque in January 2013 and had a "beautiful meeting" where "the mediators could speak about the potential of mediation for all involved parties to have a good dialogue and outcome."[22] More practically, the municipality now deemed it necessary to get involved by assisting in polling the neighborhood about the azan.

Alderman Swart wanted to agree on a fixed volume to prevent confusion in the future, but critical residents like Pascal were not reassured: "Whether we like or dislike the call is not the point. The feeling dominates that this has already been decided, while participation is feigned and [there is a pretense] that we are being heard. . . . A missed chance for the mosque, really bad for its image, and they certainly don't have to come to me again with one of their markets, eating together in the neighborhood, or whatever." Those who received a letter about the poll had a month to respond.[23] Alderman Swart and the mosque chairman asked a notary to oversee the polling process to ensure that it was "anonymous and fair."[24] Michael, one of the residents who said he was against public religion, told me that he thought the poll was biased toward the azan. He protested the inclusion of Muslim residents among those polled, and also that the right to vote for or against the azan was determined by measuring locations (homes and streets) where the azan could be heard rather than a simple radius around the mosque. The municipality had prepared a chart of the azan's soundscape and published the map with exact sound levels in the local newspaper. Michael spoke against this acoustic model, which meant that not everybody could vote against the azan: "Why can't they just use the old fashioned method of asking everybody who lives in the neighborhood?"

Indeed, the supposedly objective "acoustic model"—following Christian Bröer's terminology (2006: 25)—that was employed by the municipality had serious shortcomings. Bröer's comparative study of noise pollution caused by Amsterdam and Zurich airports shows how state policies affect perceptions of noise pollution, and that the same sound levels can lead to very different reactions depending on time and place. In past decades, the expectation in the Netherlands has been that noise pollution caused by airplanes can be fully accounted for by the so-called acoustic model of explaining noise pollution. Bröer, however, shows that from the time that Dutch Royal Airways began operation, and with increasing passenger flights from the 1960s, nonacoustic factors have had a decisive impact on the perception of noise pollution. This argument does not underplay the impact of acoustic (physical) aspects of noise pollution, but stresses that noise pollution can only be fully understood by merging perspectives from the natural sciences with approaches from the social sciences and humanities. He concludes his book with the statement that, for sounds below extreme decibel levels, "policy determines nuisance." In our case of the azan, it is not so easy to arrive at a similar conclusion that it is state policy that has determined nuisance, because the degree to which the state has been involved in Dutch aviation is of a different, much greater, order than its regulation of Muslim soundscapes. But the broader thesis that politicized perceptions have a decisive impact on the experience of noise pollution does apply in the case of the azan. From this perspective, state policies and media affecting Muslims in general, from guest workers to Muslim and "allochthonous" citizens, have co-shaped the language and aesthetic sensibilities toward Islam and its embodiment in the forms of headscarves, mosques, and also the azan.

In the history of Dutch aviation and noise pollution, municipalities employed the so-called objective acoustic model because it enabled normative judgments in a concealed way. The mapping of sound levels fits a "planological" approach (Bröer 2006: 80) that was dominant in the twentieth century, a strategy employed by the Netherlands state in cooperation with appointed experts, without serious consultation with local citizens. Similarly, in Deventer, the complexity of complaints against the azan was reduced to a single measure, namely the approximate extent to which one could hear it in one's living environment. The planological approach produced a map that determined who had a right to protest (or support) the azan and who did not. Opposed residents, who admitted that they did not always hear the azan, saw this as an exclusionary move by the municipality. Rather than being against the azan because it was too loud, they objected to the azan because it constituted sounds that they considered "out of place," sounds that did not belong to their town. The "objective" approach thus hid cultural struggles over the definition of community boundaries.

While during the informational evenings protesting residents avoided a moral debate on the place of Islam in the Netherlands and insisted on the right to be indifferent toward the azan, when the municipality employed an objectivist approach, they grumbled because it would be indifferent to their halfheartedly expressed symbolic objections to public Islam. In other words, the symbolic debate dominated the azan negotiations, exploring new limits of religious toleration, even though this was sometimes denied for the strategic reason of complaining about noise pollution rather than about Islam. Complaining too explicitly about religion would have exposed azan opponents as bigots. Nevertheless, there clearly was a slippage between nonreligious, profane noise and religious, sacred noise (cf. Weiner 2014: 28). Weiner observed a similar situation among American Catholics in the nineteenth century, who believed that opponents to their church bells were concerned not simply about noise but much more specifically about their "high church ritualism" (2014: 54). Their Protestant opponents thought that church bells were old fashioned, but considered other profane sounds such as emerging factory noises to be inevitable and necessary. In comparable fashion, azan opponents in Deventer insisted that the azan was not "necessary." The recurring question of why Muslims cannot just use pocket watches (Chapter 1) implied that a distinction could be made between sounds that belong to "contemporary time" and can be regulated but not completely silenced, such as those made by cars and motorcycles, and sounds which are "out of time" and should therefore be silenced—or never made into an object of discussion at all—such as the azan. The nostalgia felt by Muslims for the azan was hence seen as a longing for sounds that are not *of* Dutch space *and* time. In a way, then, the desire to disallow the azan was a wish to evade the ethics of memory that come with nostalgia (cf. Margalit 2011) and to silence not just a Muslim ritual but also the yearning of Turkish-Dutch fellow citizens for a Turkish homeland.

Another complaint about the poll was that it required only those against the azan to vote. In other words, if one did not return the municipality's mailed letter, that would be counted as a vote for the azan. If less than half of those who received a letter responded, the municipality would automatically allow the azan. Michael thought this was a manipulative process, and expressed indignation that an alderman of the Liberal Party had agreed with this format, which placed the mosque in the comfortable position of being portrayed as open to objections and yet rather likely to get what it wanted in the first place:

> One would expect a dirty political tactic like this from the GreenLeft or the Labor Party, the parties who have 'multi-culty' [a pejorative way of saying multiculturalism] on their priority lists. But no, it is the Liberal Party that is playing this dirty game with the mosque board. I think that the VVD alderman has been indoctrinated by the Muslims. . . . This way the alderman can give the neighborhood the impression that they are heard, while in the meantime he can shape the poll in such a way that the outcome is favorable to the Muslims.[25]

Ironically, it was a local representative of the Labor Party who expressed worries about alderman Swart's approach by asking, does not the azan need greater and explicit support?[26] Not all residents, however, were worried by the poll's format, and there were no serious, organized complaints about the polling process. Joyce, for example, said:

> I live two blocks behind the mosque and I have never had a complaint about the azan on Friday. I did attend the meetings out of curiosity, and did send an e-mail to the mosque that, in principle, I am not looking forward to a daily azan. I did that also because it seemed at the time that the mosque would simply go ahead with their plan without consulting us. I found out that there were people in the neighborhood who did have complaints about the sound of the azan on Friday. They spread a letter calling us to "resist the daily broadcasting of the azan!" During the meetings, I noticed that there were many misunderstandings, and

not wanting to understand each other. It was clear to me though that the mosque wanted to have good relations with the neighborhood. . . . Afterwards I heard that there would be an investigation about the wishes of the neighborhood. If the majority does not want the daily azan, it will not be carried out. I don't know what the current status is. . . . My neighbors did not attend the meetings, and they are not worried about the matter.

During the second meeting I realized again that the problem is not so much with the azan, but the inability of certain people to see things from someone else's perspective. But also clinging on to the old and not moving with the new. In that sense, the elder autochthonous neighbors looked much like the older mosque members. Both desperately want to hold on to what was in the past, leaving no space for a compromise. During these meetings, I have seen something of what is going on in the Netherlands: the intolerance towards each other caused by a fear of the new. Unfortunately, the scared people [religious and non-religious] make a little more noise than those without such anxieties, making the problem look much bigger than it is. I have also met other neighbors and mosque goers who think like I do, and we tried to use the microphone to make the others consider our way of thinking. Many seemed deaf [to our words], but it was still a hopeful experience for me.

Joyce's view was shared by Matthijs, who lives in the neighborhood and believes that the ruckus around the mosque was "making an elephant out of a mosquito." He went a step further by writing to the local newspaper that "the argument that public expressions of religion should not be allowed is not tenable."[27]

In March 2013, the independent notary announced the results at City Hall.[28] Of the 495 homes that were offered the opportunity to speak out anonymously against the daily azan, 167 took the trouble to do so. Although not everybody who disliked the azan may have filled out the polling form, and though the neighborhood also has Muslim residents, azan opponents did mobilize a third of those polled. Because they did not meet the 50 percent requirement, the Center Mosque's wish to amplify the azan every day sometime between noon and 2:00 p.m. was honored. Part of the agreement was the installation of a sound limiter to make sure that the azan would not be heard beyond the mosque's immediate surroundings. A few dissatisfied residents threatened to take the matter to court and the local Liberal Party supported them, supposedly for the purpose of clarifying what was allowed and what was not, even though the sound regulations were well known. Perhaps because of a weak legal position, or simply a wish to put the issue to rest, no further actions were taken. In fact, azan controversies in the Netherlands have so far never made it into a courtroom.[29]

The fire

Over the years, mosques in the Netherlands have repeatedly been vandalized (Van der Valk 2012). The Center Mosque also fell victim to an attack in August 2013, a few months after the azan negotiations came to an end.[30] An explosion on a summer night damaged the entrance to the mosque association's grocery market and caused the collapse of one of the decorative domes. The leaders of the mosque, as well as Deventer's police and mayor, tried to avoid media attention as they did not want to escalate the situation in an otherwise quiet and peaceful neighborhood. According to the mosque chairman and the police, there was no evidence that it was an act of arson and there was no proof that it was because of the azan. Skeptics, however, pointed to the fact that the mosque's cameras did not cover that part of the building and there were all kinds of conspiracy theories in the neighborhood, for instance that it was "because of the competition the Turkish grocery market at the mosque posed to [non-Turkish] shops in the neighborhood," while others said that "the atheists" had done it, probably because a local group called the Atheist Secular Party had protested the azan (Chapter 3). It was indeed easy for a potential culprit to evade detection; the mosque chairman confirmed that the video cameras had not captured any perpetrators but added that one side of the mosque did not have a camera. The police said that no combustive substances were found, but the firemen told the chairman that it was possible that someone could have set the fire. In any case, a security video did show an explosion, and the chairman said that because of the extensive damage they initially believed that a Molotov cocktail or even a hand grenade had been used.

When I visited the mosque after the attack, Yücel showed me the damage and suggested that the fire had probably been ignited "by itself." He also mentioned, however, that the mosque's community was trying to find an explanation: "Is it because of the azan, they wondered." How a concrete wall, with no connections to gas pipes or electricity cables, could suddenly explode into a huge fire remained mysterious. I frowned with disbelief, but Yücel assured me that the event had nothing to do with hatred against the mosque or the azan: "To be honest, I have been through a lot because of the azan but no such threats." He felt that the incident was just an unfortunate accident. Nevertheless, Yücel said the mosque intended to install not one or two but four new cameras. When the mosque was constructed, he said, "we didn't want to give people the feeling that we are looking into their living room," but the fire pushed the mosque toward increased surveillance.

The whole episode of the azan had exhausted the chairman:

Do you realize what it meant to be the person on whom the azan of a community of Muslims depended? . . . People have noted that my hair has gone grey in the past two years. It was very stressful. I was not trained for such a job. This is something for politicians, religious scholars, people who are trained to speak before an audience. I am just a business man, and an allochthon.

The chairman also informed me about his plan to return to Turkey, to a country "where the azan can be heard everywhere five times a day" he joked. When I asked why he was leaving, he explained as follows:

We have a good life here, our own house, a store with employees and so forth. After twenty-three years, I have seen enough here, I have learned and experienced a lot here. Luckily I'm young enough to go to Turkey with my children. I have seen that the pressure on allochthonous people here has increased and the economy is not in great shape. Here we are shoved to the side in a very gentle way. I have seen that with my two elder children, one fourteen and the other ten years old . . . I have packed our belongings, and am ready to go this week. . . . Of course it was nostalgic to do away with belongings and such. . . . It was a very hard decision, but I believe that life in Turkey will be much easier.

Yücel deduced from conversations with one of his younger sons that he did not feel one hundred percent safe with his Dutch teacher in school. He somehow felt excluded. In response, Yücel sent his son to school in Turkey, and said that the boy had remarked that the teacher there was kinder to him:

You don't notice these things. Your children go to school and they are too young to explain these things well. But then you realize that the child had felt something [a subtle form of being excluded]. . . . It is not like it used to be. Tolerance is gone. And everything just gets more difficult and my children are very important to me. . . . I have no illusions about Turkey. My sons, who are there already, have remarked that there is more dust in their new school than in the Netherlands. But even though facilities may not be always better—Turkey has many such problems—I have made the decision to go.

The chairman was satisfied that the mosque did not receive new complaints since daily azan amplification had begun, but still lamented the loss of "tolerance." The history of mosque construction and azan negotiations had made him skeptical, and he considered himself lucky to be able to repatriate to Turkey. "There are many others who would like to go back to Turkey, but they can't [because of the financial costs and their children's ties to the Netherlands]."

Alongside his complaints about intolerance and discrimination, Yücel also remarked that the social fabric of Turks in the Netherlands was not what it used to be. People lived too individualistically, he said, in comparison with his home town in Turkey where community bonds were still strong. He also found the Netherlands too liberal. There were "too many atheists," and he did not like the fact that gay teachers worked in schools. Yücel cited a sexual culture that was too open, where people "kiss each other in public," among the reasons for his desire to leave. He insisted however that the primary reason for wanting to leave was the inability to feel at home as he did in Turkey, a country "where we will not face discrimination." On the other hand, the Turkish-Dutch community, he reiterated, was here to stay because it had become rooted in the Netherlands. Those who stayed, the chairman said, should have the right to hear the azan at least once a day:

> It was not our intention to call to prayer from a great distance. . . . For example, last week I was going to the mosque by bike and then heard the azan. I've tried to convey that feeling during our informational evening. But that is something that cannot be said in words, you have to experience it. In Turkey I hear the azan everywhere. Even when you do not pray, the azan shakes you awake.

For his last deed as chairman, Yücel wanted to initiate the construction of a small building across the mosque for the ritual washing of the dead. It would be on mosque terrain, but the municipality had already objected:

> It's like the azan all over [again]. This time they say that ten years ago there was an agreement that no additional structures would be built. I have already had many conversations about this, because there is insufficient space in the hospital and there are other practical problems. This is my last project here. It's just a small building of about twenty square meters in a very quiet area surrounded by trees. It's to wash the dead and pray for them before their burial. We don't want to do it on the other side of the mosque where there is a snack bar. . . . We applied for a construction permit, but it has been rejected. I have visited the municipality and they said that they can't do anything for me, and that I just have to accept that the project cannot be realized. I replied that I would not accept that. It is not my request, but the request of the people living here. Then I was told that I needed to go higher up, I have again been in contact with alderman Marco Swart. . . . Not everybody is willing to invest so much time in these things. The last [mosque] chairman sent a letter six years ago requesting a construction permit. He didn't get the permission and that was the end of it. But I have said that I will make a political issue out of it for our community in the

next municipal elections. . . . They are simply picking on us. I will do whatever
I need to do to apply for a construction permit. . . . They are scared that others
will come here as well [to wash their dead] and talk about lack of parking spaces.

The chairman was moving to Turkey, but retaining his business in the
Netherlands. His children would continue to attend school in Turkey while he
planned to travel back and forth, also to finish his duties for the mosque. He had
a lot on his mind, but agreed to meet me a final time so that the story of the azan
in Deventer could be committed to writing. When we finished our conversation,
during which the daily azan was coincidentally broadcast, the chairman and
I shook hands and he departed for the quiet streets of Deventer on his bicycle.

Beyond integration and recognition?

After the azan negotiations in Deventer, I was invited to present the story
at the Cultural Anthropology department of the University of Amsterdam.
The audience criticized me for presenting a somber black and white image
of misunderstandings and conflicting demands. The narrative about Deventer
had become too stereotypical. One of the objections was that the multicultural
town had once again been portrayed as a site of crisis, while another professor
thought that Mary Douglas's concept of pollution was problematic because
it assumed simplistic notions of group boundaries. An anthropologist, I was
advised, should look for the particular overlaps and complex identities of the
individuals in the field. By showing the multidimensionality and hybridity
of particular identifications, the anthropologist could undo the stereotype.
Paul Gilroy offers a similar critique of ethnographic portrayals of groups in
stereotypical ways; he questions the analytical value of contrasting groups with
each other and suggests that scholars begin by showing the contradictions
within rather than between groups. One could do so by writing narratives
of cross-cultural understanding and fluid boundaries of identity, engaging in
micro-ethnographies that dissolve facile notions of the self and the other. I
conclude this chapter by acknowledging the complexity within the groups of
this study, but argue that this does not justify ignoring conflicts between groups.
I will leave it to the reader to reflect on the possible effects of an anthropology
that describes dichotomous relations between competing groups. What is
certain, however, is that we must be careful to avoid steering our fieldwork
observations toward normatively desired outcomes.

One obvious way to deconstruct the opposition between "autochthonous" non-Muslim citizens and "allochthonous" Muslim believers would be to describe members of the former group who do not object to the azan, or would even like to hear the call to prayer on a daily basis. Of course, such individuals are found in Dutch society. A more interesting manner in which we can complicate group boundaries, however, is by destabilizing the very idea of the allochthonous Muslim. Dutch anthropologists have shown little to no interest in individuals with Somalian, Moroccan, Turkish, and Iranian backgrounds, among others, who have never been religious, or who are in the process of rapidly losing their religion. How do they—minorities within the Dutch "allochthonous" and "Muslim" minorities[31]—feel and think about an amplified azan in their neighborhood?

Many Iranian-Dutch with whom I spoke during my fieldwork, for example, reacted critically to the azan or to mosques in general. They were skeptical about the status of disbelievers in Muslim communities, symbolized for them in Qur'anic verses such as 2:171, "The example of those who disbelieve is like that of one who shouts at what hears nothing but calls and cries cattle or sheep—deaf, dumb and blind, so they do not understand." And yet, these azan opponents, who range from outspoken atheists to non-Muslims who still claim a form of Islamic spirituality, can nonetheless describe the call to prayer as beautiful or even nostalgic. As post-Muslims, they have different relations to the azan than nonbelievers or non-Muslims with a longer Dutch and Christian background. This can also hold for individuals who are part of groups known to identify more strongly with Islam, such as the Turkish-Dutch community. I can mention the example of Ayhan and Deniz, two young Turkish-Dutch men who were born and raised in the Netherlands. Ayhan told me that he was not really a Muslim, but a "deist" or "theist" (after consulting Wikipedia on his smartphone). "I don't feel anything when I hear the call to prayer," he once exclaimed. He did not oppose mosques that wanted to call to prayer, but it was not an issue that he felt strongly about either. Deniz, on the other hand, reported strongly negative emotions in relation to the azan, but even he could interpret the call more positively at times. Excerpts from an interview with him show that a complex emotional relation to the azan exists not only within groups, but can even be found within a single individual:

> D: The feeling that I have is that Islam was forced onto me . . . forced down my throat. . . . The azan is "in your face." When I hear the azan, I feel slightly anxious. I'm reminded of the fact that I am not what the community wanted me to become.

PTA: Do you feel this every time you hear the azan?

D: No, for example when I was in Istanbul recently, I thought to myself that it is actually beautiful. But when I was a child visiting my family in Turkey it sometimes gave me an unpleasant feeling, and when you asked me about the azan it reminded me of how the Turkish community would treat me. They would push you, and ask "Are you a Muslim or not?" At the time I often didn't dare to say no. You had to believe. If one has such ambivalent feelings towards Islam, like I do, then the azan can be experienced in a negative way.

PTA: Do you feel the same when you see a mosque in the Netherlands?

D: Not anymore, but when I was a kid, mosques made me feel uncomfortable. But now, maybe if I heard the azan while sitting in my living room, I would even like the sound. I am more mature now, and can distance myself from the past. I'm not scared of religion. If I want to read the Qur'an, I can do that. If I want to visit a mosque, that's possible as well. But when I was a teenager, I could not identify with Islamic things. I did not fit in the groups of young Turkish-Dutch boys. I liked to read English comics, and they didn't, for example. But, I also didn't believe in God, and they did.

PTA: If Turkish-Dutch people want to use loudspeakers for the azan today, do you have an opinion on that?

D: The [white, autochthonous] Dutch feel anxious about it, like I felt when I was a child, probably also because of ignorance. Some may be even more scared than I was when I was a child, because I did have an idea of what the azan was about, because in a way I am a "Muslim." I don't think that religion should be pushed into everybody's face all the time. I think that the azan should not bother others in society. . . . So even if Muslims say that it is their right to use loudspeakers for the azan, I am against it.

The point of this digression is not to argue that some minorities within minorities also reject the azan, but that complex emotions toward the Muslim call to prayer are a social fact. These can go in multiple directions, for or against the azan, and are felt by people of different ethnicities and backgrounds. What does this say, however, about pluralism in the Netherlands and stereotypical conflicts between groups? How, in other words, should social scientists write about the existing diversities in the Netherlands, and to what extent must we analytically diversify diversity?

By overemphasizing the feelings of "autochthons" and "allochthons," giving these populist feelings and categorizations too much analytical credit, I risk blaming diversity itself as causing feelings of nostalgia rather than, for instance, criticizing the racism of the autochthonous population and its moral incapacity to feel more sympathy for their neighbors, or analyzing other broader and structural causes of feelings of alienation (cf. Gilroy 2005: 150). Duyvendak's *The Politics of Home* opens by claiming that "it is precisely this increased diversity" which must explain the nationalist obsession with cultural homogeneity (2011: 1). The border between empirical analysis and normativity is extremely vague here. That is why I appreciate my anthropologist colleagues' concern about portraying the site of the multicultural as one that is essentially in crisis. One of the problems with accounts that seem to blame conflict as inevitably arising from diversity is that they implicitly suggest a previous situation of homogeneity and do not explicitly criticize the imagined nostalgic past in which peace and order prevailed. As I showed in Chapter 2, when it comes to religious pluralism, no such previous situation ever existed. When nostalgia creates a false image of the past, it channels a "desire to purify groups and homogenize communities" (Gilroy 2005: 37). Duyvendak too distances himself from the argument that diversity is the cause of melancholy by describing it as the "alleged" (2011: 85) cause of a crisis of home feelings among Dutch autochthons and as a "dominant framing" of the issue (2011: 96).

In contrast, Scheffer reifies the populist discourse by presenting alienation at home as caused by diversity, an unfortunate melancholic reality of immigrant societies. In his documentary on the arrival of guest workers in Western Europe, plurality is lamented in this way as inevitable but harmful. This style of reasoning largely ignores that pluralism is a fact, as Rawls believed, but also that it is a product of liberal democratic societies. Religious pluralism is the necessary outcome of freedom. To lament multiculturalism and increased pluralism as inevitably causing discord and conflict, as Scheffer does, is therefore highly misleading, turning the fact of pluralism into the problem of pluralism. That said, based on my fieldwork I think it would be a mistake to deny that, despite subtleties within groups such as the autochthonous population living around the Center Mosque, the demand to amplify the azan resulted in a conflict between groups, only to be settled bitterly and undoubtedly scarring those who live together in that neighborhood. As we have seen, the grand ideals of brotherhood, conviviality, and cosmopolitanism were not the decisive factors that shaped the outcome of the azan negotiations. Normative calls to transcend too simplistic categories of the self and the other therefore do not take away the reality that, in fact, such easy categorizations can be made and felt strongly, as was the case in Deventer. While anthropologists may write about going beyond discourses of cultural assimilation and integration on the one hand, and cultural recognition on the other, such visions should not underestimate the power of the politics of home and the multiple, and competing, nostalgias of nativism. As the azan case study shows, there is still much room for the folding, unfolding, and refolding of these dialectics.

The question is then forced on us: what if people are not interested in fully overcoming easy categorizations of themselves and others? And what if they do not even speak of a "clash of civilizations" or a "crisis of multiculturalism" but demand simply to practice and tolerate what they consider familiar? Of course, not everyone was dead set against the azan, not even all of the azan opponents. In 2015, one of the mosque's neighbors summed this up by saying, "I don't mind the azan, as long as the Dutch culture is dominant here." The group conflict did allow us to better grasp how constitutional secularism actually functioned on the ground when people asserted competing conceptions of home by demanding or resisting the azan. While populist discourse may emphasize the emotions and while social scientists such as Duyvendak may take these emotions seriously, this did not, nor should it, undermine the normative priority of civil rights over the passions of the multitudes. On the other hand, the reader may have noted that constitutional secularism as a concept was barely the issue in this chapter, though popular phrases about the proper (private) place of religion and the so-called separation of church and state were sometimes used by respondents. Constitutional secularism functioned above competing demands for integration and recognition, and above competing nostalgic memories of home. It was the gorilla in the room, preventing critics of the amplified azan from disregarding the local Muslims' wishes but only for as long as the latter actively insisted on their rights.

After Deventer, azan negotiations are ongoing in other towns and cities, and calling for prayer on a daily basis has again been contested. A mosque in Zutphen, a town in the province of Gelderland, has asked to amplify the call on a daily basis,[32] while the spokesman of the recently built Ulu Mosque in Utrecht has insisted on amplifying the azan twice a day.[33] The Turkish Cultural Center of Enschede, a mosque only 60 kilometers from Deventer, also announced a daily azan. A statement of intent was drafted when it sought a construction permit, stating that calls to prayer will be limited to a "minimum," but the mosque changed its opinion in 2015 and proceeded to demand a daily azan.[34] As I finalized these words, residents in Zutphen and Enschede protested and attended informational evenings about the azan. Despite their proximity, the agreement made in Deventer in 2013—to use loudspeakers once a day to amplify the call to prayer—was deemed impossible in Enschede in 2016. An alderman of the Liberal Party, Jeroen Hatenboer, was charged with the thankless task of ameliorating tensions between local Muslims and opponents of the azan, which included members of his own party, local autochthons who proclaimed that church bells were part of Dutch culture, but also citizens affiliated with the Syriac Orthodox Church. This time, protests against the azan were much more intense and better organized. Hundreds of citizens attended not one or two but three sound tests, debated with each other in closed meetings and in rather grueling public hearings at the municipality, two of which lasted over four hours. Several local political parties explicitly asked the mosque to give up its ambition to amplify the azan for the sake of preserving the peace. The Labor Party was among them, announcing on its website that in "the community of Enschede, there is currently no support for calls to prayer" and that "the Labor Party does not object to the construction of a mosque . . . but does object to a call to prayer that can be heard in public space."[35] Despite intense criticism, the mosque nevertheless continued to negotiate for the azan through discussions of such minute details as whether they would amplify three times a week with a volume of 57 decibels or only one time with a volume of 63 decibels.[36] Only the social-liberal GreenLeft party and the city's mayor explicitly defended the right to call to prayer as constitutional. The mayor, a member of the liberal Democrats 66, warned local politicians that he would "defend the Constitution" in case they tried to ban the call to prayer.[37] In the final agreement with the Turkish Cultural Center, three years after the discussions about the azan in Deventer had been concluded and begun in Enschede, the mosque would amplify the call only once per week and with a maximum of 57 decibels. This result was disappointing for the Turkish community, who initially hoped for an outcome similar to Deventer. Some azan opponents also felt disappointed that the call would be amplified at all, and spoke of a Pyrrhic victory after the "countless hours and conversations with the municipality and the mosque board." These feelings of disappointment reveal that, despite formal agreements, the larger question of religious tolerance and the ethics of hearing remains unresolved.

Epilogue

The Right to Tolerance

All eyes and ears were on Imam Ibrahim Çavdar. He had arrived from Turkey just a few months ago to lead the prayers at the Fatih Mosque in Amsterdam's city center, and found himself performing the azan at one of the most iconic sites in Dutch history: the former St. Martin's Cathedral in Utrecht, now called the Dom Church. Standing at the back of the church, in a corner of the balcony housing the organ, Çavdar lifted his right hand to his right ear and recited the azan into a microphone. The call echoed from the speakers through the medieval church in a city that had once played a pivotal part in the dramatic religious conflicts that finally led to an independent Dutch state.

The country that is now called the Netherlands was founded de facto through the Union of Utrecht of 1579, which sought to guarantee freedom of conscience. It was, Rainer Forst explains, the "first time in the history of toleration," that this freedom was demanded as "an individual basic right" (2013: 164). In this early stage of the development of modern tolerance, it was strongly associated not only with protest and resistance but also with violence: The St. Martin's Cathedral was attacked during the Iconoclastic Fury or *Beeldenstorm* (lit. "statue storm"), which involved destruction of religious images and was a sobering testimony to the enduring religious strife in the region. Visitors to the Dom Church today can see an altar piece from which the heads of saints and even of God the Father were hacked off, and small mourning statues on a tomb that were likewise decapitated. As a result of this dark episode, which came to be known as part of the European Wars of Religion, William of Orange famously proposed a *Religions-Vrede* or "peace between religions." Tolerance in this period was a "toleration of difference as long as it remained silent: *haereticus quietus*" (Forst 2013: 132). As these events unfolded, tolerance—an ancient concept, first introduced by the Stoics as a virtue of brave endurance—gained traction in the emergence of the modern world, and contrary to prevailing assumptions, *it* contributed to the eventual formation of liberal democracies rather than vice versa.[1]

The Turkish imam's call to prayer in the Dom Church was part of the city of Utrecht's 2013 historical celebration of the tricentennial of the 1713 Treaty of Utrecht. According to the festival organizers, the treaty was a "turning point in world history": statesmen of the most powerful European nations came together in Utrecht to effectively end two centuries of religious wars. A grand yearlong program of events, including music, theater, festivals, conferences, and exhibitions, was organized to teach all and sundry about the treaty, the "art of making peace," and "respect for diversity."[2] On April 11, 2013, Queen Beatrix opened the festivities in the Dom Church after a preliminary concert named "Perpetual Peace" after Kant's famous essay. The program notes portrayed Utrecht as central to the development of the principle of tolerance, a fact that the organizers hoped would inspire the Dutch today to seek interreligious understanding and to care for each other, not only for their own national citizens but also for refugees, migrants, and fellow Europeans, through an attitude of inspired openness. The next day, on April 12, the audience listened attentively to Imam Çavdar's call to prayer and responded with staggering applause.

I was moved. I know that my respondents from the Fatih Mosque—who are by now friends as well as neighbors—were likewise touched. In this moment, the azan had come to stand for a universalist harmony between religions. And yet, I could not resist a skeptical thought: what would happen if Amsterdam's Fatih Mosque in the city center, where Imam Çavdar worked, amplified the call to prayer? In this book, we have seen how azan amplification is often viewed as crossing a red line of tolerance. Whither tolerance? I end with some thought relevant to this unresolved question, about intolerance, religious harmony, and the notion that one has the right to be tolerated.

The intolerance of "schizophonia"

Following Jan Willem Duyvendak (2011), this study not only attended to Muslim minorities' perspectives on the azan, but also to those of the non-Muslim, white majority who reject Islamic sounds on nativist grounds. White opponents of the Islamic call to prayer in the Netherlands, in particular, experience "schizophonia." Musicologist Raymond Murray Schafer introduced this concept to express the dislocation of sounds in time and space due to (competing) soundscapes being (mechanically) reproduced in new locations or times. Schafer's critique of schizophonic soundscapes was inspired by romantic notions of primordial belonging, originality, and nature. The notion of schizophonia, however, needs to be problematized for it can easily be put to use to silence minority soundscapes in a globalizing world, such as the azan in the Netherlands.[3] This same romanticism led Schafer to assert that "Islam waned when it became necessary to hang loudspeakers on the minarets" (1994: 216). He was also negative about loudspeakers in general: "The loudspeaker was . . . invented by an imperialist, for it responded to the desire to dominate others with one's own sound. As the cry broadcasts distress, the loudspeaker communicates anxiety" (1994: 91).

To my ears today, an unamplified call to prayer recorded in the early twentieth century[4] may certainly sound more human than the loud call to prayers in contemporary Istanbul, instrumentalized by the increasingly authoritarian President Tayyip Erdoğan in nationalist and Islamist discourses.[5] Nonetheless, a generalized interpretation of the use of loudspeakers, disregarding the cultural context, betrays a simplified understanding of the processes of secularization and innovative uses of new media in religion. In any case, resistance to the azan in Europe is not merely a matter of deciding whether or not to use loudspeakers; it is not primarily an act of resisting noise, but a form of resisting Islamic soundscapes. In a global media context in which the phrase *Allahu akbar* has come to be widely associated with violence, non-Muslim ears are anxious about Islamic sounds, which simply *do not belong*, amplified or not. This book's findings therefore resonate with conclusions drawn by Martha Nussbaum on a more general, pan-European, level:

> European nations tend to conceive of nationhood and national belonging in ethno-religious and cultural-linguistic terms. Thus new immigrant groups, and religious minorities, have difficulty being seen as full and equal members of the nation. All these nations are the heirs of romanticism, with its ideas of blood, soil, and natural belonging. (2012: 94)

Romanticism underlies excessive resistance to the azan in the Netherlands, and informs people's nationalist sentiments. This is summed up in the idea of nativism, which I used to describe the intolerance toward Islamic aesthetics in European societies.

The azan as a technique of unifying religious plurality

To undo the intolerance of religious schizophonia, the call to prayer has been employed as a focal point around which to realize a form of religious pluralism.

Not only did Imam Ibrahim Çavdar recite the azan in the Utrecht church, he also sang a classic Jewish hymn and verses from a Sufi mystic together with Lies Müller, who is Jewish and a friend of the Fatih Mosque in Amsterdam. In poetic verses by Yunus Emre such as "Searching, I roam from land to land/ In all tongues I ask for the Friend"—a characterization of God—the emphasis was on the unity of religions in their plurality. While the imam had begun with the azan in Arabic, Müller finished solo in Hebrew with a poem that evoked both despair and the hope that human prayer will endure. Tellingly, the poem was written by Hannah Szenes, a Jewish-Hungarian heroine of the Zionist movement who was tortured and later executed by firing squad in Nazi-occupied Hungary in 1944.

In contrast to the unwanted amplified azan in Dutch cities, the audience shared an intimate experience and was touched by what was heard because of a willingness to listen together. The fusion of religious acoustics—and let's not forget the majestic acoustics of the medieval church—was employed as a technique to unify religious pluralities. But little did the public know that there had been some bickering behind the scenes, a small crack in the much longed-for unity. According to Mehmet Yamali, spokesperson of the Fatih Mosque, the imam preferred not to sing Szenes's poem because of the "[Zionist] background" of the poet. A duet of a classical Jewish hymn was chosen instead, because it was strictly monotheist, unrelated to contemporary politics, and in those respects an easier choice. The public performance of unity required careful preparation and selection.

The azan, the Jewish hymn, and poems accompanied a lecture by author Karen Armstrong, who was touring the world to bring attention to the "urgent need for a treaty of compassion." Armstrong advocated that we must go far beyond a religious peace treaty. This could be achieved by going back to the essence of all religions: compassion. By compassion she did not mean pity, but self-knowledge in relation to religious others as reflected in the Golden Rule: "Do not do unto others what you do not want others to do unto you." This solution to intolerance is an old, indeed ancient, strategy. Among its many sources are those from Europe, when *una religio in varietate rituum* was proclaimed at least as early as the Humanism of the Renaissance era. Armstrong's approach was popular in segments of the Enlightenment too, as in Gotthold Ephraim Lessing's vision that God loves all his children—Moses, Jesus, and Muhammad—equally.[6]

Such essentialist conceptualization of religions and philosophical traditions achieves unity by reducing the truth of religion to a common core: the Golden

Rule. It is also a path that pluralizes unity because different religions are said to grasp the same divine truth (cf. Forst 2013: 75, 409), though it is not clear what is considered incidental in religion or what should happen to those who do not want to fit their religion or worldview into such a scheme. Armstrong's approach can also be seen as achieving a unity by a fusion of different faiths (including Buddhism, Daoism, and other non-Abrahamic traditions) into a single, universal religion. The problem with this strategy is that intolerance is overcome through "religious dedifferentiation" (Forst 2013: 408) rather than through a respectful conception of tolerance for differences that refuse to be effaced.

Armstrong not only defended religious unity, she flatly rejected the concept of tolerance on the grounds that it is rooted in bearing something or enduring a kind of pain, rejecting the concept for being "too tough." The fact, however, is that in tactile practice an azan in a Dutch town requires some toleration, just like an interreligious encounter or cooperation requires careful preparation as well as a willingness to explore the boundaries of tolerance. The imam was being tolerant by playing a role in the performance of religious unity. As a representative of the Turkish State's Directorate of Religious Affairs, he expressed public respect for his Jewish counterpart's voice. He went even further and participated in a duet, but did so selectively, without revealing religious or political differences to the audience. Armstrong's approach required much more: a radical familial love and compassion. She urged an active interest in and engagement with the other, presupposing not only respect for the dignity of the other, which is also a fundamental requirement of tolerance, but also esteem for the other's differing practices, beliefs, and ethical-aesthetic judgments, not just in theory but in practice. Opinions on the extent to which this was achieved in the Dom Church can differ without downplaying the continued importance of being tolerant. For the imam, his assistant told me, "It was already a big step to sing a prayer in Hebrew."

Armstrong's other objection to tolerance, beside it being too tough, was that it fostered an unethical way of living with religious others. Tolerance, in her view, was ultimately rooted in unequal power relations. The powerful tolerate the deviants, who are liberated only to become simultaneously stigmatized by the disciplining power of being tolerated. Indeed, going back in time, none other than Immanuel Kant spoke of the "arrogant name of tolerance." He rejected the authoritarian implications of the concept and wrote in his famous essay on Enlightenment that "complete freedom" was in contradiction with a ruler or state that grants toleration to religious others (Kant [1784] 1999: 27). The problem with Armstrong's approach, however appealing it may sound, is not her rehearsal of Kant's critique of tolerance, but the fact that she hastily dismisses all forms of toleration rather than selectively reject authoritarian or paternalistic conceptions of tolerance.

Nevertheless, Armstrong's strategy is popular. The use of the azan as a symbol and means for interreligious "dialogue" is a transnational phenomenon, practiced for instance also at an interfaith event in a Los Angeles church. In his study of religious sounds in the United States, Isaac Weiner too expresses reservations about using the azan in this way. His main worry is that the azan is not accepted as an exclusively Muslim practice, but instrumentalized as a symbol of American unity in plurality. The azan then functions to "celebrate and bridge religious differences," writes Weiner, but in the process risks "effacing differences altogether by diminishing their significance" (2014: 185). This strategy leaves little space for Muslims "who might not embrace the pluralistic message that the adhān was purported to announce" (Weiner 2014: 187). We may add other groups to those excluded in this way, such as Dutch nonbelievers or critics of humanism, who would not automatically feel comfortable with Armstrong's prophetic discourse. Because of these thoughts, as I was listening to the azan in Utrecht's Dom Church, I could not help question what it meant to play a part in techniques of unifying religious pluralism. Was this performance comparable to spiritualization strategies that tone down differences, as we saw for the transduction of the azan in Chapter 1?

As an anthropologist weary of cultural essentialism, I do not want to make the normative claim that the azan should stand for its "original" or "authentic" functions at the time of the Prophet Muhammad, for instance to distinguish Muslims from other believers and to create a distinctly Islamic identity. This is, in my view, an interpretive matter to be determined through interactions among believers, Muslim thinkers, and religious authorities. It could be said that to criticize such unorthodox practices as calling to prayer in the Dom Church or transducing the azan is to succumb to orientalist nostalgia for an unchanging Islamic past. This study, however, has shown that the production of Islamic sound- and lightscapes is part and parcel of the politics of home. Therefore, any innovation of the azan that is undertaken to support questionable motives of "integration" should be subjected to critical scrutiny. Religious pluralism can only be pluralistic in the strict sense of the word if it makes space for religious particularity.

Tolerance is best anchored in equal rights

Grand appeals to the Golden Rule also miss the point that protecting religious minorities from discrimination and exclusion requires tolerance (in society) and equal rights (in law). In situations of intolerance, justice requires a political conception of belonging to determine how the state may regulate competing sentiments—overriding excessively strong, romantic, investments in "culture" or "autochthony." As we saw in Chapter 3, the state may regulate religious presence within the bounds of constitutional safeguards; if pressed, the state must and often does exclude nativist arguments in favor of equal civil rights. In the Netherlands, "belonging" is thus not only a matter to be decided by romanticism, but a political ideal of citizenship codified in law. In Chapter 2, I argued that this understanding is based on a historical move away from Protestant hegemony toward religious pluralism. The Public Manifestations Act of the 1980s not only definitively ended the archaic Procession Prohibition, devised to limit and control Catholic processions in the nineteenth century, it also enabled amplified Islamic calls to prayer and the sounds of any other religious newcomers. However, this development toward equal rights is not unanimously celebrated, not even among the mainstream political parties. Nevertheless, the equality that comes with Dutch citizenship has enabled the azan to slowly become part of public spaces in the Netherlands, even if often only in modest ways. We saw this in Chapter 4, where the local government intervened and mediated between a population that wants to preserve an "autochthonous" Dutch soundscape and another that wants to reproduce familiar experiences associated with the Turkish homeland. Rather than culture, citizenship rights determined how these competing demands were to be regulated, effectively steering how people's feelings of belonging can be managed in the process. This intervention, not only in law but also practiced by municipalities, is necessary because when non-Muslim citizens demand attention for feeling alienated due to the presence of Islam in public life, this does not automatically translate into a willingness to also empathize with disrupted home feelings experienced by their Muslim counterparts.

Besides the constitution standing in the wings, what proved to be decisive for the actualization of equal rights, in the form of amplified calls to prayer, was a practical learning process for both sides as negotiating parties. Citizens did not have to begin with the impossible task of reaching agreement on a conceptual framework of either minimalist tolerance or maximalist compassion. These practical interactions pushed the limits of what could be expected of each other and designated the boundaries of each other's rights. Often, it was a painful and agonistic process. The anthropological emphasis on what people actually do in such situations can save theorists from foolishly rejecting constitutional secularism without providing alternatives that are successfully implemented in the field. The facts on the ground are that some mosques have amplified the azan in the Netherlands and that some people have learned to tolerate its presence after lengthy negotiations with the local government and the mosque. For such a modus vivendi to be achieved requires some kind of consensus between those involved, rather than any strong moral sense of accepting the azan, or even viewing oneself as tolerant. In addition, only if a mosque actively persists on its right to broadcast the azan will its right be realized. Given the difficulties involved, most mosques do not bother to even try amplifying the azan. Mosque representatives have also not taken the issue to a Dutch court, but have so far preferred to negotiate and compromise. Protests against the azan are thus effective in limiting the practice of calling to prayer, including the number of times that an azan can be heard as well as its volume. The daily azan is especially resented in Dutch society because it reconstitutes the rhythm of *everyday* life, unlike the incidental azan for congregational prayers on Friday (cf. Beekers 2015: 226).

Despite a strong resistance to the azan, the "on the ground" realization of equal rights has enabled Dutch Muslims to overcome being tolerated in the paternalistic sense of the word. When an azan is amplified, Muslims are not granted the right to perform a ritual that some state authorities may actually consider out of place. Rather than being tolerated—the way soft drugs are tolerated in the Netherlands, floating between legality and illegality—tolerance for the azan is not based on a policy of *gedogen,* turning a blind eye (or a deaf ear), as it had been when Catholics were not permitted to construct churches and had to congregate clandestinely (in *schuilkerken,* hidden churches). Instead, equal rights ensure that the state cannot easily ban amplified calls to prayer, which it never has until now. Nor can the state consider this particular style of worship as unnecessary, not truly required by religion in general or by Islam specifically. Contrary to what azan opponents often argue, the state largely based its understanding of religious difference on an insight that was defended by Locke in his *Essay on Toleration*, namely that "in religious worship nothing is indifferent" ([1667] 1997: 139). Wearing or not wearing certain garments, kneeling or not kneeling in public, worshiping in spectacular or plain ways;

none of these choices should be rejected as indifferent, but judged depending on people's own chosen styles of worshiping, in private spaces and also outside in the streets. Because the Constitution grants equal rights to all religions, the state can make only nonreligious arguments to limit, or in extreme cases ban, public forms of worship or religious expression, even as subtle forms of (Protestant) bias may remain operative.

But why do we need tolerance for this kind of justice or fairness in treating religions equally? Why don't rights suffice (cf. Brown and Forst 2014: 16)? This book shows that, in practice, the accommodation of the azan does not rely on a discourse of tolerance. Actual tolerance for the azan was legitimized first and foremost by equal rights, preempting a complete regression into a conception of tolerance in which Muslims would have to seek permission for the azan. This means that equal rights, achieved through longstanding processes of rationalizing power, can function for citizens to self-discipline and behave tolerantly, and to effectively regulate aversion (cf. Brown 2006). In effect, public deliberations on amplifying the azan daily disciplined citizens to practice tolerance, but because opponents of the daily azan were not given an *unequal* opportunity to grant permission for the azan to the mosque, the deliberations for them quickly led to feelings of disempowerment. Therefore, rather than strictly separating rights from tolerance, what is still relevant today is Locke's ambiguous formulation of "the right to tolerance" (in the *Third Letter for Toleration*, cited in Forst 2013: 231). Tolerance is in this view more than simply a public discourse or a virtue to be practiced by people on their own accord; it is also a right that can be actively promoted by the state.

***

Not unlike the admirable ideal of the Golden Rule, intertwining equal rights and tolerance cannot offer a guaranteed solution for overcoming intolerance. At best, it can only legitimize a trend toward the acceptance of a religious sound in society. Indeed, whether the opportunity to broadcast the Muslim call to prayer without censure, not only in the Netherlands but also in the United States, the United Kingdom, Germany, and Sweden, will culturally "integrate" the azan into the soundscape of the Global West remains to be seen. Rather than demanding that citizens listen attentively to the azan in the spectacular setting of a historic Cathedral, thus setting the azan apart from everyday life, it requires a normalized presence to become accepted within the context of Dutch urban life. Instead of being heard, it would also need to become inaudible as part of the background sounds of the Netherlands (cf. Weiner 2014: 206).

Reflections on religious sound and tolerance as a casus belli equally point toward the importance of hearing loss, instead of active attention. From those places in the world today, such as Nigeria, where conflicts over religious sounds have led to fatal violence, we can perhaps learn in humility that one does not require religious agreement or unity to be able to tolerate each other's sounds. In such situations, "techniques of inattention" (Larkin 2014) can be vital for groups to live with each other at peace with religious difference. These techniques are relevant because they combine objections to religious sounds with other ideas that require the simultaneous acceptance of the same sounds. In doing so, a delicate balance can be maintained in tension, which is by its nature difficult to practice. Comportments so excellent are bound to be rare. Not all citizens are always capable or willing to accept the azan despite their objections, for peace, to say nothing of higher-level reasons of justice or a philosopher's sense of fairness. They can nevertheless learn fairness in practice by cultivating the modest virtue of minding one's own business, as much as they can, when confronted with an azan that agitates them.[7] While this kind of tolerance fails in fully overcoming the "toxicity" of practices such as calling to prayer, it can at least have an immunizing effect that ameliorates tensions. Learning this virtue of inattention, an inversion of the pious virtue of Islamic listening (cf. Hirschkind 2006), is a process that involves both public deliberation and the moderate disciplining of citizens' unreasonable emotions.

Figure 13 Breitman-Breitman Architecture. The Western Mosque, Amsterdam. Photograph by the author, Spring 2016.

Figure 14 First Friday prayer at the Western Mosque, Amsterdam. April 1, 2016. Photograph by Yusuf Burlage.

No doubt, strong sentiments about amplifying Islam will be stirred again in the near future in the Netherlands. The recently built Western Mosque, finally open after two decades of controversies (Figures 13 and 14), has not yet decided to broadcast the call from its minaret alongside an Amsterdam canal. Former District Mayor Henk van Waveren (Labor Party) thinks a weekly azan on Friday would be an "excellent" idea, but that "it should stay at that":

> What I have said as District Mayor is that if a church can sound its bells, then a mosque must also be able to make itself heard in its own way. But as the Western Church does not ring bells for each moment of the day, a mosque also does not need to call to prayer all day long.[8]

It is true that the Western Church does not ring bells all day long for religious purposes, but anyone living in the neighborhood also knows that it chimes every fifteen minutes, twenty-four hours per day, seven days per week. Besides its sacred and secular clock functions, the bells are also used on occasions of national importance. In short, the sound of the Western Church determines and is very much part of the ambience and character of the capital's city center. The Fatih Mosque, only a few hundred meters away (Figure 15), has stood silent for over thirty years. In order to arrive at a comparative judgment that the church bells do not ring all the time, one needs to take their aural presence for granted, but the nearby mosque's silence and minimal visibility as such also needs to

Figure 15 The Fatih Mosque and the Western Church, Amsterdam. Photograph by the author, Winter 2015.

escape notice. From this majority perspective, an amplified azan stands out, unlike the background ambience created by the bells of the Western Church. Thus, if it is really true that religious soundscapes in the Netherlands are changing, as this book suggests, it also remains evident that the azan is widely regarded as remarkable, if not out of place.

Notes

Introduction

1 I spell the call to prayer as *azan* instead of *adhan* throughout this book, except in book quotations, because the Dutch pronounce it with the *z* sound rather than the *dh* sound, following the Turkish rather than the classical Arabic pronunciation.

2 On Top of the World. Saudigazette.com, March 6, 2012.

3 Kant discusses the sublime in his *Critique of Judgment*, published in 1790.

4 This argument is worked out in Kant's *Religion Within the Limits of Reason Alone*, published in 1793.

5 All Qur'an citations in this book are taken from the Saheeh International translation.

6 Kant uses this phrase several times in his writings, for example in the *Religion Within the Limits of Reason Alone* (Part 3, Division 1, Section 3), referring clearly to the Bible, for example Acts 1:24: "Thou, Lord, which knowest the hearts of all men . . ." or Luke 16:5: ". . . but God knoweth your hearts."

7 Kant, Immanuel. 1886 [1785]. *The Metaphysics of Ethics*, trans. J. W. Semple, ed. with introduction by Rev. Henry Calderwood. Edinburgh: T. & T. Clark, Part 1, Chapter 3, Sec. 15.

8 Kant makes this remark at the end of his essay *On the Miscarriage of all Philosophical Trials in Theodicy* of 1791, published in: Kant, Immanuel. 2001. *Religion and Rational Theology*. Translated and edited by Allen W. Wood and George di Giovanni. Cambridge: Cambridge University Press, p. 37.

9 Malaysian astronaut says his miracle in space "hearing call to prayer." www.worldbulletin.net, February 14, 2012.

10 Kant's famous description of philosophical wonder can be found in the *Critique of Practical Reason*, published in 1788: "Two things fill the mind with ever new and increasing admiration and reverence, the more often and more steadily one reflects on them: *the starry heavens above me and the moral law within me.* I do not need to search for them and merely conjecture them as though they were veiled in obscurity or in the transcendent region beyond my horizon; I see them before me and connect them immediately with the consciousness of my existence" (Kant 1997: 133, 5:162).

11 See, for example, Corbin 1998, Schmidt 2000, de Vries 2001, Hirschkind 2006, Meyer 2006, 2009, 2012, Eisenlohr 2009a, Latour 2010.

12 Mentalism is a strand of thought in the philosophy of language. One of its famous proponents is Jerry Fodor (b. 1935). While Meyer and Hirschkind rightfully criticize

the mentalist bias in the study of religion, Fodor's arguments are more subtle than at first meets the eye. However, it is not relevant for the scope of this book.

13   Hegel's lectures on aesthetics and the history of art were held at the University of Berlin, between 1820 and 1830. They have been widely criticized by art historians, for example Donald Preziosi: "His notion of art, however, was strikingly less complex or subtle than those which had developed in the aesthetic philosophy of the latter half of the eighteenth century. He regarded art as basically a secondary or surface phenomenon, the presentation of common (inner) ideas in diverse (outer) sensual forms—thus harking back to a pre-Baumgarten and pre-Kantian ideology which privileged the Ideal or Thought by *devalourizing* visual knowledge, and by relegating it once again to the realm of confused intelligibility or primitive rationality" (1998: 66).

14   This view has been criticized, among others, by Birgit Meyer, for example in Meyer 2012, note 14. She refers to recent anthropological studies of Christianity that question "the privileging of 'inward' belief above 'outward' ritual practices, content above form, texts above objects" (2012: 12).

15   I have in mind works such as those by the jurist Abu Hanifa (699–767 AD), the philosopher Al-Farabi (872–950 AD), and the poet Hafez (1325/26–89/90 AD), to mention just a few. Distinctions between religious content or essence and nonessential or secondary forms return in various ways and require close comparative reading.

16   Part 3 of Kant's *Religion Within the Limits of Reason Alone* is titled "Concerning the victory of the good over the evil principle and the founding of a Kingdom of God on earth."

17   The term *hadith* refers to historic narratives passed on in Islamic tradition that are accounts of the words and deeds of the Prophet Muhammad.

18   The Prophet Muhammad himself is said to have chosen Bilal ibn Rabah as the first *muezzin*, the person appointed to recite the call to prayer (*Encyclopaedia of Islam*, Brill Online, 2014). Bilal was a dark-skinned slave who was freed by the Prophet's companion Abu Bakr. Honored by being chosen to call to prayer, his story has inspired Muslims in modern times to promote a conception of universal racial equality. Though connected to an Islamic message of universalism, the call to prayer has also assisted in the construction of a particular Muslim identity, to be differentiated from Jewish and Christian calls to prayer. Bukhari describes how an agreement was reached on the call to prayer. There were several suggestions, including bell ringing and a light signal or fire (translation by Muhsin Khan, Nr. 580), but in the end a specific set of verses was chosen to be called out loud by the human voice:

> Narrated Ibn 'Umar: When the Muslims arrived at Medina, they used to assemble for the prayer, and used to guess the time for it. During those days, the practice of Adhan [azan] for the prayers had not been introduced yet.

Once they discussed this problem regarding the call for prayer. Some people suggested the use of a bell like the Christians, others proposed a trumpet like the horn used by the Jews, but 'Umar was the first to suggest that a man should call (the people) for the prayer; so Allah's Apostle ordered Bilal to get up and pronounce the Adhan for prayers. (translation by Muhsin Khan, Nr. 578)

There are also other similar or related stories about the origin of the call to prayer. In one of these, the Prophet is taught the azan by none other than the angel Gabriel himself. Gabriel is best known in Christianity for the annunciation of the coming of the Christ, while in Islam the archangel also delivers God's revelation to the Prophet Muhammad. The word *azan*, or *adhan*, means "announcement," and can be interpreted not only as a practical call to prayer, but also as a divine announcement.

The content of the call to prayer can vary slightly depending on the religious school and time (Howard 1981). For example, for the first prayers of the day at dawn, the line "prayer is better than sleep" is added. Though most Muslims follow a Sunni tradition, Shi'ites may add Imam 'Ali as having the authority of God after pronouncing the *shahada*, bearing witness that there is no deity except God and that Muhammad is His Messenger. Another important (and generally accepted) addition is the *iqama*, a second call to prayer, which is recited when everyone has already gathered in a mosque for prayer and which includes the line "prayer has started." In most cases, the azan is structured as follows:

Allahu akbar, Allahu akbar (God is greatest, God is greatest—intoned twice)

Ashhadu an la ilaha illa Allah (I bear witness that there is no deity but God— intoned twice)

Ashhadu anna Muhhammadan rasool Allah (I bear witness that Muhammad is the Messenger of God—intoned twice)

Hayya 'ala's-Salat (Hurry to prayer—intoned twice)

Hayya 'ala 'l-Falah (Hurry to salvation—intoned twice)

Allahu akbar (God is greatest—intoned twice)

La ilaha illa Allah (There is no deity but God; intoned once).

19 I am indebted to Kambiz GhaneaBassiri for this formulation.
20 See, for example, Appadurai 1996, McAlister 2005, Tweed 2006, Levitt 2007, Csordas 2009.
21 See, for example, Bull and Back 2003, Erlmann 2004, Feld and Brenneis 2004, Augoyard and Torgue 2005, Helmreich 2007, 2010, Kheshti 2009, Eisenberg 2010, LaBelle 2010, Samuels et al. 2010, Wilf 2012; for studies of religious soundscapes see Hirschkind 2006, Oosterbaan 2008, Eisenlohr 2009b, Jouili and Moors 2014, Larkin 2014.
22 See Metcalf 1996, Lee 1999, Perkins 2010, Khan 2011, Weiner 2014.
23 *Moskee mag luidspreker gebruiken. Leidsche Courant*, January 24, 1986.

24 According to the Netherlands Institute for Social Research, in 2012 roughly 5 percent of the country's total population of 17 million could be considered "Muslim" (Maliepaard and Gijsberts 2012). This figure, however, lumps together a variety of Muslim identifications, including those who do not or barely engage in Islamic ritual life and those who do not believe in (a) God at all. In general, the 2012 study found that the majority considers itself Muslim, regardless of mosque attendance trends, but did not find a linear "secularization" among second-generation Turks and Moroccans migrants. Around three hundred thousand Dutch Muslims have a Turkish background and another three hundred thousand a Moroccan background, together accounting for roughly 70 percent of the total Muslim population. Other large Muslim groups are Surinamese (34,000), Afghan (31,000), Iraqi (27,000), and Somalian (20,000). The number of Iranians identifying as (Shi'ite) Muslims has exceptionally sharply declined to around 12,000 (from an earlier estimate of 34,000, based on nationality alone), but despite the documented drop in Iranian believers the figures remain misleading as many Iranian nonbelievers identify as Muslim in some situations and will vehemently resist the label in others. Finally, there are small to very small pockets of Muslims from countries such as Pakistan, Egypt, Indonesia, and Tunisia and a very small percentage (less than 1 percent) of Dutch converts (Maliepaard and Gijsberts 2012: 44–45).

25 Gebedsoproep "is een grondrecht" en klinkt in zeker 12 steden. *Trouw*, March 20, 2013.

26 Calling the faithful and getting complaints. www.nytimes.com, February 25, 2007.

27 Ottawa's Muslim call to prayer: There's an app for that. www.ottawacitizen.com, August 30, 2012.

28 Granada rediscovers its Muslim roots. www.theguardian.com, December 6, 2003.

29 Historic prayer call heard at Stockholm mosque. www.thelocal.se, April 26, 2013.

30 L'appel à la prière et le Coran pour la première fois sur une télévision française! www.islametinfo.fr, July 10, 2013.

31 Channel 4 to air daily Muslim call to prayer during Ramadan. www.theguardian.com, July 2, 2013.

32 Salat, www.johannesgees.com, August 5, 2007.

33 Het gevaar is niet ons gebrek, maar ons teveel aan geloof. www.joop.nl, August 6, 2010.

34 Communalism aloud: how loudspeakers spark hate in UP. www.hindustantimes.com, July 7, 2014.

35 The Revolution is over. *The Economist*, November 1, 2014.

36 Uproar over loud prayer calls in Muslim Morocco. www.washingtonpost.com, August 9, 2008.

37 Debate heats over calls for banning mosque microphones in Morocco. english. alarabiya.net, August 29, 2011.

38 The *muezzin* is the person appointed to recite the call to prayer.

39 After controversy, Muslim call to prayer sounds from front of Duke University Chapel. *The Washington Post*, January 16, 2015.

40 Laroui was referring to the seventh and final thesis of Wittgenstein's *Tractatus-Logico Philosophicus*: "Whereof one cannot speak, thereof one must be silent."

41 Jeroen Vullings. Volgens: Fouad Laroui. *Vrij Nederland*, October 14, 2006.

42 In fact, in the early days of Islam when minarets had not yet been constructed, the first muezzin, Bilal, literally called believers to prayer from the rooftop.

43 Kant's views on universal ethics and religion are discussed in his *Religion Within the Limits of Reason Alone*. Gandhi's notion of pure religion can be found for example in his autobiography, where he writes that the essence of religion is morality.

44 Casanova famously divided the modern thesis of secularization into three claims: secularization entails (1) a decline of religious beliefs and practices, (2) institutional differentiation that weakens overall religious institutional power, and (3) the retreat of religion into the private sphere. By showing that these three aspects do not always accompany each other, Casanova could argue that secularization did not automatically imply the decline of public religion. Instead, he described a process of de-privatization of religion that can occur in one country whereas privatization becomes the norm and practice in another. His critique was never a total rejection of the thesis of secularization as a process of modernity, but made a deeper point about history itself: the "mythical account" of secularization should be thoroughly disenchanted, indeed "desacralized" as Casanova put it (1994: 17). By viewing human history as contingent (1994: 39), rather than as a teleological process, he could better account for the persistent presence, declines, revivals, and transformations of collective worship as well as varieties of private religious experiences (e.g., Casanova 2001, Beyer 2006, Taylor 2002, 2007).

45 See, for example, Audi and Wolterstorff 1997, Rorty 2003, Rawls 2005, Habermas 2007, An-Nai'm 2010. Besides debates in which Rawls, Habermas, and Rorty are major figures (less known to anthropologists, for example, are reflections by Michael Sandel (Baxter 2011) and Cristina Lafont (2009) on the same topic), other philosophers took the renewed academic interest in religion in a very different direction and actively (re)appropriated religious language for their secular political philosophies, crafting a "faith of the faithless" (Badiou 2003, Critchley 2007, 2012).

46 See, for example, Knott 2005, Braidotti 2008, de Haardt 2010, Kong 2010, Wilford 2010, Molendijk, Beaumont and Jedan 2010, Beaumont and Baker 2011, Beckford 2012, Woods 2012.

47 The research perspectives on mosque construction include institutional history and governance (e.g., Feirabend and Rath 1996, Schmitt 2003, Knippenberg 2005, 2009, Maussen 2009, Sunier 2009), stylistic analysis (e.g., Dechau 2009, Roose 2009, Vandermarliere et al. 2011), stylistic criticism (e.g., Avciogly 2002, Welzbacher 2008, Erkoçu and Bugdaci 2009, Jackle and Türetken 2011), and ethnography

(Buijs 1998, Strijp 1998, Lindo 1999, Landman and Wessels 2005, Verkaaik 2010, 2012, Rijken 2014).

48 The list is too long to be cited in full here; notable are Bhargava 1999, Bader 2007, Bowen 2007, Srinivasan 2009, Warner et al. 2010, Calhoun et al. 2011, Bowen et al. 2014, Cohen and Laborde 2015.

49 A version of this chapter was published in *Material Religion* (Tamimi Arab 2015).

Chapter 1

1 By transduction, I mean here to alter the physical nature or medium of a religious call, or perhaps more abstractly a religious "signal." To convert its pattern into corresponding patterns in a new medium is to transduce it. Silverstein (2003) and Helmreich (2007) have used the term in relation to cultural meaning and translation. Keane (2013) employs it to describe how the "religious work of transduction" can use materiality to create the impression of dematerialization. These different characteristics of transduction—the production of meaning, the possibility of cultural or religious translation, and dematerialization—intersect in this chapter in relation to the conversion of the call to prayer from sound to light signals.

2 Moskee gaat gelovigen met lichtsignalen oproepen. *Leidsch Dagblad*, February 26, 2005.

3 The idea of "sacroscapes" or "religioscapes" has been picked up in the last decade by a host of cultural thinkers (Knott 2005; McAlister 2005; Tweed 2006; Thomas 2007; Petersen 2010; Oosterbaan 2011), because they perceive a defining role for changing land- and soundscapes in the construction of how we think about globalization.

4 Een oproep tot het gebed uit Mekka. *Rotterdamsch Nieuwsblad*, September 19, 1934.

5 Moroccan ritual practices of Islam have prompted anthropologists of Islam, Clifford Geertz and, recently, John Bowen, to use words such as "aggressive" and "patriarchal" in their descriptions.

Geertz: "Islam in Barbary was—and to a fair extent still is—basically the Islam of saint worship and moral severity, magical power and aggressive piety, and this was for all practical purposes as true in the alleys of Fez and Marrakech as in the expanses of the Atlas or the Sahara" (1971 [1968]: 9).

Like Geertz, Bowen contrasts Moroccan and Indonesian Islamic practices and describes the former as "patriarchal," for example in the case of the ritual sacrifice of an animal, which in the Moroccan case signifies the "virility, power, and self-sufficiency of the male, as opposed to the female" (2012: 83). Geertz's use of the term "aggressive" may be problematic but not wholly disconnected from Bowen's descriptions of "patriarchal" practices.

6 Statistieken 2012 Tweede Kamerverkiezingen. www.stemwijzer.nl.

7 "Geen gebedsoproep via luidspreker." *Algemeen Dagblad*, March 28, 2007.

8 Swiss Ban Building of Minarets on Mosques. *The New York Times*, November 30, 2009.

9 Wat is belangrijker: monumentale status oude kerk of nieuwe moskee? www.elsevier.nl, February 2, 2016.

10 French Mosque's Symbolism Varies With Beholder. *The New York Times*, December 27, 2009. Also see the mosque's website: www.lamosqueedemarseille.com.

11 The idea that glass and the color white stand for transparency is popular in the Netherlands, where the city halls of Amsterdam and The Hague and also recently constructed public libraries such as in Amsterdam or Delft are designed to reflect such an "open experience." Tourists also often find the lack of drawn curtains and extensive use of glass in Dutch residential buildings striking. While the ideological connection of ideas of transparency with the architectural use of glass may be dominant in several European countries or simply reflect global trends, it is particularly strong in the Netherlands. Protestant churches in the Netherlands, however, cannot be characterized by a similar use of glass.

12 Nota van B&W. 25 April 2006. Registratienummer 2006 I 13038. Gemeente Haarlemmermeer.

13 Ayaan Hirsi Ali is a former member of the House of Representatives on behalf of the Liberal Party. She made the film *Submission*, a highly controversial critique of Islam, together with Theo van Gogh, who was murdered by a radical Muslim.

14 Moskee gaat gelovigen met lichtsignalen oproepen. *Leidsch Dagblad*, February 26, 2005.

15 Isaac Weiner has documented a comparable understanding of Christian calls to prayer where a man defended the right to ring church bells in court, saying: "I do not know anything more touching or more thoughtful than that arrestation, even for a moment, which a man will involuntarily make when he hears these bells, reminding him that the Saviour took upon him our flesh for our advantage" (Weiner 2014: 62). Precisely because of the element of hearing the call involuntarily, thus creating a public community of listening religious subjects, it could never be replaced by pocket watches.

16 William J. T. Mitchell defends the interesting thesis that "all media are mixed media" (2005: 260). There are no purely visual media, but also no purely auditory media. This observation does not foreclose the possibility to distinguish visual from auditory media, but reveals that a phenomenon such as the call to prayer tradition from mosque buildings is much more than merely an auditory experience. In Chapter 4, for example, we see in more detail that the azan is also experienced as tactile.

17 I contacted Repaux in 2012, and fellow anthropologist Corina Duijndam interviewed him on my behalf by video call.

18 For example, see Ibn Sina's short *Treatise on Love* (Fackenheim 1945).

19 Butler, Alfred J. 1880. The ancient pharos at Alexandria. *The Athenaeum*, November 20, p. 681.

20 More recently, Robert Hillenbrand has argued the contrary, namely that in the early Islamic period the word *manar* was semantically disconnected from fire or light, and that it indicated a place that could signal without the presence of a literal light signal (1992: 132).

21 Azhar rejects light adhan. *The Siayasat Daily*, March 8, 2012. www.siasat.com.

22 Dit is 'm dan, de nieuwe moskee in Enschede. www.tubantia.nl, February 18, 2014.

23 Enschedese buurt witheet na moskeetest. www.tubantia.nl, November 26, 2015.

Chapter 2

1 Bijna miljoen kijkers voor The Passion. ANP, April 22, 2011.

2 1,7 miljoen kijkers voor The Passion. ANP, April 6, 2012.

3 The word *procession* is more generic in the English language than its equivalent in Dutch, which refers more specifically to a religious ritual. Because The Passion is different from the traditional procession, it raises the question of whether such an event, in which even nonbelievers are also welcome, is a "real" procession. However, it must be noted that processions have always been subject to change and that there is not a single archetypical procession that would be more real or authentic than The Passion, which can also be described as a musical, a popular media form of our time. Peter van Rooden (1996: 40) described a comparable process in the nineteenth century: religious mobilizations were enabled by the use of what were then newly available media, for example "organizations, magazines, mass meetings, petitions, political parties, and unions." The Passion, since 2011, has annually made use of the media of its time. If we indeed view religions as *media*, as so many scholars of religion do (Meyer 2009; Eisenlohr 2009a; Weiner 2014), then the question is not whether The Passion is a real procession but how contemporary Christianity is developing in European countries like the Netherlands. One commentator noted, for example, that The Passion is strongly based on a secular "events culture" (*evenementencultuur*), and that it symbolizes the new role of Christianity in a mainly de-churched and secularized country: "Christianity is not presented as a ritual way of life with fixed habits (such as going to church on Sunday) but as a single special event" (Emiel Hakkenes. Kerst als tv-spektakel: is dit het nieuwe Christendom? Trouw.nl, December 24, 2013).

4 Since 2004, the Dutch Reformed Church merged with other Protestant churches to form the Protestant church in the Netherlands (*Protestantse Kerk in Nederland*, PKN).

5 Wel Nederlands, geen Nederlander. *De Volkskrant*, June 22, 2002.

6 The term "public worship" is used in *A Letter Concerning Toleration*, written by Locke during his exile in Holland.

7 The societal distinction between private and public churches ensured that a single church had a monopoly over the public manifestations of worship. The public church, however, was not a state church that each subject of the Republic was automatically a member of.

8 Ivan Kalmar made a similar remark based on a comparison of nineteenth-century Jewish struggles to build synagogues in Europe with that of Muslims today (2013: 172).

9 Toespraak Maxime Verhagen over populisme. www.nrc.nl, June 28, 2011.

10 Maxime Verhagen is a Roman Catholic and member of the Christian Democratic Appeal (CDA). For his speech, see CDA Symposium Populisme, June 28, 2011.

11 Sarkozy joins multiculturalism attack. *Financial Times*, February 10, 2011.

12 Ultimately, this also requires rethinking how Enlightenment philosophers were influenced by the Global West of their time, being more familiar with religious others, Buddhists, Muslims, and others, than is sometimes recognized. Locke and Voltaire, for instance, already included Islam and Muslims in their understanding of "universal toleration" (e.g., Forst 2013: 292).

13 The northern provinces of the Netherlands have been historically known as roughly more Protestant while the southern provinces close to Belgium are known as more Catholic.

14 Corbin (1998) describes, for example, how French soldiers executed citizens in the countryside unwilling to hand over their church bells, or the rather violent silencing of the Notre Dame in Paris, which could not ring bells for ten years after the French Revolution. He writes that in the dark episodes following the French Revolution, church bell sounds could evoke emotions such as "fear, exhilaration, panic, and horror" (1998: 196). In the nineteenth century, "Through bells an individual was better able to apprehend the identity of the group to which he belonged. They helped him locate himself in space and time. They audibly proclaimed to him the order of the society within which his life unfolded, and made manifest the power of the constituted authorities" (Corbin 1998: 158). Thus, for Catholics in the nineteenth-century French countryside, "A bell tower without bells served as a constant reminder of a painful lack" (1998: 201).

15 The practice of carrying a cross was initiated by Emperor Justinian II and made mandatory after the Second Council of Nicaea.

16 The Catholic Church did not officially accept democracy until 1944, and only for states but not for the Vatican itself (Bader 2011: 32).

17 The Dutch government organized the State Commission Van Schaik to produce recommendations for a significant number of constitutional revisions deemed necessary after World War II. Major areas of concern were revisions

to parliamentary procedures, decolonization, and the European Coal and Steel Community.

18 The State Commission Cals-Donner was mainly preoccupied with suggestions for renewing the Dutch electoral system, and delivered its final report in 1971.

19 Handelingen II, 1987–88, 41, January 27, 1988, p. 2238.

20 Ibid., p. 2250.

21 Ibid., p. 2245.

22 There was some pressure, not only to allow a plurality of religious sounds, but also to limit the power of churches to enforce quiet. The so-called Sunday Law (*Zondagswet*) was criticized, but survived the constitutional disestablishment of the 1980s. In 2012, the Dutch House of Representatives (*De Tweede Kamer*) accepted an amendment proposed by Democrats 66 and the Liberal Party to grant municipalities the right to determine for themselves whether they wanted to enforce Sunday quiet, instead of assuming that the Sunday Law should apply to the entire country. Although Dutch constitutional secularism may be biased in favor of Protestant notions of proper religion, it has the capability to reform itself to lessen such biases. Similarly, Weiner describes how churches in nineteenth-century United States were faced with limitations due to increasingly secular governance: "Just as their right to make noise was being called into question, so too was their right to enforce quiet, at least on Sundays, and the shifting responses to these auditory practices mediated, in part, how Protestant Americans experienced the dramatic changes of the nineteenth century" (Weiner 2014: 21). It is therefore important not to conflate political and constitutional secularism with Protestantism (see Chapter 3), even though there are historic crossings, exchanges, and overlaps between these general concepts.

23 Handelingen II, 1987–88, 41, January 27, 1988, p. 2252.

24 Weiner (2014) describes a similar development in the United States, where court cases in the twentieth century affirmed cities' rights to regulate religious sounds but not to ban them.

25 Moderne Islam. Gebruik van microphoon. *Het Vaderland: staat- en letterkundig nieuwsblad*, October 8, 1938.

26 Een oproep tot het gebed uit Mekka. *Rotterdamsch Nieuwsblad*, September 19, 1934.

27 De muezzin is verdwenen. *Het Vaderland: staat- en letterkundig nieuwsblad*, March 14, 1930.

28 The recordings have been recently digitized by Leiden University, but have not yet been made available to the public. Anne van Oostrum has published on the recorded music (2012). On at least one of the recordings, street musicians can be heard playing together with the call to prayer.

29 De moskeeën van Kairo. *De Tijd: godsdienstig-staatkundig dagblad*, August 14, 1936.

30 Moderne Islam. *Nieuwe Leidsche Courant*, October 10, 1938.

31 Turksch en Arabisch. *De Indische courant*, November 25, 1932.

32 Oost-Java. *Het nieuws van den dag voor Nederlandsch-Indië*, January 6, 1938.

33 De Moskee: Heiligdom der Moslims. De Moskee is het Middelpunt van het Religieuze Leven. *De locomotief: Samarangsch handels- en advertentie-blad*, June 1, 1948.

34 De zilveren hamer. *Leidsch Dagblad*, September 23, 1966.

35 Moskeeën. *Limburgsch dagblad*, August 17, 1967.

36 Uitkijkpost in een moslimse wereld. *Nieuwe Leidsche Courant*, August 12, 1972.

37 Islam en kerk moeten leren samenleven. *Nieuwe Leidsche Courant*, March 4, 1968.

38 Oproep imam gelijk aan klok luiden van kerken. *Leidsch Dagblad*, January 28, 1988.

39 Moskee mag luidspreker gebruiken. *Leidsche Courant*, January 24, 1986.

40 Oproep. *Leidsch Dagblad*, October 22, 1986.

41 Nu ook luidspreker bij moskee Rembrandtstraat. *Leidsche Courant*, February 5, 1986.

42 Islamieten bij Goekoop op bezoek. *Leidsche Courant*, February 18, 1986.

43 Kerken staan tolerant tegenover oproep imam. *Leidsche Courant*, February 10, 1988.

44 Moskee heeft geen vergunning nodig voor elektronische oproep tot gebed. *Leidsch Dagblad*, October 23, 1993.

45 Haci Bayram Moskee krijgt rol in integratie Turkse gemeenschap. *Leidsch Dagblad*, December 6, 1997.

46 For the sake of brevity, this chapter largely omits the important history of pillarization in the Netherlands in the nineteenth and twentieth centuries. It should be remarked, however, that this history is quite essential to understanding the Dutch consensus model of governance (Lijphart 1999), which has also affected the governance of religious diversity, for example the right to organize schools according to religious lines including, more recently, Islamic schools (Sunier 2004). Also, the standard narrative of pillarization and de-pillarization has been recently nuanced by Peter van Dam (2011, 2014), who proposes a more gradualist account of modern Dutch history rather than the thesis and antithesis of pillarization and de-pillarization. For our purpose, it is important to note that, despite the official Procession Prohibition, pillarization, and polarization, Catholic (public) presence was normalized throughout the twentieth century, which finally also led to legal change, albeit after significant secularization of the populace and de-churching (*ontkerkelijking*) from the 1960s onward.

47 De processie is terug—katholieke emancipatie voltooid. *De Volkskrant*, June 21, 2005.

48 Een optocht voor de jarige profeet. Trouw.nl, February 14, 2011.

49 Ruim 7000 pelgrims bij Stille Omgang Amsterdam. Nu.nl, March 17, 2013.

50 www.stille-omgang.nl, accessed February 2014.

51 Sinds ontzuiling niet eerder zoveel sacramentsprocessies. Katholieknederland.nl, May 25, 2008.

Chapter 3

1 Contemporary liberals such as Kwame Anthony Appiah, Amartya Sen, and Martha Nussbaum have devoted much of their writings to refute parochial and xenophobic conceptions of liberalism that are informed by a supposed "clash of civilizations" (Appiah 2005, 2007; Sen 2007, 2009; Nussbaum 2012).

2 Geen gebedsoproep via luidspreker. www.ad.nl, March 28, 2007.

3 Henk Kamp. Immigratie en Integratie. VVD Tweede Kamer-fractie, November 12, 2007.

4 Ibid. (no page numbers).

5 Ibid. (no page numbers).

6 The European Court of Human Rights found that the SGP's position on women's political participation is "unacceptable regardless of the deeply-held religious conviction on which it is based." July 10, 2012, Staatkundig Gereformeerde Partij v. The Netherlands.

7 At the time, there was an antiblasphemy law in the Netherlands that was not applied in practice. There have been many critical debates on this archaic law, especially after the murder of filmmaker Theo van Gogh, and it was removed from Criminal Law in 2013.

8 "Straks de hele dag dat islam-gejammer." www.volkskrant.nl, April 18, 2004.

9 "Geen gebedsomroep vanaf moskee Zeist." www.digibron.nl, Kenniscentrum Gereformeerde Gezindte, August 16, 2004.

10 SGP legt zich neer bij gebedsoproep. www.trouw.nl, September 3, 2004.

11 Antwoorden op kamervragen over islamtische gebedsoproepen via geluidsinstallaties en gemeentelijke autonomie hierbij. www.rijksoverheid.nl, May 11, 2007.

12 VROM—Wet milieubeheer, Besluit woon- of verblijfsgebouwen milieubeheer, article 1.1.3.

13 De klokkenluider van Tilburg. www.omroepbrabant.nl, December 13, 2007; Tilburgs klokkenluiden aan banden gelegd. www.omroepbrabant.nl, April 20, 2009.

14 Pastoor mag Tilburgse klok ook van Raad van State niet luiden. www.omroepbrabant.nl; Uitspraak Raad van State, zaaknummer 201011441/1/H3, July 13, 2011.

15 Oproep vrijdaggebed moskee Middelburg doet "pijn en verdriet." www.pzc.nl, September 29, 2015.

16 ASP Kenmerk: Dagelijkse gebedsoproep Deventer Centrum Moskee. October 26, 2012.

17 Antwoorden op de Kamervragen van de leden Van Klaveren en Wilders (PVV) over "de dagelijkse imperialistische moskeeoproep." April 8, 2013, referentie 2013-0000042786.

18 Pim Fortuyn was a politician whose critical views of multiculturalism, and Islam in the Netherlands in particular, significantly impacted the Dutch political landscape.

He was assassinated in 2002 by Volkert van der Graaf, an environmental and animal rights activist who said that he murdered Fortuyn for targeting Muslims. Theo van Gogh was a film director who criticized the position of women in Islam in a film entitled *Submission* that he coproduced with Somali-born politician Ayaan Hirsi Ali. He was murdered in 2004 by Mohammed Bouyeri, a Moroccan-Dutch Muslim. Peter van der Veer has analyzed the impact of these murders on Dutch debates surrounding Islam and religious tolerance (2006).

19 It is questionable whether labels of left and right are so easily applicable to Dutch politics, as the Liberal Party has stances that would be understood in other contexts as left-wing, such as their affirming of the rights to abortion and euthanasia. The same can be said about the Party for Freedom, which occasionally defends civil and social rights ordinarily associated with the left such as gay marriage or better pensions for retired citizens. In the Netherlands, however, these parties are described in public debates as right wing.

20 SP Zutphen: dagelijkse azan voorkomen. www.destentor.nl, August 11, 2014.

21 Marokkaanse opent wijnbar in Rotterdam: "Ik ben de regisseur van mijn eigen leven." *Metro*, February 8, 2014.

22 Küçük and Boulayoun showed me the correspondence between the Islam Democrats and the mayor's advisor.

23 Moskee heeft geen vergunning nodig voor elektronische oproep. *Leidsch Dagblad*, October 23, 1993.

24 "Dat de gebedsoproep een recht is, betekent nog niet dat je er gebruik van moet maken." www.wijblijvenhier.nl, March 3, 2013.

25 Gebruik het recht op de gebedsoproep! www.wijblijvenhier.nl, April 5, 2013.

26 Gebedsoproep, thuisgevoel voor moslims. April 5, 2013. www.moslimvandaag.nl, Jaargang 1, Nummer 1.

27 "Gebedsoproep goed voor integratie." www.telegraaf.nl, February 7, 2013.

28 For explanations by Bhargava and Bader of what is meant by weak and strong "establishment" and, for example, the differences between a church and a religion that could be established, see Bhargava 2010a, b, and Bader 2007.

Chapter 4

1 The idea of "practical schemas" as a methodological framework for studying contingencies and multilayered interactions between European states and their Muslim citizens has been recently worked out by Bowen et al. (2014). We read that "... schemas classify persons, erect boundaries, and inform practices" (p. 256), that schemas have "grammars of justification" (p. 12), that they include "... complexes of ideas, norms, values, and emotions" (p. 3). Practical schemas remind the reader of Wittgenstein's pragmatic philosophy of language. Wittgenstein described

the phenomenon of how social practices, "language games," shape meanings. In philosophical language, practical schemas not only contain certainties, epistemological backgrounds from which one can head out, but also determine what counts as a candidate for being true or false.

2   While the belief in Rousseau's Noble Savage has declined considerably, the discipline of cultural anthropology itself can also be viewed as still too nostalgic for "endangered cultures." It is important to take seriously the emotions of the indigenous white Dutch majority, as Duyvendak does. However, researchers of the politics of home should not apply traditional anthropological nostalgia to the "natives" who are now "endangered" in the Netherlands. This is not because white majorities deserve less hermeneutic charity than supposedly weak black minorities, of course, but because anthropological nostalgia itself is too orientalist a mode of interpretation to begin with. Anthropological nostalgia, despite its good intentions, has always been closely linked to colonial nostalgia and exaggerated cultural relativism which turns the other into a radical other. A new generation of anthropologists interested in the question of preserving heritage, however, has criticized their discipline's nostalgic presuppositions (e.g., Silverstein 2004; Bissel 2005; Özyürek 2006; Kendall 2009; Berliner 2012). In our case, preserving heritage is a matter of competing nostalgias. While one group wants to preserve a "Dutch landscape" and demands "cultural integration," the other desires to transport heritage in the form of the mosque and azan, demanding "cultural recognition."

3   In Chapter 1, the concept of transduction was used to describe the proposal to transform the azan from sound to light signals. The azan is also transduced, however, as it enters the human body. The penetrating aspect of sound is itself a form of transduction, but what is involved here cannot be reduced to a step from the auditory to the tactile because the meaning of the azan, depending on context, affects listeners on a broader multisensory and visceral level.

4   Moskee is prima, dagelijks gebed niet. *de Stentor*, June 29, 2012.

5   Dagelijkse oproep tot gebed is stap te ver. *de Stentor*, June 30, 2012.

6   Just like Protestant Christianity, Islam is complex and multifaceted. In some instances, Muslims refuse to separate form and content, such as in the required bodily movements while praying, and at other times they separate what is in the heart from what is done by the body. One would need to simplify general concepts such as "Protestant Christianity" and "Islam" to an extreme, covering a great number of countries and millions of people, to arrive at a simplistic conclusion that Protestants make a fundamental distinction between the invisible church of the heart and the church as building, whereas Muslims would not distinguish hearing the call to prayer from their belief in Allah.

7   Moskee een week op proef met azan. *de Stentor*, July 19, 2012.

8   Internal letter from the municipality to the VVD councillor Ledeboer. Kenmerk BDO/722397. Onderwerp: Schriftelijke vragen ex art. 45 RvO over minaretspeakers.

9   Scheffer, Paul, and Roelofs, René. *Land van Aankomst.* International Documentary Film Festival Amsterdam 2013.

10 For a critical history of Dutch immigration policies, see: de Jong, Lammert. 2011. *Being Dutch, more or less.* Amsterdam: Rozenberg Publishers.

11 Bouw moskee laat op zich wachten. *Deventer Dagblad*, September 28, 1999.

12 Bezwaren tegen moskee ongegrond. *Deventer Dagblad*, October 30, 1999.

13 Verzet tegen de moskee gaat door. *Deventer Dagblad*, November 5, 1999.

14 Een wedloop van moskeeën. *NRC Handelsblad*, November 5, 1999.

15 Nog even geen dagelijkse azan. *de Stentor*, July 3, 2012.

16 College maant moskee tot overleg. *de Stentor*, June 30, 2012.

17 Samsom: "azan" in harmonie oplossen. *de Stentor*, July 20, 2012.

18 Bloomberg on Mosque: "A Test of Our Commitment to American Values." Blogs.wsj.com, August 24, 2010.

19 Obama Strongly Backs Islam Center Near 9/11 Site. *The New York Times*, August 13, 2010.

20 I thank anthropologist Manon Tiessink for her notes and recordings of this evening, which I could not attend.

21 Promoting "moderate" Islam, and therefore trying to influence definitions and practices of Islam, is a fluctuating policy of Dutch secular local governance. Justus Uitermark, Jan Willem Duyvendak, and Jan Rath describe how local government in the capital has tried to utilize and promote a "moderate Islam" versus "radical Islam." In Foner et al. 2014, Chapter 6.

22 Resultaat discussie bewoners en bestuur van de moskee. Deventer Mediators, February 13, 2013.

23 Peiling over dagelijkse azan. Website Gemeente Deventer, January 21, 2013.

24 Notaris bewaakt proces rond azan. *de Stentor*, January 22, 2013.

25 Weiner describes how the Hamtramck demand for the daily azan resulted in a poll in which a "No" vote would count as upholding Muslims' rights to the azan, whereas a "Yes" vote would leave the azan question unresolved. Local council members were keen on avoiding the courtroom and used this deliberately confusing method to let the people speak in democratic fashion, although Weiner adds "it was not clear what the people had said!" (2014: 190). Nevertheless, the result by a narrow margin was that the daily azan was allowed and the issue never made it to court.

26 Vragen bezorgde PvdA over azan-enquête. *de Stentor*, January 31, 2013.

27 Geschreeuw doet azan verstommen. *de Stentor*, July 7, 2012. J. Mostert reacted to this article a few days later, stating that the sound of the church and the azan produce different sonic experiences. In: Oproep tot gebed niet te vergelijken met

lawaai trein. *de Stentor*, July 13, 2012. The chairman of the mosque reacted to these criticisms by explicitly defending the analogy with church bells, not because he thought that the experience of hearing church bells was exactly the same as hearing the azan, but with a reference to "equal rights in a multicultural society."

28 Moskee Deventer mag dagelijks azan laten klinken. *de Stentor*, March 8, 2013.

29 Weiner similarly describes how disputes over religious sounds were brought to American courts in the nineteenth and mid-twentieth centuries. As a result, when Muslims in the twenty-first century wanted to amplify the azan, jurisprudence and law had already been shaped to the extent that taking the matter to court would be futile (since mosques in the United States have the right to amplify the azan). The azan controversy in the town of Hamtramck therefore never made it to a US courtroom (2014: 14).

30 Ever since the agreement, the mosque had generally amplified the call to prayer every day. On some days there was no muezzin available so the call was not amplified. Only about four to five people are allowed to call to prayer, and when they are not available the call is not amplified.

31 Also see Eisenberg, Avigail, and Spinner-Halev, Jeff (eds.). 2005. *Minorities Within Minorities. Equality, Rights and Diversity.* Cambridge: Cambridge University Press.

32 Zutphens college wil dialoog over azan. *De Stentor*, March 6, 2014.

33 Oproep tot gebed blijft. *Algemeen Dagblad*, November 11, 2013.

34 Moskee Kuipersdijk wil elke dag van zich laten horen. www.tubantia.nl, July 5, 2013.

35 PvdA voor bouw moskee, maar tegen hoorbare oproep tot gebed. Enschede.pvda.nl, February 10, 2016.

36 Een moskee vindt Enschede prima, maar hoe ga je de geluidsoverlast tegen? *De Volkskrant*, April 22, 2016.

37 Burgemeester wijst Enschedese raadsleden op stemgedrag moskee: "Ik verdedig de Grondwet." www.tubantia.nl, March 23, 2016.

Epilogue

1 This view is defended in detail by Rainer Forst in his book *Toleration in Conflict* (2013), in which he makes a systematic-philosophical analysis of the development of the concept of tolerance throughout European history.

2 Vrede van Utrecht magazine. September 2012, and www.vredevanutrecht2013.nl.

3 On the other hand, schizophonia can also be appropriated as an empowering concept, for example to criticize the leveling effect of one master azan for the entire city of Cairo instead of the cacophony of voices, which are also mechanically reproduced through loudspeakers.

4 I am thinking of the wax cylinder recordings of the call to prayer in Jeddah in 1908 and 1909 (Chapter 2, note 28).

5 Islam center stage as Turkish election campaign enters final week. www.reuters. com, May 30, 2015.

6 In Lessing's parable of the rings, God desired to bestow the ring of true revelation to his sons, so he had two identical copies made which were crafted so perfectly that He himself could not anymore identify which of the three was the original. The result was the impossibility to distinguish whose faith is the true faith, born out of the equal love of God for his children.

7 Of course, when the religious other is an object of racism, as when a person objects not merely to the azan but discriminates against people who have the cultural phenotype of "Muslim" in daily life, tolerance is not the solution. In practice, however, the line between subtle forms of racism and intolerance toward religious sounds can be difficult to determine.

8 Moskee in de Stad. Een multiculturele droom anno 2014. Interactive online documentary: moskeeindestad.nl, episode 5.

Bibliography

Akhtar, Salman. 1999. The Immigrant, the Exile, and the Experience of Nostalgia. *Journal of Applied Psychoanalytic Studies*, 1(2): 123–30.

Althusser, Louis. 2006. *Politics and History: Montesquieu, Rousseau, Marx*. New York: Verso.

Amin, Ash. 2010. The Remainders of Race. *Theory, Culture & Society*, 27(1): 1–23.

Anderson, Benedict. 2006. *Imagined Communities: Reflections on the Origin and Spread of Nationalism*. London and New York: Verso.

An-Na'im, Abdullahi. 2010. *Islam and the Secular State. Negotiating the Future of Shari'a*. Cambridge, MA: Harvard University Press.

Appadurai, Arjun. 1996. *Modernity at Large. Cultural Dimensions of Globalization*. Minneapolis, MN: University of Minnesota Press.

Appiah, Kwame A. 2005. *The Ethics of Identity*. Princeton: Princeton University Press.

Appiah, Kwame A. 2007. *Cosmopolitanism, Ethics in a World of Strangers*. New York: W.W. Norton & Co.

Asad, Talal. 2003. *Formations of the Secular: Christianity, Islam, Modernity*. Stanford: Stanford University Press.

Asad, Talal. 2011. Muhammad Asad Between Religion and Politics. Paper presented at the symposium entitled 'Dr. Muhammad Asad—A Life for Dialogue,' Riyad, King Faisal Center for Research and Islamic Studies.

Audi, Robert, and Wolterstorff, Nicholas. 1997. *Religion in the Public Square: The Place of Religious Convictions in Political Debate*. Lanham: Rowman & Littlefield.

Augoyard, Jean-Francois, and Torque, Henri. 2005. *Sonic Experience: A Guide to Everyday Sounds*. Montreal: McGill-Queen's University Press.

Avciogly, Nebahat. 2002. Identity-as-Form. The Mosque in the West. *Cultural Analysis*, 6: 91–112.

Bader, Veit. 2007. *Secularism or Democracy? Associational Governance of Religious Diversity*. Amsterdam: Amsterdam University Press.

Bader, Veit. 2010. Constitutionalizing Secularism, Alternative Secularisms or Liberal-Democratic Constitutionalism? A Critical Reading of Some Turkish, ECtHR and Indian Supreme Court Cases on 'Secularism.' *Utrecht Law Review*, 6(3): 8–35.

Bader, Veit. 2011. Religions and Liberal Democracy: Reflections on Doctrinal, Institutional and Attitudinal Learning. In Monica Mookherjee (ed.). *Democracy, Religious Pluralism and the Liberal Dilemma of Accommodation*. London and New York: Springer, 17–46.

Bader, Veit. 2012. Post-secularism or Liberal-Democratic Constitutionalism? *Erasmus Law Review*, 5(1): 5–26.

Badiou, Alain. 2003. *Saint Paul. The Foundation of Universalism*. Stanford: Stanford University Press.

Bangstad, Sindre. 2009. Contesting Secularism(s): Secularism and Islam in the Work of Talal Asad. *Anthropological Theory*, 9(2): 188–208.

Baxter, Hugh. 2011. Sandel on Religion in the Public Square. *Boston University Law Review*, 91(4): 1339–45.

Beaumont, Justin, and Baker, Christopher (eds.). 2011. *Postsecular Cities: Space, Theory and Practice*. London: Continuum.

Becker, Jos, and de Hart, Joep. 2006. *Godsdienstige veranderingen in Nederland, Verschuivingen in de binding met de kerken en de christelijke traditie*. Den Haag: Sociaal en Cultureel Planbureau.

Beckford, James A. 2012. Public Religions and the Postsecular: Critical Reflections. *Journal for the Scientific Study of Religion*, 51(1): 1–19.

Beekers, Daan. 2014. Pedagogies of Piety: Comparing Young Observant Muslims and Christians in the Netherlands. *Culture and Religion: An Interdisciplinary Journal*, 15(1): 72–99.

Beekers, Daan. 2015. *Precarious Piety: Pursuits of Faith among Young Muslims and Christians in the Netherlands*. PhD dissertation, VU University Amsterdam.

Beekers, Daan, and Tamimi Arab, Pooyan. 2016. Dreams of an Iconic Mosque: Spatial and Temporal Entanglements of a Converted Church in Amsterdam. *Material Religion*, 12(2): 137–64.

Berliner, David. 2012. Multiple Nostalgias: The Fabric of Heritage in Luang Prabang (Lao PDR). *Journal of the Royal Anthropological Institute*, 18(4): 769–86.

Bernstein, Richard J. 2009. The Secular-Religious Divide: Kant's Legacy. *Social Research*, 76(4): 1035–48.

Beyer, Peter. 2006. *Religions in Global Society*. New York: Routledge.

Bhargava, Rajeev (ed.). 1999. *Secularism and Its Critics*. New Delhi: Oxford University Press.

Bhargava, Rajeev (ed.). 2010a. *What is Political Theory and Why do We Need It?* New Delhi: Oxford University Press.

Bhargava, Rajeev (ed.). 2010b. States, Religious Diversity, and the Crisis of Secularism. *The Hedgehog Review*, 12(3): 8–22.

Bilgrami, Akeel. 2014. *Secularism, Identity, and Enchantment*. Cambridge, MA: Harvard University Press.

Bissel, William Cunningham. 2005. Engaging Colonial Nostalgia. *Cultural Anthropology*, 20(2): 215–48.

Bosnak, Marije. 1998. Wie niet luisteren wil . . . een sociaal wetenschappelijke benadering van geluidshinder. *Amsterdams Sociologisch Tijdschrift*, 25: 479–510.

Bouma, Gary. 1999. From Hegemony to Pluralism. *Australian Religion Studies Review*, 12(2): 7–27.

Bowen, John. 2007. *Why the French Don't Like Headscarves: Islam, the State, and Public Space*. Princeton: Princeton University Press.

Bowen, John. 2012. *A New Anthropology of Islam*. Cambridge: Cambridge University Press.

Bowen, John, Bertossi, Christophe, Duyvendak, Jan Willem, and Krook, Mona Lena (eds.). 2014. *European States and their Muslim Citizens. The Impact of Institutions on Perceptions and Boundaries*. Cambridge: Cambridge University Press.

Boym, Svetlana. 2001. *The Future of Nostalgia*. New York: Basic.

Braidotti, Rosi. 2008. In Spite of the Times, The Postsecular Turn in Feminism. *Theory, Culture & Society*, 25(6): 1–24.

Bröer, Christian. 2006. *Beleid vormt overlast: hoe beleidsdiscoursen de beleving van geluid bepalen*. Amsterdam: Aksant.

Brown, Wendy. 2006. *Regulating Aversion: Tolerance in the Age of Identity and Empire*. Princeton: Princeton University Press.

Brown, Wendy. 2007. Idealism, Materialism, Secularism? *The Immanent Frame. Secularism, Religion and the Public Sphere*. October 22, http://blogs.ssrc.org.

Brown, Wendy, and Forst, Rainer. 2014. *The Power of Tolerance. A Debate*. Edited by Luca Di Blasi and Christoph F. Holzhey. New York: Columbia University Press.

Buijs, Frank. 1998. *Een moskee in de wijk: De vestiging van de Kocatepe Moskee in Rotterdam-Zuid*. Amsterdam: het Spinhuis.

Bull, Michael, and Back, Les (eds.). 2003. *The Auditory Culture Reader*. Oxford: Berg.

Butler, Alfred J. 1880. The Ancient Pharos at Alexandria. *The Athenaeum*, November 20: 681.

Byrne, Bridget. 2007. England—whose England? Narratives of Nostalgia, Emptiness, and Evasion in Imaginations of National Identity. *Sociological Review*, 53: 509–30.

Calhoun, Craig. 2010. Rethinking Secularism. *The Hedgehog Review*, 12(3): 35–48.

Calhoun, Craig, Juergensmeyer, Mark, and VanAntwerpen, Jonathan (eds.). 2011. *Rethinking Secularism*. Oxford and New York: Oxford University Press.

Cannell, Fenella. 2010. The Anthropology of Secularism. *Annual Review of Anthropology*, 39: 85–100.

Casanova, José. 1994. *Public Religions in the Modern World*. Chicago: The University of Chicago Press.

Casanova, José. 2001. Religion, the New Millenium, and Globalization. *Sociology of Religion*, 62(4): 415–41.

Casanova, José. 2009. The Secular and Secularisms. *Social Research*, 76(4): 1049–66.

Casanova, José. 2012. The Politics of Nativism: Islam in Europe, Catholicism in the United States. *Philosophy and Social Criticism*, 38(4–5): 485–95.

Cesari, Joycelyne. 2005. Mosque Conflicts in European Cities: Introduction. *Journal of Ethnic and Migration Studies*, 31(6): 1015–24.

Clifford, James. 1986. Introduction: Partial Truths. In James Clifford and George E. Marcus (eds.). *Writing Culture: The Poetics and Politics of Ethnography*. Berkeley: University of California Press, 1–26.

Cohen, Jean, and Laborde, Cecile (eds.). 2015. *Religion, Secularism, and Constitutional Democracy*. New York: Columbia University Press.

Constable, Olivia Remie. 2010. Regulating Religious Noise: The Council of Vienne, the Mosque Call and Muslim Pilgrimage in the Late Medieval Mediterranean World. *Medieval Encounters*, 16: 64–95.

Corbin, Alain. 1998. *Village Bells: Sound and Meaning in the Nineteenth-Century French Countryside*. Translated by Martin Thom. New York: Columbia University Press.

Critchley, Simon. 2007. *Infinitely Demanding, Ethics of Commitment, Politics of Resistance*. London and New York: Verso.

Critchley, Simon. 2012. *The Faith of the Faithless: Experiments in Political Theology*. New York: Verso.

Csordas, Thomas J. (ed.). 2009. *Transnational Transcendence: Essays on Religion and Globalization*. Berkeley: University of California Press.

Dabashi, Hamid. 2013. *Being a Muslim in the World*. New York: Pallgrave Macmillan.

van Dam, Peter. 2011. *Staat van Verzuiling. Over een Nederlandse mythe*. Amsterdam: Wereldbibliotheek.

Dechau, Wilfried. 2009. *Mosques in Germany/Moscheen in Deutschland*. Tübingen/Berlin: Ernst Wasmuth Verlag.

Doomernik, Jeroen. 1991. *Turkse moskeeën en maatschappelijke participatie: de institutionalisering van de Turkse Islam in Nederland en de Duitse Bondsrepubliek*. Nederlandse Geografische Studies, nr. 129. Universiteit van Amsterdam.

Douglas, Mary. 2002 [1966]. *Purity and Danger: An Analysis of Concepts of Pollution and Taboo*. London and New York: Routledge.

Duyvendak, Jan Willem. 2011. *The Politics of Home. Belonging and Nostalgia in Western Europe and the United States*. New York: Pallgrave Macmillan.

Eisenberg, Avigail, and Spinner-Halev, Jeff (eds.). 2005. *Minorities Within Minorities. Equality, Rights and Diversity*. Cambridge: Cambridge University Press.

Eisenberg, Andrew J. 2010. Toward an Acoustemology of Muslim Citizenship in Kenya. *Anthropology News*, 51(9): 6.

Eisenlohr, Patrick. 2006. The Politics of Diaspora and the Morality of Secularism: Muslim Identities and Islamic Authority in Mauritius. *Journal of the Royal Anthropological Institute*, 12(2): 395–412.

Eisenlohr, Patrick. 2009a. *What is a Medium? The Anthropology of Media and the Question of Ethnic and Religious Pluralism*. Inaugural Lecture, Utrecht University.

Eisenlohr, Patrick. 2009b. Technologies of the Spirit: Devotional Islam, Sound Reproduction, and the Dialectics of Mediation and Immediacy in Mauritius. *Anthropological Theory*, 9(3): 273–96.

Eisgruber, Chrisopher L., and Sager, Lawrence G. 2010. *Religious Freedom and the Constitution*. Cambridge, MA: Harvard University Press.

Erkoçu, Ergün, and Bugdaci, Cihan. 2009. *De Moskee. Politieke, architectonische en maatschappelijke transformaties*. Rotterdam: NAi Uitgevers.

Erlmann, Veit. 2004. But What of the Ethnographic Ear? Anthropology, Sound, and the Senses. In Veit Erlmann (ed.). *Hearing Cultures. Essays on Sound, Listening and Modernity*. Oxford and New York: Berg, 1–20.

Essed, Philomena, and Hoving, Isabel (eds.). 2014. *Dutch Racism*. Thamyris/
    Intersecting Vol. 27. Amsterdam: Rodopi.

Fackenheim, Emil. 1945. A Treatise on Love by Ibn Sina [translation]. *Mediaeval
    Studies*, 7(1): 208–28.

Fainstein, Susan. 2010. *The Just City*. Ithaca: Cornell University Press.

Feirabend, Jeroen, and Rath, Jan. 1996. Making a Place for Islam in Politics: Local
    Authorities Dealing with Islamic Associations. In Wasif A. R. Shadid and Pieter S.
    van Koningsveld (eds.). *Muslims in the Margin. Political Responses to the Presence of
    Islam in Western Europe*. Kampen: Kok Pharos, 243–58.

Feld, Steven, and Brenneis, Donald. 2004. Doing Anthropology in Sound. *American
    Ethnologist*, 31(4): 461–74.

Foner, Nancy, Rath, Jan, Duyvendak, Jan Willem, and van Reekum, Rogier (eds.). 2014.
    New York and Amsterdam. Immigration and the New Urban Landscape. New York
    University Press.

Forst, Rainer. 2013. *Toleration in Conflict. Past and Present*. Translated by Ciaran
    Cronin. Cambridge: Cambridge University Press.

FORUM Verkenning. 2012. *Moslims in Nederland 2012*. Utrecht: FORUM Instituut
    voor Multiculturele Vraagstukken.

Foucault, Michel. 1984 [1967]. Of other Spaces, Heterotopias. *Diacritics*, 16(1): 22–27.

Fraser, Nancy. 2009. *Scales of Justice: Reimagining Political Space in a Globalizing World*.
    New York: Columbia University Press.

Frembgen, Jurgen Wasim. 2012. The Horse of Imam Hoseyn: Notes on the Iconography
    of Shi'i Devotional Posters from Pakistan and India. In Pedram Khosronejad (ed.).
    *The Art and Material Culture of Iranian Shi'ism: Iconography and Religious Devotion
    in Shi'i Islam*. New York: I.B. Tauris, 179–94.

Frishman, Martin, and Khan, Hasan-Uddin (eds.). 2002. *The Mosque: History,
    Architectural Development and Regional Diversity*. London: Thames & Hudson.

Gazzah, Miriam. 2008. *Rhythms and Rhymes of Life: Music and Identification Processes
    of Dutch-Moroccan Youth*. Amsterdam: ISIM/Amsterdam University Press.

Geertz, Clifford. 1971 [1968]. *Islam Observed: Religious Development in Morocco and
    Indonesia*. Chicago: The University of Chicago Press.

Geschiere, Peter. 2009. *The Perils of Belonging. Autochthony, Citizenship, and Exclusion
    in Africa and Europe*. Chicago: The University of Chicago Press.

GhaneaBassiri, Kambiz. 2010. *A History of Islam in America*. Cambridge: Cambridge
    University Press.

Ghorashi, Halleh. 2003. *Ways to Survive, Battles to Win: Iranian Women Exiles in the
    Netherlands and the United States*. New York: Nova Science.

Gilroy, Paul. 2005. *Postcolonial Melancholia*. New York: Columbia University Press.

Grotius, Hugo. 1945. *Over Goede Trouw en Onbetrouwbaarheid (De Fide et Perfidia)*.
    Translated by Alexander Stempels. The Hague: L.J.C. Boucher.

de Haardt, Maaike. 2010. Making Sense of Sacred Space in the City. In Christoph Jedan, Justin Beaumont and Arie L. Molendijk (eds.). *Exploring the Postsecular: The Religious, the Political and the Urban.* Boston and Leiden: Brill, 163–82.

Habermas, Jürgen. 2007. *Notes on a Post-Secular Society.* Nexus Lecture, Tilburg University.

Hacking, Ian. 1981. Was There Ever a Radical Mistranslation? *Analysis,* 41(4): 171–75.

Harvey, David. 2008. The Right to the City. *New Left Review,* 53: 23–40.

Helmreich, Stefan. 2007. An Anthropologist Underwater: Immersive Soundscapes, Submarine Cyborgs, and Transductive Ethnography. *American Ethnologist,* 34(4): 621–41.

Helmreich, Stefan. 2010. Listening Against Soundscapes. *Anthropology News,* 51(9): 10.

Hillenbrand, Robert. 1992. *Islamic Architecture: Form, Function and Meaning.* Edinburgh: Edinburgh University Press.

Hirschkind, Charles. 2006. *The Ethical Soundscape. Cassette Sermons and Islamic Counterpublics.* New York: Columbia University Press.

Hollinger, David. 2003. Religious Disestablishment in Western Europe: An Undervalued Step. *Responsive Community,* Spring, 25–30.

Howard, Ian K. A. 1981. The Development of the Adhan and Iqama of the Salat in Early Islam. *Journal of Semitic Studies,* 26: 219–28.

Huizinga, Johan. 1924. *The Waning of the Middle Ages. A Study of the Forms of Life, Thought and Art in France and the Netherlands in the Fourteenth and Fifteenth Centuries.* Translated by F. Hopman. London: Edward Arnold & Co.

Jackle, Justin, and Türetken, Füsun. 2011. *Faith in the City: The Mosque in the Contemporary Urban West.* London: The Architecture Foundation.

Jäncke, Lutz. 2008. Music, Memory and Emotion. *Journal of biology,* 7(21): 1–5.

Jansen, Yolande. 2013. *Bedriegelijk prisma. Voorbij de tegenstelling tussen religie en seculariteit.* Inaugural Lecture, Vrije Universiteit Amsterdam.

de Jong, Lammert. 2011. *Being Dutch, More or Less.* Amsterdam: Rozenberg Publishers.

Jouili, Jeanette S., and Moors, Annelies. 2014. Introduction: Islamic Sounds and the Politics of Listening. *Anthropological Quarterly,* 87(4): 977–88.

Juslin, Patrick N., and Sloboda, John A. (eds.). 2010. *Handbook of Music and Emotion: Theory, Research, Applications.* Oxford: Oxford University Press.

Kalmar, Ivan. 2013. The Israelite Temple of Florence. In Oskar Verkaaik (ed.). *Religious Architecture: Anthropological Perspectives.* Amsterdam: Amsterdam University Press, 171–84.

Kaplan, Benjamin J. 2007. *Muslims in the Dutch Golden Age. Representations and Realities of Religious Toleration.* Amsterdam centrum voor de studie van de Gouden Eeuw: University of Amsterdam.

Kant, Immanuel. 1886 [1785]. *The Metaphysics of Ethics,* translated by J. W. Semple, edited with introduction by Rev. Henry Calderwood. Edinburgh: T. & T. Clark.

Kant, Immanuel. 1997 [1788]. *Critique of Practical Reason.* Edited by Gregor, Mary, introduction by Andrews Reath. Cambridge: Cambridge University Press.

Kant, Immanuel. 1999. *Was ist Aufklärung? Ausgewählte kleine Schriften.* Hamburg: Felix Meiner.

Kant, Immanuel. 2001. *Religion and Rational Theology.* Translated and edited by Allen W. Wood and George di Giovanni. Cambridge: Cambridge University Press.

Keane, Webb. 2013. On Spirit Writing: Materialities of Language and the Religious Work of Transduction. *Journal of the Royal Anthropological Institute,* 19(1): 1–17.

Kendall, Laurel. 2009. The Global Reach of Gods and the Travels of Korean Shamans. In Thomas J. Csordas (ed.). *Transnational Transcendence. Essays on Religion and Globalization.* Berkeley: University of California Press.

Khan, Naveeda. 2011. The Acoustics of Muslim Striving: Loudspeaker Use in Ritual Practice in Pakistan. *Comparative Studies in Society and History,* 53(3): 571–94.

Kheshti, Roshanak. 2009. Acoustigraphy: Soundscape as Ethnographic Field. *Anthropology News,* 50(4): 15–19.

Khorsandi, Aida, and Saarikallio, Suvi. 2013. Music-Related Nostalgic Experiences of Young Migrants. In Geoff Luck and Olivier Brabant (eds.). *Proceedings of the 3rd International Conference on Music & Emotion.* Jyväskylä, Finland: University of Jyväskylä, 11th–15th June 2013.

Klop, Cornelis J. 1999. Religie of etniciteit als bindmiddel? *Migrantenstudies,* 4: 246–54.

Knippenberg, Hans. 2005. The Netherlands: Selling Churches and Building Mosques. In Hans Knippenberg (ed.). *The Changing Religious Landscape of Europe.* Amsterdam: Het Spinhuis, 88–106.

Knippenberg, Hans. 2009. Secularisation and the Rise of Immigrant Religions: The Case of The Netherlands. *Geographica,* (1–2): 63–82.

Knott, Kim. 2005. *The Location of Religion, a Spatial Analysis.* London and Oakville: Equinox Publishing.

Kong, Lily. 2010. Global Shifts, Theoretical Shifts: Changing Geographies of Religion. *Progress in Human Geography,* 34(6): 755–76.

Kuppinger, Petra. 2010a. Factories, Office Suites, Defunct and Marginal Spaces: Mosques in Stuttgart. In Michael Guggenheim and Ola Söderström (eds.). *Mobility and the Transformation of Built Form.* London: Routledge, 83–99.

Kuppinger, Petra. 2010b. Vibrant Mosques: Space, Planning and Informality in Germany. *Built Environment,* 37(1): 78–91.

LaBelle, Brandon. 2010. *Acoustic Territories. Sound Culture and Everyday Life.* New York: Continuum.

Labuschagne, Bart C. 1994. *Godsdienstvrijheid en niet-gevestigde religies. Een grondrechtelijk-rechtsfilosofische studie naar de betekenis en grenzen van religieuze tolerantie.* Groningen: Wolters-Noordhoff.

Lafont, Cristina. 2009. Religion and the Public Sphere. What are the Deliberative Obligations of Democratic Citizenship? *Philosophy & Social Criticism,* 35(1): 127–50.

Landman, Nicolaas. 1992. *Van mat tot minaret: De institutionalisering van de Islam in Nederland.* Amsterdam: VU Uitgeverij.

Landman, Nico, and Wessels, Wendy. 2005. The Visibility of Mosques in Dutch Towns. *Journal of Ethnic and Migration Studies,* 31(6): 1125–40.

Larkin, Brian. 2014. Techniques of Inattention: The Mediality of Loudspeakers in Nigeria. *Anthropological Quarterly,* 87(4): 989–1015.

Laroui, Fouad. 2006. *Over het Islamisme. Een persoonlijke weerlegging.* Breda: Uitgeverij De Geus.

Latour, Bruno. 2010. *On the Modern Cult of the Factish Gods.* Durham: Duke University Press.

Laurence, Jonathan. 2012. *The Emancipation of Europe's Muslims: The State's Role in Minority Integration.* Princeton: Princeton University Press.

Lee, Tong Song. 1999. Technology and the Production of Islamic Space: The Call to Prayer in Singapore. *Ethnomusicology,* 43(1): 86–100.

Lefebvre, Henri. 1991. *The Production of Space.* Oxford and Cambridge, MA: Blackwell.

Lefebvre, Henri. 1996. *Writings on Cities.* Translated and edited by Eleonore Kofman and Elizabeth Lebas. Cambridge, MA: Blackwell.

Levitt, Peggy. 2007. *God Needs no Passport: Immigrants and the Changing American Religious Landscape.* New York: The New Press.

Lijphart, Arend. 1999. *Patterns of Democracy. Government Forms and Performance in Thirty-Six Countries.* New Haven: Yale University Press.

Lindo, Flip. 1999. *Heilige Wijsheid in Amsterdam: Ayasofya, stadsdeel De Baarsjes en de strijd om het Riva-terrein.* Amsterdam: Het Spinhuis.

Locke, John. 1689. *A Letter Concerning Toleration.* 1983, edited by James H. Tully. Indianapolis: Hackett Publishing Company.

Locke, John. 1997. *Political Essays.* Edited by Mark Goldie. Cambridge: Cambridge University Press.

Mahmood, Saba. 2015. *Religious Difference in a Secular Age: A Minority Report.* Princeton: Princeton University Press.

Mahmood, Saba. 2010. Can Secularism Be Other-wise? In Michael Warner, Jonathan VanAntwerpen, and Craig Calhoun (eds.). *Varieties of Secularism in a Secular Age.* Cambridge, MA: Harvard University Press, 282–99.

Maliepaard, Mieke, and Gijsberts, Mérove. 2012. *Moslims in Nederland 2012.* Den Haag: Sociaal en Cultureel Planbureau.

Maly, Michael T., Dalmage, Heather M., and Michaels, Nancy. 2013. The End of an Idyllic World: Nostalgia Narratives, Race, and the Construction of White Powerlessness. *Critical Sociology,* 39: 757–79.

Margalit, Avishai. 2011. Nostalgia. *Pyschoanalytic Dialogues,* 21(3): 271–80.

Margry, Peter Jan. 2000. *Teedere Quaesties: Religieuze Rituelen in Conflict. Confrontaties tussen katholieken en protestanten rond de processiecultuur in 19e-eeuws Nederland.* Hilversum: Verloren.

Margry, Peter Jan, and te Velde, Henk. 2003. Contested rituals and the battle for public space: the Netherlands. In Christopher Clark, and Wolfram Kaiser (eds). *Culture Wars. Secular-Catholic Conflict in Nineteenth-Century Europe.* Cambridge: Cambridge University Press, 129–51.

Massey, Doreen. 2007. *World City.* Cambridge, UK: Polity Press.

Massumi, Brian. 2002. *Parables for the Virtual: Movement, Affect, Sensation.* Durham: Duke University Press.

Maussen, Marcel. 2009. *Constructing Mosques, the Governance of Islam in France and the Netherlands.* PhD dissertation, Amsterdam School for Social Science Research.

Mayer, Jean-Francois. 2011. A Country without Minarets: Analysis of the Background and Meaning of the Swiss vote of 29 November 2009. *Religion,* 41(1): 11–28.

McAlister, Elizabeth. 2005. Globalization and the Religious Production of Space. *Journal for the Scientific Study of Religion,* 44(3): 249–55.

Mendieta, Eduardo, and VanAntwerpen, Jonathan (eds). 2011. *The Power of Religion in the Public Sphere.* New York: Columbia University Press.

Mepschen, Paul. 2016. *Everyday Autochthony: Difference, Discontent and the Politics of Home in Amsterdam.* PhD dissertation, University of Amsterdam.

Metcalf, Barbara Daly (ed.). 1996. *Making Muslim Space in North America and Europe.* Berkeley: University of California Press.

Meyer, Birgit. 2006. *Religious Sensations. Why Media, Aesthetics and Power Matter in the Study of Contemporary Religion.* Amsterdam: Inaugural Lecture, Vrije Universiteit.

Meyer, Birgit. (ed.). 2009. *Aesthetic Formations, Media, Religion, and the Senses.* New York: Palgrave MacMillan.

Meyer, Birgit. 2012. *Mediation and the Genesis of Presence. Towards a Material Approach to Religion.* Utrecht: Inaugural Lecture, Utrecht University.

Mitchell, William J. T. 2005. There are no Visual Media. *Journal of Visual Culture,* 4(2): 257–66.

Modood, Tariq. 2014, accessed from Modood's academia.edu webpage. State-Religion Connexions and Multicultural Citizenship. Forthcoming in Cohen, Jean, and Laborde, Cecile (eds). *Beyond Post-Secularism: Political Secularism, Legal Pluralism and Democratic Constitutionalism.* New York: Columbia University Press.

Molendijk, Arie L., Beaumont, Justin, and Jedan, Christoph (eds). 2010. *Exploring the Postsecular: The Religious, the Political and the Urban.* Leiden and Boston: Brill.

Muus, Philip J. 1986. *Terugkeren of Blijven, een onderzoek onder Turkse werknemers van het bedrijf Thomassen & Drijver-Verblifa NV naar aanleiding van het instellen van een vertrekpremie.* Amsterdam: Instituut voor Sociale Geografie, Universiteit van Amsterdam.

Nasr, Seyyed Hossein. 1987. *Islamic Art and Spirituality.* Albany: State University of New York Press.

Needham, Anuradha Dingwaney, and Sunder Rajan, Rajeswari. 2007. *The Crisis of Secularism in India.* Durham: Duke University Press.

Nussbaum, Martha. 2012. *The New Religious Intolerance: Overcoming the Politics of Fear in an Anxious Age.* Cambridge, MA: Harvard University Press.

Oosterbaan, Martijn. 2008. Spiritual Attunement: Pentecostal Radio in the Soundscape of a Favela in Rio de Janeiro. *Social Text,* 26(3): 123–45.

Oosterbaan, Martijn. 2011. Virtually Global: Online Evangelical Cartography. *Social Anthropology,* 19(1): 56–73.

van Oostrum, Anne. 2012. Arabic Music in Western Ears: An Account of the Music of the Hejaz at the Turn of the Twentieth Century. *Quaderni di Studi Arabi,* 7: 127–44.

Ormsby, Eric. 1984. *Theodicy in Islamic Thought: The Dispute over al-Ghazali's "best of all possible worlds."* Princeton: Princeton University Press.

Overdijk-Francis, Joyce E., van den Eijnden, Pien M., Martens, Roelof, and Gerritsen, Jan D. 2009. *Tweeluik religie en publiek domein. Handvatten voor gemeenten.* The Hague: Ministerie van Binnenlandse Zaken en Koninkrijksrelaties.

Özyürek, Esra. 2006. *Nostalgia for the Modern. State Secularism and Everyday Politics in Turkey.* Durham: Duke University Press.

Penninx, Rinus. 1979. *Etnische Minderheden.* Wetenschappelijke Raad voor het Regeringsbeleid.

Perkins, Alisa. 2010. Negotiating Alliances. Muslims, Gay Rights and the Christian Right in a Polish-American City. *Anthropology Today,* 26(2): 19–24.

Petersen, Jesper A. 2010. Heart of Darkness? The "Satanic Milieu" as Religioscape. Paper presented at the Chaos symposium Religion and Geography arranged by the University of Tromsø (downloaded from www.academia.edu).

Pickering, Michael, and Keightley, Emily. 2006. The Modalities of Nostalgia. *Current Sociology,* 54(6): 919–41.

Preziosi, Donald (ed.). 1998. *The Art of Art History: A Critical Anthology.* Oxford: Oxford University Press.

Putnam, Hillary. 2002. *The Collapse of the Fact/Value Dichotomy and Other Essays.* Cambridge, MA: Harvard University Press.

Rath, Jan, Penninx, Rinus, Groenendijk, Kees, and Meyer, Astrid. 2001. *Western Europe and its Islam.* Leiden: Brill.

Rawls, John. 1987. The Idea of an Overlapping Consensus. *Oxford Journal of Legal Studies,* 7(1): 1–25.

Rawls, John. 2005. *Political Liberalism.* New York: Columbia University Press.

Rijken, Kemal. 2014. *De Westermoskee en de geschiedenis van de Nederlandse godsdienstvrijheid.* Amsterdam and Antwerp: Atlas Contact.

Robertson, Roland. 1995. Glocalization: Time-space and Homogeneity-heterogeneity. In Michael Featherstone, Scott Lash and Roland Robertson (eds). *Global Modernities.* London: Sage, 25–43.

van Rooden, Peter. 1996. *Religieuze Regimes. Over godsdienst en maatschappij in Nederland, 1570-1990.* Amsterdam: Bert Bakker.

Roose, Eric. 2009. *The Architectural Representation of Islam: Muslim-commissioned Mosque Design in The Netherlands.* PhD dissertation, ISIM/Amsterdam University Press.

Rorty, Richard. 2003. Religion in the Public Square: A Reconsideration. *The Journal of Religious Ethics,* 31(1): 141–49.

Rousseau, Jean-Jacques. 1997. *The Social Contract and other Later Political Writings.* Edited by Victor Gourevich. Cambridge: Cambridge University Press.

Routledge, Clay, Arndt, Jame, Hart, Claire M., Vingerhoets, Ad J. J. M., Juhl, Jacob, and Schlotz, Wolff. 2011. The Past Makes the Present Meaningful: Nostalgia as an Existential Resource. *Journal of Personality and Social Psychology,* 101(3): 638–52.

Roy, Oliver. 2004. *Globalized Islam: The Search for a New Ummah.* New York: Columbia University Press.

Samuels, David W., Meintjes, Louise, Ochoa, Ana Maria, and Porcello, Thomas. 2010. Soundscapes: Toward a Sounded Anthropology. *Annual Review of Anthropology,* 39: 329–45.

Schafer, Raymond Murray. 1994 [1977]. *The Soundscape: Our Sonic Environment and the Tuning of the World.* Rochester: Destiny Books.

Scheffer, Paul. 2007. *Het land van aankomst.* Amsterdam: De Bezige Bij.

Schinkel, Willem. 2009. De productie van marginaliteit. In Ergün Erkoçu and Cihan Bugdaci (eds). *De Moskee. Politieke, architectonische en maatschappelijke transformaties.* Rotterdam: NAi Uitgevers, 70–78.

Schmidt, Leigh Eric. 2000. *Hearing Things: Religion, Illusion, and the American Enlightenment.* Cambridge, MA: Harvard University Press.

Schmitt, Thomas. 2003. *Moscheen in Deutschland. Konflikte um ihre Errichtung und Nutzung.* Flensburg: Deutsche Akademie für Landeskunde.

Schuemer, Rudolf, and Schreckenberg, Dirk. 2000. Änderung der Lärmbelästigung bei maßnahme-bedingter, stufenweise veränderter Geräuschbelastung. Hinweise auf einige Befunde und Interpretationsansätze. *Zeitschrift für Lärmbekämpfung,* 47: 134–43.

Schwally, Friedrich. 1898. Lexikalische Studien. *Zeitschrift der Deutschen Morgenländischen Gesellschaft.* Bd. 52: 145.

Scott, Joan. 2009. *Sexularism.* Ursula Hirschmann Annual Lecture on Gender and Europe, Florence: European University Institute.

Sedikides, Constantine, Wildschut, Tim, Routledge, Clay, Arndt, Jamie, and Zhou, Xinyue. 2009. Buffering Acculturative Stress and Facilitating Cultural Adaptation: Nostalgias as a Psychological Resource. In Robert S. Wyer, Chi-yue Chiu and Ying-yi Hong (eds). *Understanding Culture: Theory, Research, and Application.* New York: Psychology Press, 361–78.

Sen, Amartya. 2007. *Identity and Violence. The Illusion of Destiny.* London and New York: Penguin.

Sen, Amartya. 2009. *The Idea of Justice.* Cambridge, MA: Harvard University Press.

Shatanawi, Mirjam. 2014. *Islam at the Tropenmuseum.* Utrecht: LM Publishers.

Silverstein, Michael. 2003. Translation, Transduction, Transformation: Skating Glossando on Thin Semiotic Ice. In Paula Rubel, and Abraham Rosman (eds). *Translating Cultures: Perspectives on Translation and Anthropology.* Oxford: Berg, 75–105.

Silverstein, Paul A. 2004. Of Rooting and Uprooting. Kabyle Habitus, Domesticity, and Structural Nostalgia. *Ethnography*, 5(4): 553–78.

Soja, Edward. 2010. *Seeking Spatial Justice.* Minneapolis: University of Minnesota Press.

Spinoza, Baruch. 2002. *Spinoza: Complete Works.* Edited by Michael Morgan. Indianapolis: Hackett Publishing Company.

Spinoza, Baruch. 2007. *A Theologico-Political Treatise, and a Political Treatise.* New York: Cosimo.

Srinivasan, Thirukodikaval Nilakanta (ed.). 2009. *The Future of Secularism.* Oxford: Oxford University Press.

Strijp, Ruud. 1998. *Om de moskee. Het religieuze leven van Marokkaanse migranten in een Nederlandse provinciestad.* Amsterdam: Thesis Publishers.

Stüssi, Marcel. 2008. Banning of Minarets: Addressing the Validity of a Controversial Swiss Popular Initiative. *Religion and Human Rights*, 3: 135–53.

Sunier, Thijl. 2004. Naar een nieuwe schoolstrijd? *Bijdragen en Mededelingen betreffende de Geschiedenis der Nederlanden*, 119(4): 552–76.

Sunier, Thijl. 2009. Houses of Worship and the Politics of Space in Amsterdam. In Lisa Nell and Jan Rath (eds). *Ethnic Amsterdam: Immigrants and Urban Change in the Twentieth Century.* Amsterdam: Amsterdam University Press, 159–77.

Sunier, Thijl, and Landman, Nico. 2015. *Transnational Turkish Islam. Shifting Geographies of Religious Activism and Community Building in Turkey and Europe.* New York: Pallgrave.

Tamimi Arab, Pooyan. 2012. (Dis)Entangling culturalism, nativism, racism. *Krisis*, 2: 68–74.

Tamimi Arab, Pooyan. 2013a. The Biggest Mosque in Europe! A Symmetrical Anthropology of Islamic Architecture in Rotterdam. In Oskar Verkaaik (ed.). *Religious Architecture: Anthropological Perspectives.* Amsterdam: Amsterdam University Press, 47–61.

Tamimi Arab, Pooyan. 2013b. Mosques in the Netherlands: Transforming the Meaning of Marginal Spaces. *Journal of Muslim Minority Affairs*, 33(4): 477–94.

Tamimi Arab, Pooyan. 2015. "A Minaret of Light": Transducing the Islamic Call to Prayer? *Material Religion*, 11(2): 136–63.

Taylor, Charles. 2002. *Varieties of Religion Today: William James Revisited.* Cambridge, MA: Harvard University Press.

Taylor, Charles. 2007. *A Secular Age.* Cambridge, MA: Harvard University Press.

Thomas, George M. 2007. The Cultural and Religious Character of World Society. In Peter Beyer and Lori G. Beaman (eds). *Religion, Globalization, and Culture.* Leiden: Brill, 35–56.

Tweed, Thomas A. 2006. *Crossing and Dwelling: A Theory of Religion.* Cambridge, MA: Harvard University Press.

Vandermarliere, Katrien, Kanmaz, Meryem, De Kesel, Ruth, Welzbacher, Christian, Kör, Mustafa, and Duman, Abdul-Vahit. 2011. *Nieuwe moskeeën in Vlaanderen: tussen heimwee & werkelijkheid.* Brussel: MANAvzw.

van der Valk, Ineke. 2012. *Islamofobie en Discriminatie.* Amsterdam: Amsterdam University Press.

van der Veer, Peter. 2001. *Imperial Encounters: Religion and Modernity in India and Britain.* Princeton: Princeton University Press.

van der Veer, Peter. 2006. Pim Fortuyn, Theo van Gogh, and the Politics of Tolerance in the Netherlands. *Public Culture,* 18(1): 111–24.

van der Veer, Peter. 2008. Spirituality in Modern Society. In Hent de Vries (ed.). *Religion: Beyond a Concept.* New York: Fordham University Press, 789–97.

Verkaaik, Oskar. 2009. *Ritueel Burgerschap. Een Essay Over Nationalisme en Secularisme in Nederland.* Amsterdam: Aksant.

Verkaaik, Oskar. 2010. Tussen Marrakech en Theater De Flint: ideologie en praktijk in moskeebouw. *Justitiële Verkenningen,* 36(6): 20–26.

Verkaaik, Oskar. 2012. Designing the "Anti-mosque": Identity, Religion and Affect in Contemporary European Mosque Design. *Social Anthropology,* 20(2): 161–76.

Verkaaik, Oskar. (ed.). 2013. *Religious Architecture: Anthropological Perspectives.* Amsterdam: Amsterdam University Press.

Verkaaik, Oskar, and Tamimi Arab, Pooyan. 2016. Managing Mosques in the Netherlands: Constitutional versus Nativist Secularism. *Journal of Muslims in Europe,* 5(2), forthcoming.

Vess, Matthew, Arndt, Jamie, Routledge, Clay, Sedikides, Constantine, and Wildschut, Tim. 2012. Nostalgia as a Resource for the Self. *Self and Identity,* 11: 273–84.

de Vries, Hent. 2001. In Media Res: Global Religion, Public Spheres, and the Task of Contemporary Religious Studies. In Hent de Vries and Samuel Weber (eds). *Religion and Media.* Stanford: Stanford University Press, 3–42.

Warner, Michael, VanAntwerpen, Jonathan, and Calhoun, Craig (eds). 2010. *Varieties of Secularism in a Secular Age.* Cambridge, MA: Harvard University Press.

Weiner, Isaac. 2014. *Religion Out Loud. Religious Sound, Public Space, and American Pluralism.* New York: New York University Press.

Welzbacher, Christian. 2008. *Euroislam-Architektur. Die neuen Moscheen des Abendlandes.* Amsterdam: SUN.

Wildschut, Tim, Sedikides, Constantine, Arndt, Jamie, and Routledge, Clay. 2006. Nostalgia: Content, Triggers, Functions. *Journal of Personality and Social Psychology,* 91: 975–93.

Wilf, Eitan. 2012. Rituals of Creativity: Tradition, Modernity, and the Acoustic "Unconscious" in a U.S. Collegiate Jazz Music Program. *American Anthropologist,* 114(1): 32–44.

Wilford, Justin. 2010. Sacred Archipelagos: Geographies of Secularization. *Progress in Human Geography*, 34(3): 328–48.

Woods, Orlando. 2012. The Geographies of Religious Conversion. *Progress in Human Geography*, 36(4): 440–56.

Young, Iris Marion. 1990. *Justice and the Politics of Difference.* Princeton: Princeton University Press.

Zentner, Marcel, Grandjean, Didier, and Scherer, Klaus R. 2008. Emotions Evoked by the Sound of Music: Characterization, Classification, and Measurement. *Emotion*, 8(4): 494–521.

Index